MONEY, FINANCE, and MACROECONOMIC PERFORMANCE in JAPAN

MONEY, FINANCE, and MACROECONOMIC PERFORMANCE in JAPAN

Yoshio Suzuki

Translated by Robert Alan Feldman

Yale University Press
New Haven and London

Designed by Susan P. Fillion
and set in Times Roman type by Rainsford Type.
Printed in the United States of America by
Edwards Brothers, Ann Arbor, Mich.

Library of Congress Cataloging-in-Publication
Data
Suzuki, Yoshio, 1931-
  Money, Finance, and macroeconomic per-
formance in Japan.

  Rev. translation of: Nihon kin'yū keizairon.
  Bibliography: p.
  Includes indexes.
  1. Finance—Japan. 2. Money supply—Ja-
pan. 3. Monetary policy—Japan. I. Title.
HG187.J3S96 1986 332'.0952 85-26375
ISBN 0-300-03387-7

*The paper in this book meets the guidelines for
permanence and durability of the Committee on
Production Guidelines for Book Longevity of the
Council on Library Resources.*

Figures in chapters 2 and 3 originally appeared
in the Bank of Japan's *Journal of Monetary and
Economic Studies*, volume 1, no. 2, and volume
2, no. 1.

10 9 8 7 6 5 4 3 2 1

Contents

Figures and Tables

Figures

Tables

Preface

This book analyzes changes in Japan's monetary and financial system and monetary macroeconomic performance focusing on the period since 1973, when the transition to a floating exchange rate system and the first oil crisis fundamentally altered the economic history of postwar Japan. As part of its analyses, the book covers recent developments in financial innovation and deregulation and speculates on future developments. In addition, the book surveys the literature on recent macroeconomic performance by Bank of Japan research economists and Japanese academics.

The present book is in some respects a sequel to my *Money and Banking in Contemporary Japan* (Yale University Press, 1980, originally published in Japanese in 1974). The enormous changes in the Japanese economy and Japan's financial conditions since 1974 have made new analysis necessary. It is hoped that this new book will help foreign readers become further acquainted with specific trends within the Japanese financial system and economy while emphasizing Japan's increased dependence on international developments.

The book consists of two parts, each of which has been subdivided into four chapters. In part I, Evolution of the Financial System, chapter 1 provides historical background for the recent structural modifications of the financial system and establishes a bridge from my earlier book to the new book. It delineates how factors behind several important features of Japan's financial structure described in the earlier book have faded, and describes the new forces that are still changing the financial and monetary characteristics of Japan.

Chapter 2 presents statistical analyses on recent changes in the accumulation and selection of financial assets and on the resultant changes in the flow of funds. These analyses reveal a recent decline in the trend of the share of private financial intermediaries, especially deposit banks, in the total flow of funds. This decline is one of the essential forces behind financial deregulation and reform.

Chapter 3 treats the same subject from a different point of view. Here financial innovation is considered from an international perspective and the conditions of financial innovation in Japan are compared with those of other economies. The chapter also discusses the impact of financial changes on the implementation of monetary policy.

Chapter 4 highlights the implications of recent financial developments for the effectiveness of monetary policy. It analyzes the relationship between the pattern of the financial system and the available set of financial assets, and speculates on how innovations in financial assets, services, and institutions affect the transmission channels of monetary policy.

In part II, Money and Macroeconomic Performance, chapter 5[1] surveys the inflation debate in postwar Japan, emphasizing the last decade, and investigates recent changes in macroeconomic performance from an international perspective. The successes and failures of price stabilization in Japan are explored. Chapter 6 introduces the results of empirical tests of the major contemporary hypotheses about macroeconomic behavior in Japan. The chapter explores the potential explanations for the improvement of Japan's macroeconomic performance since the first oil price shock. Chapter 7 presents the results of theoretical and empirical analyses of yen exchange rate movements since the transition to a floating rate regime in 1973. Finally, chapter 8 focuses on monetary control by the Bank of Japan, and emphasizes an international perspective. I conclude that Japan has been less monetarist in rhetoric than either the United States or Great Britain, but far more monetarist in practice.

Chapters 2 and 3 originally appeared in *Monetary and Economic Studies* (in English, published by the Bank of Japan). Chapters 1 and 4 through 8 are partly drawn from my *Nippon kin'yuu keizai ron* (in Japanese, published by Tooyoo Keizai Shimpoo Sha, Tokyo, 1983), which discusses the financial aspects of recent changes in the Japanese economy and offers an interpretation of Japanese macroeconomic performance based on contemporary theoretical analysis. However, these chapters have all been at least partially revised so as to help foreign readers understand recent monetary and financial aspects of the Japanese economy. Wherever possible, comparisons have been drawn with characteristics of the economies of the United States and Europe so as to place the discussion in a context

---

1. Portions of this chapter originally appeared in English in *Japanese Economic Studies*, Fall 1982, translated there by David Spackman.

familiar to foreign readers. In addition, statistics in both the tables and figures have been updated where appropriate.

This English version would not have appeared but for the efforts of Dr. Robert Alan Feldman of the International Monetary Fund. Dr. Feldman's exceptional knowledge of Japanese, of the Japanese economy, and of macroeconomics have made him an ideal translator. I would also like to acknowledge the financial assistance for the translation process provided by the Suntory Foundation and The Forum for Policy Innovation. I am, therefore, greatly obliged to both Dr. Feldman and the two institutions for making it possible to offer my ideas to readers of English.

I am also grateful for the advice afforded me by Professors Hugh T. Patrick and Thomas F. Cargill during the editing process. The final form of this English version owes very much to them.

Acronyms and Abbreviations

BA   Banker's acceptance
BOP   Balance of payments
CD   Certificate of deposit
CP   Commercial paper
CPI   Consumer price index
EC   European Community
EMS   European monetary system
FY   Fiscal year
GNP   Gross national product
INS   Information network system
IS   Investment-savings
LM   Liquidity-money
MMMF Money market mutual fund
M1   Narrow money
M2   Broad money
M2 + CDs Broad money plus
      certificates of deposit

M3   Broad money plus postal
      savings
NBER National Bureau of
      Economic Research
NOW   Negotiable order of
      withdrawal
OECD Organization for
      Economic Cooperation
      and Development
OPEC Organization of
      Petroleum Exporting
      Countries
RP   Repurchase agreement
RPC   Relative power
      contribution
TB   Treasury bill
WPI   Wholesale price index

xvii

MONEY, FINANCE, and MACROECONOMIC PERFORMANCE in JAPAN

I

EVOLUTION OF
THE FINANCIAL
SYSTEM

1

Historical Developments and Resultant Conflicts in the Financial System

$\mathbf{T}$he Japanese financial system has exhibited several special characteristics in the period since the end of World War II. I have previously described these as (1) overloan, (2) overborrowing, (3) skewness of funding, and (4) predominance of indirect financing. The environment for these characteristics included three basic elements—export/investment-led high growth, the artificially low interest rate policy, and barriers to internationalization. (See Suzuki 1974, part I.) The first and third of these elements disappeared because of historical developments after 1974, which resulted in the subsiding of overborrowing and change in the nature of skewness of funding and overloan. (See Suzuki 1981, chapter 4). The artificially low interest rate policy continues to be influential even today, however, and, as a result, the fourth characteristic, predominance of indirect financing, stands at a major crossroads. The direction the Japanese financial system takes from here on depends on how the artificially low interest rate policy and the indirect financing structure interact. This chapter evaluates the pros and cons of the artificially low interest rate policy and considers the direction of development of the financial system.[1]

I. High Growth and the Artificially Low Interest Rate Policy

1. Exports, Investment, and Economic Strategy

Modern economics textbooks tell us that the final object of economic policy is to maximize international economic welfare. To that end, scarce

1. For a recent treatment of pros and cons of the artificially low interest rate policy, see Teranishi 1982, and for a treatment of evolution of the financial system see Royama 1982.

3

resources must be used *efficiently* to enlarge the pie, and the pie must be distributed *fairly*. In the postwar era, labor was abundant, but shortages of capital equipment and raw materials severely constrained the size of the pie. Hence, giving priority to plant and equipment investment and to exports (used to secure imported raw materials) was the most effective way to increase the size of the pie. Moreover, this "investment/export-led growth" simultaneously absorbed latent unemployment in agricultural villages and among the poorer classes in the cities, eliminated wage and income differentials between cities and villages and between large and small firms, and thus achieved a fair distribution of the pie. This was indeed killing two birds with one stone.

Postwar economic policy was constructed with investment/export-led growth as its strategic objective. The important elements in the policy were trade and foreign exchange management, protection of industry, and tax treatment favoring saving and investment. The artificially low interest rate policy, which we will discuss below, was also oriented toward this goal. It attempted to lower the financial costs of exporting and investment by controlling interest rates at the lowest level possible.

This strategy for economic policy was possible only because Japan was a semi-industrialized country, in the process of catching up with the advanced countries of Europe and North America. Maintaining barriers to internationalization, protecting industries and the financial system under a controlled interest rate structure, and thus promoting exports are not acts that industrial countries permit among themselves. Moreover, among OECD nations current account surpluses are strongly criticized as export of unemployment.

The Japanese have taken these lessons to heart due to the many international economic frictions of the 1970s. In order to escape from the "trilemma" (imported inflation, recession, and current account deficit) brought by the two oil crises of 1973 and 1979, Japan has twice, in 1976–77 and in 1980–81, trod the path of export-led recovery. The degree of trade friction this generated was unheard of in the high growth era. Semi-industrialized status and fully industrialized status are very different, and Japan's economic strategy for today's world must also be different.

2. Dual Structure of Interest Rates

a. Controlled Rates and Free Rates.   Artificial suppression of interest rates was an element in the economic strategy of investment/export-led growth used in the period when Japan was a semi-industrialized nation. But whether it actually lowered the financial costs of Japanese corporations is unclear, because, in addition to the controlled interest rates, there formed certain financial markets in which interest rates were determined

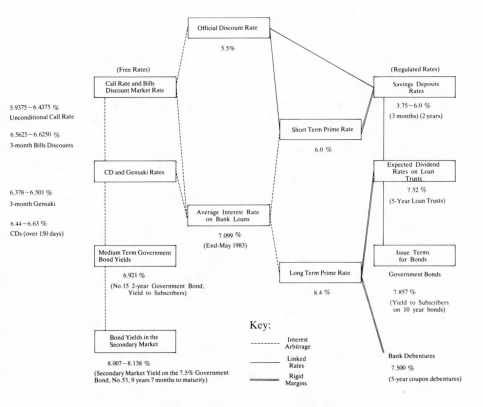

Figure 1.1.   Japan's Two-Tier Interest Rate Structure (June 1983)

freely, so that the "effective" interest rates borne by firms did not remain
low, as intended by policy.

The structure of interest rates in the high-growth period was a dual
structure of both controlled and free rates, with the free rates exceeding
controlled rates by a wide margin. I pointed this out in detail relatively
early (1974).[2] It is clear, based on current facts, that the dual structure
of interest rates continues even today.

Figure 1.1 shows Japanese interest rates as of June 1983. Controlled
rates are on the right side of the figure and free rates on the left. (The
controlled rates include those de jure set voluntarily by the financial
industry but de facto controlled by authorities.) For both controlled and

2. A detailed analysis of the dual structure of interest rates in the high growth period
is given in Suzuki 1984, section I, chapter 3, "Kinri no hishinshukusei to kinri taikei no
yugami" (Stickiness of interest rates and distortions in the structure of interest rates).

free rates, those listed near the top of the figure are shorter in maturity than those near the bottom. But the long-short differentials for the controlled rates are determined through a mechanical link, whereas those for the free rates are determined naturally, through interest rate arbitrage in the markets. The sarcastic phrase "four and a half mat interest rate structure"[3] expresses the narrow range in which controlled rates are determined, with long rates always exceeding short rates. In contrast, as the expectations theory of the maturity structure teaches, the free rates are more flexible, with short rates rising above long rates in periods of monetary tightness, and the opposite in normal times. (Figure 1.1 shows the normal case.)[4]

The central bank's discount rate and the commercial bank's loan rates lie between the controlled and free rate structures. Because the discount rate is the rate at which the central bank lends to commercial banks, the interbank call rate is quite sensitive to its movements, as are the free rates, through arbitrage relations with the call rate. Moreover, when the controlled rates are set, the discount rate displays a very close relationship with deposit rates and with the short-term prime rate; hence, it is the lever that moves the controlled rate structure.

The commercial bank loan rates are also mechanically tied to controlled rates by fixed spreads: the short prime is tied to deposit rates, and the long prime to expected yields on investment trusts and to financial debenture rates. However, actual loan rates are set freely, with these prime rates as lower limits, and arbitrage relations between short-term money markets and the secondary bond market exist.[5]

The above describes the current state of determination of interest rates. However, it is immediately clear from figure 1.1 that the free rate at each maturity is higher than the corresponding controlled rate. For example, the free short rates such as the call, bill, CD, and repurchase (*gensaki*) rates (which range in maturity from overnight to four months) are all higher than even the two-year deposit rate. The subscriber's yield on

3. Room size in Japanese houses is measured by the number of tatami mats of floor space. A "four and a half mat room" is the smallest deemed fit for habitation. An equivalent English expression would be "phone booth–sized."

4. For detailed analysis of the maturity structure of free rates in Japan, see Kuroda and Ohkubo 1981 and A. Kuroda 1982.

5. In earlier years, it was widely believed that even the rate on general loans was a type of controlled rate, and that it moved mechanically with the prime rate. But Suzuki 1968 and Bank of Japan, Research and Statistics Department 1973 first pointed out the possibility of some arbitrage between the average contracted rate on loans and the call rate, which is a free rate. This research is summarized in Suzuki 1974, chapter 7, section 2.2. Iwao Kuroda 1979a analyzes the structure of the average rate on loans, and establishes that there is arbitrage between loan rates and the free rates on the open market, such as gensaki and secondary bond rates. On this basis, he criticized Hamada et al. 1976, who emphasize stickiness of the loan rate.

medium-term (two- to four-year) bonds is higher than the rates on five-year investment trusts and money trusts. Market rates on outstanding bonds exceed subscriber yields on new bonds.

One aspect of this dual structure of interest rates is that the free rates apply to large-unit transactions which have relatively lower transactions costs than controlled rate transactions that are usually done in small units. This factor alone, however, cannot explain the large interest differentials, particularly in times of tight money. These differentials must be viewed as the effects of the artificially low interest rate policy in effect for so long in the postwar years.

b. The Limits of Reduction of Financial Costs.   The artificially low interest rate policy was responsible for the dual structure of Japanese interest rates, but there are doubts about whether it actually lowered the financial burdens on firms and promoted exports and investment, as it was originally intended to do. These doubts arise because the effective loan rates paid by firms to private financial institutions were not so low, once compensating balances are considered.

Only the long and short prime lending rates were de facto included in the controlled rate structure, while other lending rates were free. Research by I. Kuroda (1979a) shows a substantial arbitrage relation between the loan rate on the one hand and the money market and secondary bond market rates on the other. For example, even when the prime rate and the deposit rates, which are controlled rates, were lowered, the general rate on loans would not necessarily fall, due to arbitrage between it and the free rates in the markets.

On the other hand, it is undeniable that stated loan rates were lower than the free market rates. Loan conditions, however, are not limited to the stated rate on the loans, but are rather determined from a long-range, comprehensive perspective that takes into account other important conditions such as average compensating balances, foreign exchange transaction fee payments, and collateral.[6] Judging from the facts about these freely determined loan conditions, the *effective* loan rates do not appear to have been sufficiently low to promote exports or investment.

An attempt at estimation of effective loan rates was made in Suzuki 1966, as an estimate of the marginal profitability of bank loans. This is shown more clearly in Suzuki 1974. According to these estimates, effective loan rates in the 1964–73 period of high growth fluctuated between 8 and 12 percent for city banks, 9 and 13 percent for local banks, and 11 and 15 percent for credit co-ops. These levels were well above those envisioned by the artificially low interest rate policy. Moreover, the compensating balances that raised effective rates were not limited to obvious,

---

6. On the topic of maximization of long-term profits by banks and borrowers based on long-term customer relationships, see Wakita 1981 and Iwao Kuroda 1979b.

contractual practices such as *buzumi* or *ryoodate*[7] deposits, but were also part of voluntary, rational behavior of those in long-term customer relationships.[8]

Even though the artificially low interest rate policy was not successful in reducing effective interest rates once compensating balances are included, it did reduce financial costs in two ways. First, government financial institutions lent funds long term at stated interest rates well below those of private institutions, and this stimulated investment. Since of course compensating deposits were not a factor in government lending, the effective loan rates were quite low. Second, the Bank of Japan's priority discounting of export bills lowered the financial costs of exporting.[9]

c. Excess Protection of Private Financial Intermediaries. Even though artificial control of interest rates failed to lower financial costs very much, interest rate control did have a major effect of protecting private financial institutions that performed indirect finance. This was most likely the means by which the artificially low interest rate policy promoted growth. In a system of direct finance, only firms with established reputations can issue securities. Financial judgments have an inexorable tendency to become conservative. But in a system of indirect finance, based on long-term customer relations, one principle of behavior is to support medium and small firms with latent growth potential. Thus, the protection of private financial intermediaries through the controlled interest rate system gave the institutions a cushion, enabled support of high-potential firms, and thus did promote high growth.

Protection of private intermediaries through interest rate controls was extremely thorough. We can see in figure 1.1 that the interest rates available on assets held by the general populace, from deposits to investment trusts to subscribers' yields on bonds, were systematically included among controlled rates. From the first half of the 1960s, consumer price inflation exceeded these interest rates. This happened because participation in the free rate markets such as the repurchase and secondary bond markets was impossible, except for firms and for individuals with extremely large investments.

---

7. A *buzumi* deposit is a percentage (often about 5 percent) of the value of a discounted trade bill kept by the discounting bank in a regular (lowest interest) deposit account as insurance against default or to raise the effective rate of discount. A *ryoodate* deposit is similar, but is usually levied against the value of a loan collateralized by a bill, and is kept in a time (higher interest) deposit account.

8. Suzuki 1974, chapter 3, section 2.1, "Kashidashi shijoo" (The Loan Market), shows that corporations hold about 25 percent of the value of loans as deposits, independent of the usual three motives for holding money. These deposits are not coerced, but rather are voluntary and based on the long-term customer relationships as pointed out in Wakita 1981.

9. Suzuki 1981, chapter 1, discusses these historical turning points and their economic implications.

The private institutions that engaged in indirect finance obtained controls on rates paid on their liabilities, such as deposits and financial debentures; they were controlled on the asset side only on rates on new bonds and prime loans, however, and nonprime loans, which comprised their main business, were not rate-controlled. Moreover, even the controlled rates on new bonds and prime loans were always fixed spreads above those on deposits and financial debentures. In addition, the effective rates on corporate bonds and local government bonds were effectively raised by compensating balances of the borrower or issuer; hence they were substantially higher than stated rates. And national government bonds underwritten by the syndicate caused no squeeze on profits, since three-quarters of them were repurchased after only one year by the Bank of Japan, to provide "growth money" to the economy.

Hence, the private financial institutions could buy funds in a controlled market and sell them in a free one; barring spectacular bankruptcies or scandals, they had a good thing going.

II. Loss of Basis for the Low Rate Policy

1. End of Export and Investment–Led High Growth

However, the world had changed by 1973, because of two major historical transformations. The first was the change in the international monetary system, with the Nixon shocks of August 1971 and the switch to floating exchange rates by major countries in February and March of 1973. The result was the destruction of the two pillars of the Bretton Woods system, the gold exchange standard and fixed (but adjustable) exchange rates. This international monetary system had been supported by the overwhelming economic superiority of the United States; now, the economic emergence of West Germany and Japan signaled multilateralization of economic power.

From Japan's viewpoint this was a historical watershed, symbolizing completion of its metamorphosis in status from semi-industrial nation to full industrial nation. The last spurt of postwar high growth was completed, and with it the process of catching up with the West in industrialization and modernization—a process going back a hundred years to the Meiji Restoration. The implications of this change for economic policy were tremendous. A semi-industrialized country may be ignored when it pursues export-led growth with barriers to internationalization. But a fully industrialized nation, such as Japan had become, cannot.

The second historical transformation was wrought by the oil shocks of 1973 and 1979. Throughout the postwar high-growth period, Japan saw almost continuous improvement in its terms of trade. Innovations in oil extraction technique and petrochemical technology made possible low-

Table 1.1. The Marginal Capital Coefficient

	1956–60	1961–66	1967–70	1971–75	
Series A*	0.9	1.0	1.2	1.6	
			1969–72	1973–76	1977–80
Series B†			1.5	1.9	2.4

*Calculated from production function in Bank of Japan 1981a.
†Calculated from production function in Bank of Japan 1981b.

cost production of synthetic resins, fibers, and rubber. This put pressure on the markets for steel, nonferrous metals, natural fibers, and artificial rubber, and generated a downward trend in the prices of their raw materials versus the prices of industrial products. Japan, a country with few raw materials, was thus able to develop intermediate materials and equipment industries (steel, nonferrous metals, petrochemicals, textiles, paper, and pulp) that used ever-cheaper raw materials intensively along Japan's Pacific coast, and this new investment-led high growth was able to continue.

But OPEC's large increase in the price of crude oil changed the pattern dramatically. Now Japan's terms of trade began worsening, and the materials-processing industries, which use imported raw materials intensively, lost comparative advantage and fell into structural recession. In their place, high value-added assembly industries gained comparative advantage. But these industries do not use heavy equipment, and hence they do not have the power to be demand leaders for an investment boom generating high growth.

Moreover, on the supply side, the two large hikes in crude oil prices raised the marginal capital coefficient; thus, even though the savings rate remained high, the warranted rate of growth of the Harrod-Domar framework fell.[10] Even in the late 1960s, due to investments in pollution abatement and to energy-saving or materials-saving investments that were not immediately tied to productivity increases, Japan's marginal capital coefficient was steadily rising. The explosion in energy-saving investment after the two crude oil price hikes spurred this tendency. Table 1.1 shows Bank of Japan estimates of marginal capital coefficient.

Let us consider this problem from the point of view of the neoclassical theory of the firm.[11] Let us assume that the aggregate production function for an industrial country such as Japan has three factors of production: labor, capital, and imported energy. Now let the price of imported energy rise substantially. In order to reduce the cost increases this generates,

10. The warranted rate of growth is the savings rate divided by the marginal capital coefficient. For an exposition of Harrod-Domar growth theory, see Harrod 1948.

11. Articles that analyze the effects of an oil price hike on the economy from a theoretical viewpoint include Sachs 1979 and 1980, Bruno 1981, Bruno and Sachs 1979 and 1981, and Sachs and Lipton 1981.

firms will substitute relatively cheaper labor and capital for imported energy. With constant technology, the law of diminishing returns says that the marginal products of capital and labor must therefore decline. However, unless the real wage and real rate of interest also decline simultaneously and proportionally, these returns to factors will exceed their marginal products, and both employment and investment will be restrained. Hence, supply of industrial products will not be in equilibrium.

The above analysis is static, but the dynamic analysis is similar. The growth rate of capacity to supply industrial output will fall unless there is (*a*) an increase in the speed of energy saving and labor- or capital-augmenting technical progress, (*b*) a slowdown in the rate of increase of real wages, or (*c*) a fall of the long-term real interest rate.

In Japan, real wages are relatively flexible, and so real wage growth declines when the labor market softens; hence, there is the possibility of recovery of GNP growth. However, experience heretofore suggests that the speed of technical progress and the long-term real interest rate do not change so easily. And, even if they do change, the changes take time. But until they change, the downward kink in growth caused by an oil shock continues to be felt.[12]

A transitional factor constraining supply is the effect of changes in industrial structure, mentioned in reference to the demand side. That is, the structure of demand changes as relative prices of industrial products adjust to reflect the rise in oil prices. Hence, the structure of labor and capital on the supply side is in the process of change, but this takes time since mobility of labor and capital among sectors is low. In the interim, labor and capital are idle in industries in structural recession. The overall efficiency of the economy falls, the marginal capital coefficient rises, and supply capacity falls.

This framework shows us how the conditions on both demand and supply sides that underlay high growth in the years before 1973 were destroyed, and that the decline in GNP growth from 1974 is a reality very difficult to reverse.

2. New Historical Conditions

We have now seen that the Nixon shocks and the oil crises made change unavoidable in Japan's postwar growth strategy of export/investment-led high growth with barriers to internationalization.

What, then, has been the economic strategy since 1974? It is not at all clear. But no matter whether an economic strategy exists, the new his-

---

12. Suzuki 1981, chapter 4, section 1 treats the changes in Japanese financial structure accompanying lower growth and internationalization. Discussion here is limited to the bare essentials and based on figure 7.1. Interested readers are referred to Suzuki 1981 for details.

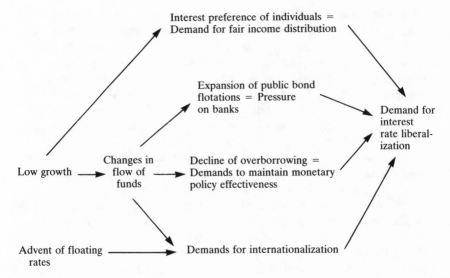

Figure 1.2. Destruction of Foundation of the Artificially Low Interest Rate Policy

torical conditions do mean that Japan must face two new realities—low growth and internationalization.

Figure 1.2 shows the reasons that these new realities require liberalization of interest rates; it clearly demonstrates that the artificially low interest rate policy has lost its historical foundation. Let us now consider these causal factors in order.

a. Financial Aspects of Low Growth. First and foremost of the financial aspects of low growth is the change in the direction of the flow of funds. Since corporate investment was the leading factor behind high growth, the share of corporate investment in GNP was extremely high. Although the share of the corporate sector in income distribution was not at all low, the investment share in GNP was so high that retained profits and depreciation (corporate saving) could not cover corporate investment. Hence, the corporate sector generated a tremendous excess investment (implying a deficit of funds). The savings surplus of the household sector was transferred almost totally to the corporate sector, and the deficits of the government and external sectors were small. With the predominance of indirect finance, this flow-of-funds structure necessarily led to overborrowing.[13]

13. For an account of the origins of "supremacy of indirect finance," "overborrowing,"

But in a period of low growth, the share of investment in GNP falls. As Harrod-Domar–style growth theory teaches, a fall in the growth rate requires a fall in corporate investment (unless the marginal capital co-efficient rises), and as a result the deficit of the corporate sector shrinks. With other factors unchanged, there is now an overall savings surplus in the nation, and the economy slows. With other factors unchanged, there is now an overall savings surplus in the nation, and the economy slows. To replace investment, the government share of GNP rises, meaning expansion of the deficit (i.e., excess investment) in the public sector.

Figure 1.3 shows the movements of these sectoral deficits and surpluses on a quarterly basis. Before 1973, the deficit of the corporate sector was overwhelming. But its share peaked in the first half of 1974, and public-sector deficits replaced it. The public-sector deficit peaked in early 1978, running at an annual rate of ¥20 trillion, whereas the corporate-sector deficit barely reached ¥1 trillion. After 1978, however, firms finished their adaptation to low growth through economization measures, and investment gradually recovered. The corporate sector's savings deficit has expanded, and hit ¥12 trillion in 1982. This is equivalent to about three-fifths of the public-sector deficit. Though tax revenue may recover and fiscal restructuring may lower expenditure, reducing the public-sector deficit below the corporate deficit will not be easy as long as low growth continues.

As we saw in figure 1.2, these alterations in flow of funds have generated three changes. The first is large-scale flotation of public bonds to finance the public-sector deficits. The subscribers' yields on these new bonds have been kept within the controlled rate structure of the artificially low interest rate policy. As will be seen below, this has put major pressure on bank profits; it also is a factor working toward elimination of the artificially low interest rate policy itself.

Second, as the corporate-sector deficit shrank, overborrowing subsided, and corporate liquidity rose. As a result, as shown in detail in chapter 4, there are now limits to the effectiveness of monetary policy based on controls, and this situation has brought demands for increasing the importance of interest rates. Here, too, the artificially low interest rate policy has lost its basis.

Third, flow-of-funds changes have brought demands for financial internationalization, and maintenance of the controlled rate structure through barriers to internationalization is becoming difficult. This topic is treated below in section II.2.b.

One final financial aspect of the fall of growth is the increased preference on the part of the public for high-yielding assets. The tempo of

and other special characteristics of the Japanese financial structure in the high-growth period, see Suzuki 1974, section 1 (chapters 1 to 4).

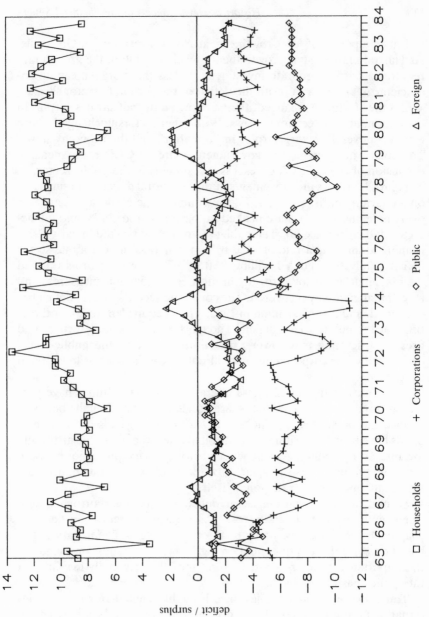

Figure 1.3. Sectoral Net Investment (Deficit) and Net Savings (Surplus) as a Percentage of GNP

□ Households + Corporations ◇ Public △ Foreign

14

asset accumulation by the public during the high-growth era was determined for the most part by the double-digit wage increases every year. But as the growth rate fell, wage hikes fell to single-digit levels, and, since people had already accumulated substantial levels of assets, they became sensitive to interest rates, particularly to real rates (i.e., nominal rates less the inflation rate). As a result, there was criticism, on grounds of fairness of income distribution, of artificially controlling rates on deposits, trusts, and subscriber yields, since such controls generate losses for creditors and gains for debtors. For example, there were arguments, which even went to court, on diminution of deposit value and reckless investment by banks. Recent controversy about postal savings deposits also reflects these arguments. These factors also make difficult the continuation of the artificially low interest rate policy's controlled interest rates. In a world of free interest rates, the rates on deposits, trusts, and so forth could of course be the expected inflation rates plus a spread (the Fisher effect), and hence would not decline in real value *ex ante*. Thus the spread, that is, the real interest rate, would be guaranteed.[14]

b. Demand for Internationalization. Financial internationalization was another of the historical factors making continuation of the controlled interest-rate policy difficult.

There is no point to detailed repetition of reasons that Japan, as an advanced country, should have an open economy. Without an open economy, Japan would be ostracized by other advanced nations, and the Japanese economy itself would become unviable. On the financial side, there are at least three requirements for internationalization. As seen in figure 1.2, these requirements derive from both flow-of-funds and from the exchange rate system.

First, due to the changes in flow of funds, banks have been faced with decline in loan demand from domestic corporations. Hence, the search for good borrowers has brought expansion into foreign markets, an expansion led by larger banks such as city banks, long-term credit banks, and trust banks. At first the banks concentrated on loans to local subsidiaries of Japanese firms in foreign countries, but they soon diversified into general international intermediation. Activity is becoming brisk in all kinds of international intermediation, including offshore (foreign-to-foreign) transactions, foreign-to-domestic transactions (such as impact loans), and domestic-to-foreign transactions (e.g., flotation of yen-denominated bonds by foreigners). Under these circumstances, it is only natural that there be stronger demands for liberalization of money and bond markets to levels seen in developed Western nations, and for easing of restrictions on transactions.

14. Empirical studies demonstrating the Fisher effect (see Fisher 1930) in Japan include Oritani 1979 and Akio Kuroda 1982, chapter 7.

Second, the functioning of the floating rate system itself requires internationalization of finance. Contrary to practice under the fixed-rate system, the Bank of Japan does not intervene in exchange markets except in smoothing operations to prevent volatile fluctuations. In principle, the Bank of Japan does not buy and sell foreign exchange in response to the day-to-day deficits and surpluses in the spot market that reflect each day's overall balance of transactions. As a result, the spot market reflects the daily demand and supply conditions, and it generates pressures pushing the yen up and down.

Moreover, a forward rate is established on the basis of expectations of market participants; when the actual rate diverges from this, speculative transactions bring the actual rate back to the expected level. In other words, as long as expectations are stable, the forward rate is also stable.

Thus, we see that the spot rate moves to reflect the overall balance. As a result, the spot-forward spread fluctuates, since the forward rate is stable. Let us assume that a shortage of exchange in the spot market weakens the yen, meaning the forward yen is at a premium, and that the spread exceeds the sum of the interest rate differential between Japan and foreign markets plus transactions costs. In this situation, there is the opportunity for a safe and certain bet.

First, an investor may borrow foreign exchange abroad, say for three months, and then sell this foreign exchange in the domestic spot market (which is short of foreign exchange). The yen proceeds of this sale are then invested in domestic financial markets (gensaki, CD, bill markets, etc.), say for three months. Simultaneously, the investor sells yen in the forward market. Once the transactions are settled three months hence, there is a safe, sure profit of exactly the excess of the yen premium over the sum of the interest differential and transaction costs.

In this fashion, the floating rate system will always absorb the day-to-day imbalances in international payments through interest arbitrage and swap transactions. In other words, without interest rate liberalization and relaxation of controls to levels equivalent to those of foreign nations, the interest rate arbitrage and swap transactions that link the four relevant markets (domestic and foreign money markets, and the spot and forward exchange markets) will not operate smoothly, and the floating rate system will not function properly.[15]

A third force for internationalization of Japanese financial markets is the rise of foreign demand for yen as a store of value, based on Japan's economic performance after the second oil shock. The OPEC nations, accumulating oil money, began raising the proportion of their assets held

15. For a description of swap arbitrage transactions and the role of swaps in the functioning of the floating rate system, see Suda and Komiya 1980 and Suzuki 1981, chapter 3, section 1.4.

in yen just after the second oil crisis, and monetary authorities of advanced nations and multinational firms have done so more recently. But because Japan's money and bond markets remain underdeveloped, there are difficulties in investing these funds, for instance problems in finding appropriate assets as well as in the functioning of interest rates. International demand for relaxation of restrictions on interest rates and transactions, and especially for development of a government bill market, is strengthening.

III. Emerging Conflicts in the Financial System

1. The Danger of Financial Socialism

We have seen that new historical developments have eroded the foundation of the artificially low interest rate policy, but that it nevertheless continues its influence in the form of a dual structure of interest rates. How is this to be explained?

First, everyone realizes that the suppression of interest rates by the artificially low interest rate policy was a link in the basic strategy of investment/export-led growth, and that this strategy has lost its raison d'être with the changes in historical conditions. We saw above how the intent to lower financial costs and promote export and investment was achieved through the two methods of low rate financing by government intermediaries and Bank of Japan priority discount of export bills. Moreover, protection of indirect finance through controlled interest rates promoted growth by supporting firms with strong potential.

But the Bank of Japan's export bill system ceased to perform its historical role long ago and in fact became a hindrance to international cooperation; this system was abolished in the early 1970s. On the other hand, cheap financing by government financial institutions was between 16 and 17 percent of total indirect finance in the high growth era; its share increased rapidly after 1974. By 1980, this share stood at 36 percent. Table 2.1 in chapter 2 shows the enlargement of public intermediation.

If the enlargement of artificially low interest financing by government institutions continues, then the business of financial intermediation in Japan will be led by government institutions that will have gained an oligopolistic position. This would amount to socialism in financial markets.[16] There are at least three problems with this.

First, it will harm the efficiency of funds allocation and squeeze the private economy, which is the source of the nation's vitality. Originally, the role of public institutions was to fund economic activity that was not

16. Iwao Kuroda 1981 was the first to point out the danger of "socialism in financial markets."

covered by private institutions based on market principles but was desirable for the national economy as a whole. Now that the nation has completed its investment/export-led high growth and achieved advanced-country status, the areas requiring protection and incubation ought to be on the decline, and certainly not on the increase. In spite of this, the large, sudden increase in the share of public intermediation shows that private finance is being pressured. This is particularly obvious in public investment and finance, which are the core of activity of the public financial institutions. The unused portions of public investment and finance budgets (3.7 percent in 1977, 9.7 percent in 1978, and 4.0 percent in 1979) reflect this. And examples of competition between private and public intermediaries on specific investment projects could fill many volumes.

From the point of view of private corporations and individuals who borrow, the squeeze of private financial institutions means that less funding will be granted on the basis of the borrower's ability to repay from expected income or corporate earnings (i.e., efficiency of the investment project), and more funding will be granted on the basis of the government's policy goals. This is an attempt to bring socialism to the general economy through finance, and it would foolishly strangle the market economy.

Second, expansion of public intermediation threatens the effectiveness of monetary policy. Public financial activity is supposed to take place in areas that the market principle has difficulty permeating, and hence monetary policy working through interest rates would not affect these areas; they are also exempted from credit controls. However, once the area to which public institutions lend expands, the effectiveness of monetary policy will clearly be reduced. And on top of this, if the decline in effectiveness is resisted, then the burden of adjustment on private institutions will only become heavier, inviting a vicious cycle of further declines in the private share of financing.

The third problem is the decline in fiscal discipline. For example, the excessive funds now in public intermediaries are seeking outlets. This situation has invited an accumulation of short-term loans extended past the end of the fiscal year from the Trust Fund Bureau to off-budget accounts of the government. Short lending past fiscal year end by the Trust Fund Bureau to the revenue-sharing (*koofu zei*) account, the welfare insurance (*koosei hoken*) account, and so forth reached ¥9.1 trillion by year-end 1980, equivalent to 9.1 percent of Trust Fund Bureau financing. However, even though these funds are called "short-term loans," they are in fact permanent bad loans financing the accumulated deficits of these accounts. It is clear that this trend represents a degradation of the quality of the portfolio of public financial institutions. Moreover, the practice hides the existence of the fiscal deficits from the eyes of the populace, and is nothing but fiscal lassitude and loss of discipline.

To resolve the problems posed by the bloating of public intermediation, the entire stance of public finance, which is based on inertia from the artificially low interest rate policy, must be reexamined. A new accommodation between public and private finance is needed to ensure that the former only augments the latter. Public funding should be restricted to those areas that cannot obtain funding from private sources, and for the present these excess demands should be covered through continued large flotations of public bonds. In the longer term, the postal savings system, which is the source of excess public funding currently, should be reformed to put it on an entirely and thoroughly equal footing with private financial institutions.[17]

2. Profit Pressure on Private Institutions

Let us now consider another aspect of the low interest rate policy: the overprotection of private financial institutions. The profits of private institutions are being lowered not only by the expansion of public intermediaries but also by the controlled interest rate structure that is supposed to protect them. That is, the artificially low interest rate policy puts a dual squeeze on the private institutions.

a. Pressure on the Underwriting Syndicate. I have described above how flotation of public bonds during the high growth period was done at artificially low rates not reflective of market conditions; these bonds were absorbed by private financial institutions through an underwriting syndicate. And even after the era of large-scale flotations began, the system has been maintained in principle. But what was possible during the high-growth era is not necessarily reasonable under today's different conditions.

The first and foremost feature of high-growth period bond flotations was their small amounts. Moreover, in the case of central government bonds, about three-fourths were repurchased by the Bank of Japan after a year outstanding, as part of the bank's provision of currency to accommodate the higher demand for money that accompanied growth. Moreover, the repurchase price was set at a level such that the original purchasers would never suffer losses on the bonds. In fact, long-term bonds were extremely liquid after a year, and hence the interest rates earned on them were not at all low. In the case of local bonds, the issuing bodies were major depositors in the banks that purchased the bonds. If we think of local bond underwriting as a type of deposit-secured lending, then the interest rates were not low.

17. This author's attitude toward the postal savings problem is given in Suzuki 1981, chapter 4, section 1. Moreover, I believe the recommendations of the Seisaku Koosoo Fooramu (The Forum for Policy Innovation), including elimination of the Fiscal Investment and Loan Program, are entirely appropriate.

In summary, underwriting of public bonds during the high-growth period by the syndicate under the low interest rate policy was not, for the members of the syndicate, a source of adverse pressure, from the viewpoint of either liquidity or profit.

However, after 1975, the amounts of public bonds floated increased tremendously. Ironically, this occurred just at the time that the Bank of Japan reduced its repurchases of bonds, to reflect the lower growth of the economy. The lion's share of bonds underwritten by the syndicate accumulated in the portfolios of financial institutions, causing severe liquidity pressure. Since the bonds were underwritten at artificially low rates, selling them in the market would almost certainly result in capital losses and lower profits. Moreover, the Bank of Japan's bond repurchase system changed to a bid system in 1978, so even these transactions could yield losses to syndicate members. And local bonds became hard to view as deposit-secured loans, since local authorities' needs for financing expanded and reduced the ratio of deposits to flotations. Local bonds resembled national ones in that liquidation in the market could result in capital losses that lowered profits.[18]

These pressures on financial institutions appear to be reaching their limit. The symbol of this limit has been the periodic refusal of the syndicate, beginning with two cases in June–August 1981 and in July 1982, to underwrite bonds for the government. The yield to subscribers offered was too low relative to market rates, and the syndicate insisted on an increase. In these cases, no agreement could be reached.

b. Pressure on Controlled Rates. The movement to interest rates that reflect market conditions is not limited to underwriting of public bonds by the syndicate. It is unfortunate that problems with controlled rates are not fully recognized even by some executives of private financial intermediaries, who have a tendency to think that all would be well if controlled rates were adhered to as before. But in fact, the controlled interest rate structure that once protected private financial intermediaries during the

18. Suzuki 1981, chapter 4, section 1.3 includes the following rough calculation on the profit squeeze caused by public bond underwriting. In 1980, the total value of bonds underwritten by syndicate members was 42 percent of the total increase in deposits in that year. Purchases of bonds by the Bank of Japan were only 10 percent of the total underwritten. To avoid liquidity problems, about 40 percent of the total underwritten would have to be sold to nonfinancial institutions and agents. Liquidation losses on these would come to about 10 or 20 percent of operating profits. Moreover, bonds held by the banks are accumulating, and continuing to pressure both profits and liquidity of financial institutions. The data on private financial institutions' portfolio composition (stock basis) show that public bonds were 5.6 percent of total funds at year-end 1973, with central government bonds 1.3 percent. By year-end 1979, these numbers had risen to 15.2 percent and 7.4 percent, respectively. Akio Kuroda 1982, chapters 1–8, gives details of the accumulations of public bonds in the hands of financial institutions that has accompanied the rise in quantities issued and decline in quantities repurchased by the Bank of Japan.

high-growth era has become the source of three problems for them over and above the syndicate underwriting problem mentioned above.

First, as we saw above, is the effect of the two-tier structure of interest rates, with the controlled rates well below the free rates. Among executives of private financial institutions, there are many who think this gap is natural, since controlled rates apply to small transactions and free rates to large ones. And it is true that the unit-transaction costs differ for large and small transactions, *and to this extent*, an interest rate gap is natural.

But let us consider the case of funds from "small," three- or six-month fixed-term deposits, handled on-line, by computers. When these funds are reinvested in call, bill, repurchase, or CD markets immediately, what are the unit transactions costs? Probably below 0.5 percent. But for argument's sake let us double this to 1 percent. In this case, an intermediary could keep its three- or six-month term-deposit rates (such term deposits correspond to money market certificates or small savers' certificates in the United States) a bit more than 1.0 percent below money market rates and secure a profit on the spread. Such accounts would be extremely popular in Japan. We know they would because, as in figure 1.1, the rates on these hypothetical accounts would be about 5.5 percent, much above the actual rates on three- and six-month fixed-term deposits—which are 3.75 percent and 5.0 percent, respectively. (These rates as of June 1983.) The same is true of funds gathered from one- or two-year term deposits, financial debentures, or money and loan trusts, when these are compared to rates in money markets and the secondary bond market.

In light of this, there is no doubt that the spreads between current controlled rates and free rates are above the levels of cost differentials. In other words, the private financial intermediaries are earning both latent and actual excess profits (latent excess profits in the form of unexploited profits from X-inefficiencies).[19]

The reason such new deposits have not appeared is, of course, that they have been suppressed by financial regulations. However, as we saw in section II.2 and figure 1.2, the populace's preference for high yields is strengthening. The existence of excess profits for banks, which imply unfair income distribution, will not be permitted forever.

In fact, there is a gradual spread of trends destructive of these excess profits. Corporations, pension funds, wealthy individuals, and other such holders of large amounts of assets are reducing holdings of fixed-term deposits, new financial debentures, and trust accounts, and raising holdings of money market instruments (CDs, repurchases, discounted trade bills) and secondary market bonds. Even in the general populace, indi-

---

19. The term "unexploited profits" includes not only latent excess profits but also latent unrealized profits in the form of inefficiencies in the firm. Such latent unrealized profits are called "X-inefficiencies."

viduals knowledgeable about finance are increasing purchases of medium-term bonds and secondary market bonds.

And this is not all. The medium-term bond funds (*chuuki kokusai fando*) of securities firms, even though their interest rates are held a bit lower than market rates by official guidance, are in essence market-rate type deposits, of the nature of money market mutual funds in the United States. Shift of funds from deposits to market-rate funds of securities firms is gradually but steadily progressing.

The private financial intermediaries must eventually realize that small leaks sink great ships. Funds are fleeing from the world of safe, excess profits under controlled rates to the world of free rates, and the speed of this movement is accelerating. Indeed, as we saw in table 2.3 in chapter 2, the share of indirect finance has been declining since 1975.

A second problem with the two-tier structure of interest rates is that the maladjustments between controlled and free rates become acute in times of tight money. This is because in times of tight money the short free rates for the period over which tightness is forecast remain above the long free rates; on the other hand, the short controlled rates always remain below long controlled rates, even in times of tightness. The gaps between free and controlled rates at both short and medium maturities can become extremely wide. Figure 1.4 shows yield curves for free rates (secondary national bond yields) and controlled rates in periods of easy money (March 1979) and tight money (March 1980). As is well known, the free short rates (three- to six-month rates in call, CD, and repurchase markets) in the period of tight money rose to 13 or 14 percent, while the controlled short rates remained at only 6 to 7 percent levels. But the figure also shows that free rates at the two- to five-year maturity rose to the 9 to 11 percent range while controlled rates were around 7 percent, a gap of 2 to 4 percent.

Recent research shows that the yield curve of free rates in Japan can be explained almost entirely by expectations theory.[20] Expectations theory states that long-term rates are equal to a weighted average of the current short rate and expected short rates over the period in question. This is based on the idea that the long rate is determined by equalization (for both borrowers and lenders) of returns no matter whether funds are invested long term or as a series of rolled-over short-term investments. So long as people act rationally, any gap between the long rate and the average of concatenated short rates will be extinguished as lenders lend

20. The excellent research of Kuroda and Ohkubo 1981 and Akio Kuroda 1982 analyzes in detail the term structure of free interest rates from the viewpoint of expectations theory, and shows that the term structure in Japan, which appears somewhat special at first glance, can in fact be explained by that theory. Older research using expectations theory is rare, but Inagaki 1974 is an example.

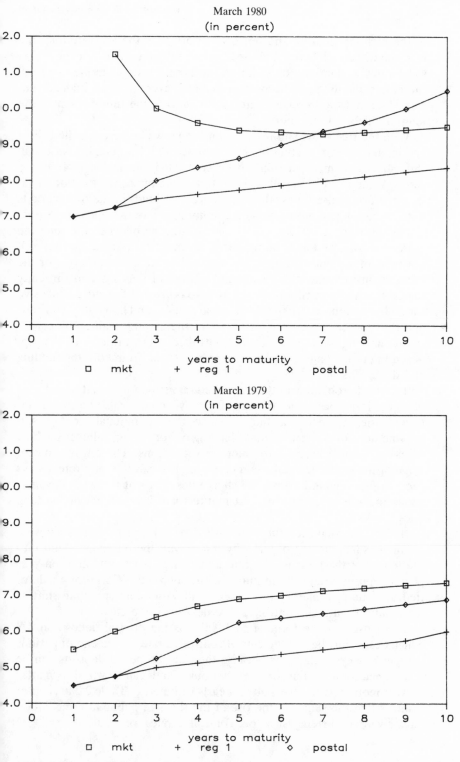

Figure 1.4. Yield Curves of Free and Controlled Rates

in the high-rate market and borrowers borrow in the low-rate one; the low rate will certainly rise and the high rate fall. Since people expect high short rates to continue only during the period of tight money and fall thereafter, the long rate becomes a weighted average of the high current short rate and the lower expected short rates of the future. Hence, the long rate is below the short.

With the free short and medium rates high while the controlled short and medium rates are still low, what will occur? Of course, investors will shift short and medium funds from controlled-rate assets to free-rate assets, while borrowers will seek to shift in the opposite direction. That is, when firms raise funds, they will leave own-funds in the free markets to the greatest extent possible and attempt to borrow as much as possible at the short prime rate, which is controlled. And between the time the funds are borrowed and the time they are used for purchases, they will not be kept as deposits but rather invested in the free markets. For the financial institutions, this means an outflow of deposits and difficulty raising funds; the institutions are forced to borrow in the more expensive call, bill, and repurchase markets, to call in loans and liquidate securities, and thus to bear losses proportionate to the earnings gained by corporations shifting funds. Though the controlled interest rate system is supposed to protect banks, it is in fact harming them, from both the funding and the profits sides.

The third problem with the controlled rate structure is that its Johnny-one-note insistence on an upward-sloping yield curve also harms the intermediaries. Expectations theory teaches that the rational agent considers whether, for a given length of lending or borrowing, rollover of short loans or a single long loan is more advantageous. The always-upward slope of the controlled rate yield curve implies that the long rate always exceeds the weighted average of short rates. Thus, it is always advantageous to raise funds in the short markets and invest them in the long ones.

In fact, the deposit composition of financial intermediaries shows a continuous lengthening of maturity. Moreover, there is even a shift into the longer of the long assets—that is, into five-year trusts and ten-year postal deposits—rather than into two-year deposits. (Corporations have fled into the free market rate assets, and so no corresponding shift to long maturity in their controlled rate deposits has occurred.)

The most extreme form of such shifts is the "postal deposit shift," which occurs just before the cuts of controlled rates at the end of periods of tight money. It happens because the rates on postal deposits can be guaranteed for up to ten years, even though funds can be withdrawn after only six months, with no penalty for early withdrawal. Table 2.3 in chapter 2 shows that the stages in the rise of the share of public intermediation have always occurred just before controlled rates were cut.

On the fund-raising side, there is a general trend in which borrowing from private financial institutions is composed increasingly of rollover of short loans, with the weight of long loans declining.

In summary, the controlled interest rate structure ignores economic rationality and has become a source of lowered earnings for private financial intermediaries.

3. A New Mix of Direct and Indirect Finance

The controlled interest rate structure based on the artificially low interest rate policy protected the private financial institutions engaged in indirect finance, and played a role in promoting high growth. But the controlled interest rate structure has become a drag on performance. On the other hand, the securities firms responsible for direct finance are displaying great vitality as dealers in open markets such as the repurchase and secondary bond markets. Given the new historical conditions, will indirect finance wane and direct finance wax?

Matters are not so simple. We must not forget that both direct and indirect finance have special functions in a financial system. Indirect finance contributes to growth of medium-sized and small companies because it raises customers from small to large size in a bilateral relationship. Small, innovative firms are not rare, even today. Indirect finance is best suited to long-term customer relationships based on bilateral transactions, and direct finance is best suited to market transactions done independently with the general public. This means that indirect finance can be carried out in either large or small transactions, but that direct finance is restricted for the most part to large transactions.

However, the types of financial transactions required by the new stage of the Japanese economy are mostly large, market-type transactions. Demands for financial internationalization are an example. International interest rate arbitrage, syndicated loans, bond flotations, and monetary authorities' investment of foreign exchange reserves are all elements of wholesale banking for large domestic and foreign banks, or are lending or borrowing activities of large corporations or public bodies. Even domestically, continued large-scale issuing of national bonds is done in lots much larger than that of corporate or financial debentures. Moreover, the own-capital of corporations is expanding, thus increasing the need for large-scale investing services.

Unless the Japanese financial system can incorporate the demands for large-scale financial transactions, it cannot meet the demands of the new era. To this end, it is necessary to develop further places for direct finance to occur, such as open money markets and bond markets. The hindrances to this development are controls on subscriber yields on Ministry of Finance bills and long-term bonds, that is, controls based on the old artificially low interest rate policy. If determination of these yields is left to demand and supply conditions in the market, the development of a financial market suitable to the new era will be guaranteed.

This does not deny a role for the private institutions engaged in indirect finance. But it will be desirable for private intermediaries and securities firms to cooperate in developing large-scale markets. And there is also a need for active promotion of development of new types of deposits and mutual funds to intermediate between free-rate, large-unit markets and bilateral, small-unit transactions.

Such developments are not at all disadvantageous to private financial intermediaries engaged in indirect finance. In fact, they constitute an excellent chance to increase opportunities for new types of intermediation by using development of large-unit transactions in both long and short markets. For example, city banks, long-term credit banks, and trust banks can actively develop wholesale banking that spans domestic and foreign markets. Local banks, mutual banks, and credit co-ops can actively develop new types of market-oriented products, and, by tie-ups with securities firms engaged in direct finance, expand small-unit financial intermediation.

The current situation is actually a golden opportunity, particularly today when asset accumulation by individuals and firms is rising and preference for high yields is strengthening. For example, as seen above, a new type of fixed-term asset could be entirely invested in repurchases, CDs, medium-term bonds, and secondary market long-term bonds, and still pay the depositor a rate above current fixed-term or trust accounts. Combining this with a regular deposit account would be very attractive. Financial innovations in the United States can serve as a veritable jewel box of examples of development of such new financial products.

But there is one major obstacle on the road to development of such accounts. Ironically, this obstacle is the artificially low interest rate policy, which is supposed to protect the indirect finance institutions. Free development of new financial products is unthinkable in a "four and a half mat" structure of controlled interest rates. Moreover, interest rate controls are not only preventing development of indirect finance and its coexistence with direct finance. They are also pressuring the performance of institutions engaging in the old type of indirect finance.

It will certainly not be easy to develop new links between free markets with large transactions and bilateral markets that mix large and small transactions. But if the institutions heretofore engaged in indirect finance fail to do so, then the securities firms will. The era demands new links. Thus, if one side refuses to develop them, then the other will not overlook the opportunity for business. Still, unilateral innovation on the part of securities firms is certainly not desirable, since it would unnecessarily agitate the credit system.

It is a good idea gradually to dismantle the fence between securities and banking business (Article 65 of the Securities Exchange Law) through joint business development by banks and securities firms. Both dealing and financial intermediation business on one hand and large-scale lending and bond underwriting on the other are pairs of businesses not cleanly separable. It is wisest to promote liberalization of transactions and interest rates gradually so that both banks and securities firms are on an equal footing.

In fact, the very distinction between indirect and direct finance will probably lose its meaning in the new era of liberalization, since direct finance (defined as intermediation between surplus sectors and deficit sectors through dealing in securities and underwriting by securities firms) and indirect finance (defined as intermediation by banks through deposits and loans) will be less distinguishable as securities firms and banks enter each other's businesses. Even more important, classifying types of financial intermediation on the basis of distinctions between market and bilateral transactions, transaction accounts and investment accounts, safe assets and risky assets, and so forth and then choosing an area in which to specialize is the way to adapt to the new type of management needed for today.

Liberalization of interest rates and liberalization of transactions are preconditions for all these changes. However, for small, bilateral transactions, there is a major information gap between intermediary and customer; thus, for customer protection, it is probably necessary to introduce formulae to determine interest rates on such transactions, through fixed links to market interest rates and to then establish a system of public posting of these rates.

Still, financial innovation should be promoted gradually, since the price of excessive speed will be instability in the financial system. The destination—a fully liberalized financial system—must be thoroughly discussed and prepared for, starting now.

2

Structural Changes
in the Financial System

$\mathbf{T}$his chapter surveys the actual changes since the end of the era of rapid growth in the buildup and composition of financial assets in the private nonfinancial sector, and how these changes have been linked with developments in financial markets and changes in the financial system. Section I.1 presents a survey of financial assets held by the private nonfinancial sector as ratios to GNP. I show how the buildup of such assets has accelerated since the second half of the 1970s and consider a few reasons for the acceleration. Section I.2 shows that, in the midst of this speedup in the accumulation of financial assets, in relative terms only holdings of currency and deposit money assets diminished; reasons for this are considered. Section II shows that there have been major changes since the second half of the 1970s in the composition of investment accounts—that is, in the composition of broader financial assets excluding cash and deposit money and in the underlying channels of these flows of funds. In brief, direct financing increased in relative importance and indirect financing decreased. Among financial institutions engaged in indirect financing, the market share of private deposit banks declined and that of private nondeposit banks and public sector financial intermediaries increased. Finally, section III presents an overview of these changes in financial asset selection and in the flows of funds from the standpoint of the financial system as a whole, and considers the causes of these changes. One major reason for the change is the two-tier interest rate structure with regulated rates and free market rates, and the irrational term structure of regulated rates. Section IV outlines the prospects for future developments in the financial system.

I. Changes in Speed of Asset Accumulation

1. The Recent Acceleration in the Accumulation of Financial Assets

The pace of financial asset accumulation in the private nonfinancial sector can be obtained from the Bank of Japan's Flow of Funds Tables, which show assets held by the personal sector and the nonfinancial corporate sector (hereafter "private nonfinancial sector") as well as the total year-end balances of financial assets ("gross financial asset balances"). These are shown in figure 2.1 as ratios to nominal GNP.

One feature common to all six sets of time series is the sharp upward spike in 1972. This resulted from a combination of huge current balance-of-payments surpluses in 1971–72 and the large deficits (i.e., net investment or dissaving) of the public sector that accompanied the expansionary fiscal policies of 1972–73. Both these influences came together in 1972, bringing about an enormous increase in the private nonfinancial sector's surplus (net savings). This observation can be confirmed by reference to figure 1.3 in chapter 1, which shows the trend in sectoral surpluses and deficits in relation to GNP. The private nonfinancial sector's surplus (and particularly the personal sector's surplus) rose to between 10 and 13 percent of GNP in 1972, and correspondingly the deficits of both the public sector and the overseas sector rose to between 2 and 3 percent of GNP.

The upward spike in 1972 is especially large for the ratio of gross balances as shown in figure 2.1; the relaxation of monetary policy in 1972 resulted in a huge increase in credit to the private sector from financial institutions. This increase was reflected in a simultaneous expansion of both financial assets and liabilities. This phenomenon was called "an excess liquidity situation" at the time; it became the domestic source of the Great Inflation of 1972–75.[1]

Leaving aside the upward spike in 1972, the gross balance ratio for the total nonfinancial private sector (the solid line in the upper section of figure 2.1) increased steeply until the early 1960s, then flattened until around 1970, and has subsequently risen sharply again. The ratio for the same sector on a net basis (the solid line in the lower section of figure 2.1) rose quite gently until around 1974; since then it has also risen steeply until recently.

Needless to say, the net financial balances of the private nonfinancial sector represent the accumulation of financial surpluses of that sector. Consequently, the steep rise in the net ratio after 1975, shown in the lower section of figure 2.1, means that the private nonfinancial sector

1. For a detailed analysis of the causes of the Great Inflation of 1972–75 in Japan, see Komiya and Suzuki 1977.

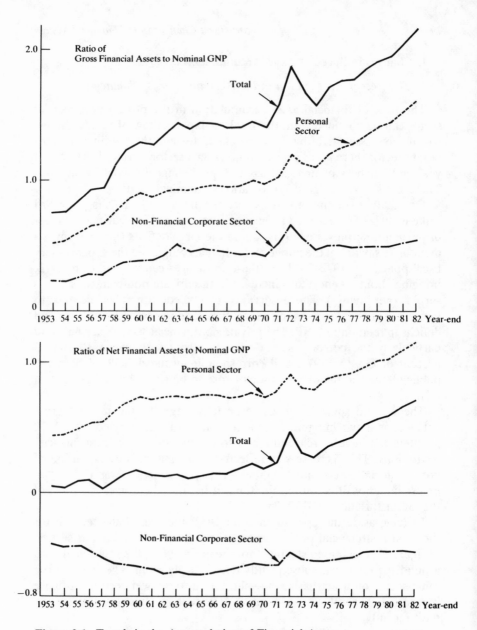

Figure 2.1. Trends in the Accumulation of Financial Assets

surpluses were increasing. This can also be seen in figure 1.3. After 1975, partly reflecting the increase in the public-sector deficit and partly reflecting the contraction in the nonfinancial corporate sector's deficit, the surplus of the whole private nonfinancial sector (including the personal sector) increased correspondingly. This dramatic change in the structure of sectoral surpluses and deficits resulted primarily from the decline in private-sector investment as a proportion of GNP (which in turn reflected the slowdown in Japan's real economic growth rate from an average of 10 percent per annum before 1973 to about 5 percent per annum subsequently); it also stemmed from the increase in the public sector's expenditure as a proportion of GNP.

The gross financial balances of the private nonfinancial sector reflect both the trends in its net financial assets described above and the trend in that part of its gross financial assets which increases in step with its financial liabilities to the financial sector. Although the net ratio (lower section of figure 2.1) rose only at a gentle pace, the gross ratio (upper section of figure 2.1) rose steeply from the early 1960s because during this period both the financial assets and liabilities of the private nonfinancial sector, especially the nonfinancial corporate sector, were increasing. In the same way, as shown in figure 2.1, the nonfinancial corporate sector's gross ratio was rising at this time despite a decline in its net ratio, on account of a simultaneous large increase in its financial assets and liabilities. At that period, which corresponds to the early part of the era of rapid economic growth, the ratio of corporate investment to GNP was still rising; the nonfinancial corporate sector's gross ratio was also rising at this time, despite a decline in its net ratio, on account of an increase in its financial assets and liabilities. In the same period, the ratio of corporate investment to GNP was still rising, and the nonfinancial corporate sector's deficit was rising steeply, as firms' dependence on external funds increased. Since securities markets in Japan were underdeveloped at that time and indirect financing was the predominant method of raising funds, most external funds for business enterprises were in the form of bank borrowings. This high degree of dependence on bank borrowing by business enterprises (called "overborrowing") meant that firms tended to maintain substantial amounts of bank deposits, and banks tended to give preferential treatment to firms with large compensating balances.[2] This explains why financial assets and liabilities in the nonfinancial corporate sector grew simultaneously.

2. A detailed description of the underdeveloped state of the securities market, the dominance of indirect financing and overborrowing, et cetera, and their causes is given in Suzuki 1980, part I. Also, according to the results of the regression analysis on p. 50 of the same book, apart from business firms' normal motives of holding deposit money, firms tended to hold the equivalent of 25 percent of their borrowings in deposits.

However, this trend slackened in the latter part of the era of rapid economic growth, as the nonfinancial corporate sector's deficit grew more slowly. With the economy entering the slow growth period, this financial deficit contracted and even disappeared for a while. After 1975, over-borrowing diminished, because firms' dependence on external financing declined. As open markets for financial instruments (e.g., the gensaki or repurchase market, the CD market, and the secondary markets for bonds) developed, the nonfinancial corporate sector's financial assets shifted from bank deposits to marketable assets. This phenomenon will be examined in detail in sections III and IV. For the present, we should note from figure 2.1 that since the mid-1960s the nonfinancial corporate sector's gross ratio has generally been fairly flat with the unwinding of the accelerated growth of financial assets and liabilities, whereas the net ratio has been on a firm upward trend.

Summarizing, the postwar accumulation of gross financial assets by the private nonfinancial sector exceeded the nominal growth rate of the economy—leaving aside the exceptional 1972 episode—both in the period up to the 1960s and in the period since 1975. In the first period (which was predominantly an era of indirect financing) the main reason was the simultaneous growth in assets and liabilities of the nonfinancial corporate sector, so that the buildup of net financial assets was not as rapid as the growth of gross financial assets. In the second period the increase in the private nonfinancial sector's surpluses or financial assets was rapid both on a net and on a gross basis. As we will see below, this has had a major impact both on developments in Japan's financial markets and on changes in the financial system.

2. Progressive Economizing of Monetary Assets

In contrast to the increase in private nonfinancial sector holdings of financial assets relative to GNP after 1975, holdings of money (cash and demand deposits, i.e., M1 relative to GNP) have tended to decline. This is shown in figure 2.2 The ratio also shows a sharp upward spike around 1972 associated with the excess liquidity at that time. Except in this period, there was a rising trend up until the early 1970s, followed by a period of flatness, and a declining trend in the early 1980s. This pattern holds for both the personal sector and the nonfinancial corporate sector, with the latter showing the more pronounced pattern.

Splitting these monetary data into cash currency and deposit money and taking the ratio of each to GNP produces the results shown in figure 2.3. For the deposit money ratio, the downturn occurs in the 1980s, whereas for the cash currency ratio the trend since 1975 has been roughly flat. These ratios demonstrate that economizing in the use of money has

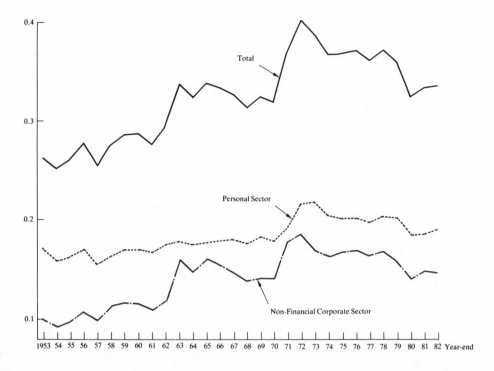

Figure 2.2.   Private Nonfinancial Sector's Holdings of Money as a Ratio to GNP

been most conspicuous in the nonfinancial corporate sector, especially in relation to deposit money.

Three factors may be considered to have caused this economizing in the use of deposit money. First, with the disappearance of overborrowing, the simultaneous acceleration of deposits and loans has begun to unwind. As dependence on borrowed funds has declined, the tendency for demand deposits to grow at the same rate as loans has given way to a relative decline in the former; the actual amount of such deposits has also declined. Figure 2.4 confirms the fact with data from the Bank of Japan's "Analysis of Financial Statements of Principal Enterprises," which shows that since 1975 both the ratio of enterprises' demand deposits to borrowed funds and the ratio of borrowings to financial assets (an indicator of overborrowing) have declined, resulting in a decrease in the ratio of demand deposits to sales revenue. Moreover, the ratio of financial assets to sales revenue (the reciprocal of the asset turnover rate) has also declined over this period, contributing to the decrease in the ratio of demand deposits

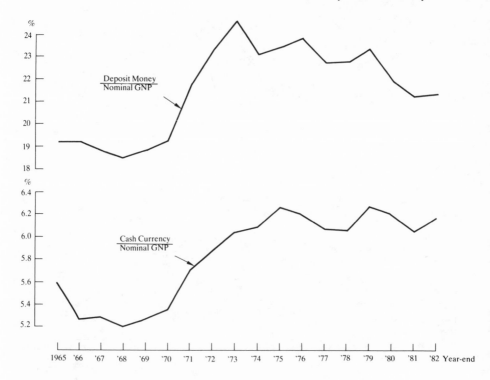

Figure 2.3. Ratio of Cash Currency and Deposit Money to GNP

to sales. This trend reflects the efforts of Japanese corporations to raise
the efficiency of capital use.

The second reason for economizing on deposit money is the increased
opportunity cost of holding deposit money balances at zero or controlled
low interest rates. This is due to the reduced transaction costs of switching
between deposit money and marketable short-term financial assets as a
result of the growth of open money markets (e.g., gensaki and CD markets) after 1975. It is also due to the maintenance of high interest rates
in the open money markets relative to returns on demand deposits
throughout the two periods of oil crisis and imported inflation and through
the period of global high interest rates in the early 1980s. We can confirm
the latter in figure 2.5.

The third factor behind economizing on deposit money in the case of
individuals was the development of the "deposit combined account" (*Soogoo kooza*), that is, demand deposit accounts with overdraft facilities
secured against fixed-term deposits or with loan trusts as collateral: such
accounts encouraged economizing on ordinary deposit balances. As of

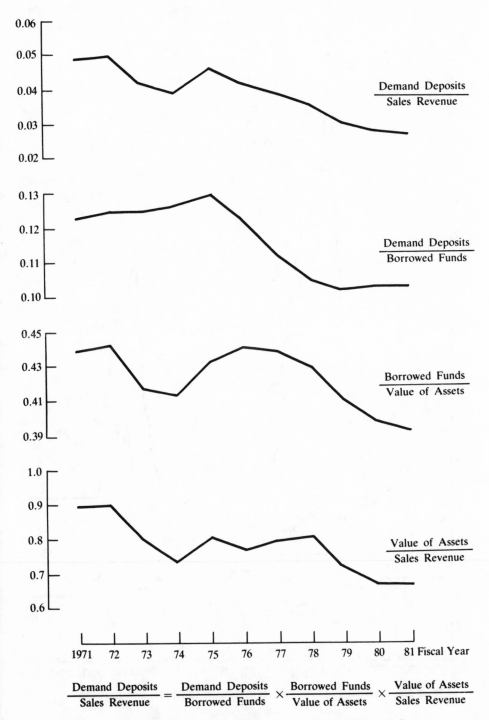

Figure 2.4. Economization of Demand Deposits by the Nonfinancial Corporate Sector

35

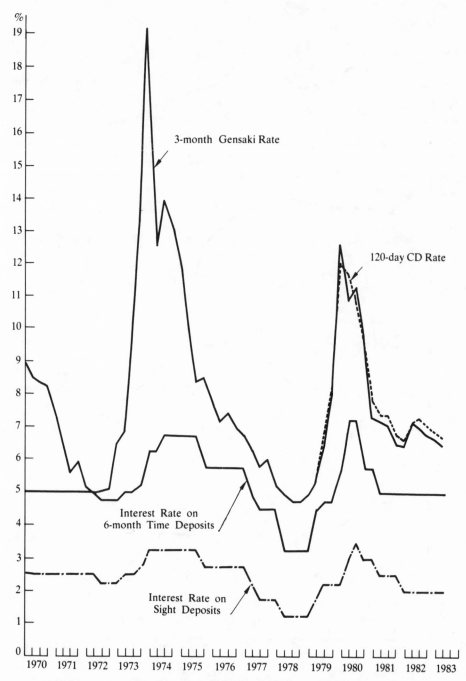

Figure 2.5. Indicators of Interest Rates Relating to Corporate Liquidity

March 1983, some 15 percent of banks' fixed-term deposits were collateralized in this way, permitting economies on this amount of ordinary deposits. This may be regarded as a kind of financial innovation corresponding to "sweep" accounts in the United States.[3]

With regard to cash currency, there has not been so much economizing as for deposit money, but the fact that the upward trend of the ratio of currency to GNP became flat after 1975 may be taken as evidence that the same kind of movement toward economizing has begun. Reasons for this may be the spread of credit cards, the increase in direct debt and automatic utility billing, and the wider availability of automated teller machines. It has also been hypothesized that in several foreign countries the reason that the ratio of cash currency to GNP has not declined may be the development of the "underground economy"; there is no statistical basis for such a proposition in Japan, however. (For further discussion in detail, see chapter 3, section II.2.)

II. Financial Asset Selection and Changes in the Flow of Funds

1. Changes in the Asset Composition of Investment Accounts

Next, we examine changes in the composition of financial assets excluding money (in the sense of transactions or checkable accounts)—that is, investment accounts. Tables 2.1 and 2.2 present data for the past thirty years for the personal sector and the nonfinancial corporate sector, respectively, showing shifts in the component elements of these investment accounts. From these two tables, we may observe some distinctive trends, which can be summarized in the following four points:

1. The proportion of fixed-term deposits at private financial institutions has been relatively stable over the long term, but it began to decline from 1975 in the personal sector and from 1971 in the nonfinancial corporate sector; the decline intensified after 1980. As we will see below, this phenomenon reflects the erosion of a distinctive feature of the Japanese financial system, namely, the predominance of indirect financing in the private sector, especially via the banks as favored intermediaries.

2. As a corollary to my first point, the proportion of personal sector assets in the Post Office savings system, in loan trusts, and in insurance has been increasing. In other words, instead of opting for financial assets offered by the private banks, people have been shifting to financial assets offered by nonbank intermediaries in the public and private sectors.

3. In both the personal sector and the nonfinancial corporate sector, holdings of securities (bonds) have increased as a counterpart of my first

3. Since American-type Super-NOW accounts paying money market rates of interest on transaction accounts do not exist in Japan, financial innovation has taken the form of economizing on transaction accounts along the lines of sweep accounts in the United States.

Table 2.1. Composition of Assets Held by the Personal Sector (Excluding Money)

	Fixed-Term Time Deposits	Private Financial Institutions	Postal Office	Loan Trusts	Insurance	Securities (excluding equities)	Government Bonds	Local Government Bonds	Public Financial and Nonfinancial Corporation Bonds	Bank Debenture	Corporate Bonds	Investment Trust Fund-Type Securities	Equities	Total
end-1953	54.5	n.a.	n.a.	2.1	8.4	6.9	3.2	0.1	0.2	0.6	0.1	2.7	28.1	100.0
1954	58.5	n.a.	n.a.	2.7	9.5	6.0	2.5	0.1	0.3	0.6	0.2	2.3	23.3	100.0
1955	58.2	n.a.	n.a.	3.9	10.1	4.6	1.8	0.1	0.4	0.7	0.2	1.4	23.2	100.0
1956	56.1	n.a.	n.a.	3.4	10.5	4.0	1.2	0.1	0.1	0.9	0.5	1.2	26.0	100.0
1957	58.1	n.a.	n.a.	3.1	11.4	4.6	0.9	0.1	0.1	0.9	0.4	2.2	22.8	100.0
1958	56.1	n.a.	n.a.	3.2	11.6	5.6	1.0	0.1	0.2	1.2	0.4	2.7	23.5	100.0
1959	52.6	n.a.	n.a.	3.3	11.3	6.3	0.6	0.2	0.2	1.7	0.4	3.2	26.5	100.0
1960	49.3	n.a.	n.a.	3.4	11.0	7.9	0.4	0.1	0.3	1.8	0.5	4.8	28.4	100.0
1961	48.5	n.a.	n.a.	3.6	11.3	10.8	0.2	0.2	0.4	1.7	0.5	7.8	25.8	100.0
1962	48.0	n.a.	n.a.	4.0	11.7	10.6	0.2	0.2	0.5	1.9	0.5	7.3	25.7	100.0
1963	48.7	n.a.	n.a.	4.5	11.7	10.1	0.2	0.1	0.6	2.2	0.5	6.5	25.0	100.0
1964	49.9	40.0	9.9	5.1	14.2	9.7	0.3	0.0	0.8	2.4	0.4	5.7	21.1	100.0
1965	51.1	40.9	10.2	5.7	14.2	8.8	0.3	0.0	1.1	2.8	0.4	4.2	20.2	100.0
1966	51.9	41.4	10.5	6.2	14.5	8.9	0.7	0.0	1.3	3.4	0.4	3.1	18.5	100.0
1967	54.0	42.7	11.3	6.6	14.9	9.0	0.8	0.0	1.5	3.8	0.4	2.5	15.5	100.0
1968	53.4	41.7	11.7	6.7	14.9	8.5	0.7	0.0	1.7	3.8	0.3	2.0	16.5	100.0
1969	52.1	40.4	11.7	6.5	14.6	8.6	0.7	0.1	1.7	3.9	0.3	1.9	18.2	100.0
1970	54.3	41.7	12.6	6.8	15.4	9.1	0.6	0.1	1.9	4.0	0.4	2.1	14.4	100.0
1971	53.6	40.4	13.2	6.9	15.5	9.6	0.6	0.1	2.0	4.4	0.4	2.1	14.4	100.0
1972	51.4	38.5	12.9	6.5	14.2	9.0	0.6	0.1	1.8	4.3	0.3	1.9	18.9	100.0
1973	56.3	41.9	14.4	6.9	14.8	9.4	0.7	0.1	1.7	4.3	0.6	2.0	12.6	100.0
1974	57.7	42.4	15.3	7.1	14.9	9.4	0.7	0.1	1.6	4.1	0.8	2.1	10.9	100.0
1975	57.2	41.5	15.7	7.0	14.3	9.6	0.6	0.2	1.5	4.4	0.9	2.0	11.9	100.0
1976	57.3	40.6	16.7	7.2	14.4	10.3	0.9	0.2	1.4	4.9	0.8	2.0	10.8	100.0
1977	58.2	40.2	18.0	7.3	14.5	10.8	1.8	0.2	1.2	4.7	0.6	2.1	9.2	100.0
1978	57.7	39.1	18.6	7.1	14.4	11.1	2.5	0.2	1.1	4.6	0.6	2.1	9.7	100.0
1979	58.5	39.4	19.1	7.1	14.7	10.7	2.6	0.2	1.0	4.3	0.6	2.0	9.0	100.0
1980	59.2	39.2	20.0	6.9	15.0	10.4	2.9	0.2	0.9	4.1	0.6	1.7	8.5	100.0
1981	58.9	38.8	20.1	7.1	15.3	10.6	3.1	0.2	1.0	4.0	0.5	1.8	8.1	100.0
1982	57.9	37.7	20.2	7.5	15.8	11.1	3.4	0.1	1.0	4.0	0.5	2.1	7.7	100.0
1983	56.0	36.2	19.8	7.5	15.9	11.7	3.4	0.1	1.0	4.0	0.5	2.7	8.9	100.0

Table 2.2. Composition of Financial Assets (Excluding Money) Held by the Nonfinancial Corporate Sector

	Fixed-Term Time Deposits (%)	Nego-tiable CDs (%)	Loan Trusts (%)	Securities (Excluding equities) (%)	Investment Trust Fund-Type Securities (%)	Equities (%)	Total (%)
end-1953	62.6	0.0	3.8	3.7	0.7	29.9	100.0
1954	65.5	0.0	4.2	4.0	0.7	26.3	100.0
1955	62.1	0.0	4.7	3.9	0.4	29.3	100.0
1956	59.0	0.0	5.2	3.2	0.4	32.6	100.0
1957	60.2	0.0	6.2	3.1	0.6	30.5	100.0
1958	59.7	0.0	6.0	3.7	0.7	30.6	100.0
1959	55.5	0.0	5.8	4.7	0.9	34.0	100.0
1960	53.2	0.0	5.8	5.4	0.8	35.6	100.0
1961	52.8	0.0	6.1	6.4	1.5	34.7	100.0
1962	54.8	0.0	6.3	6.4	0.9	32.5	100.0
1963	57.6	0.0	6.4	6.6	0.7	29.4	100.0
1964	62.7	0.0	6.9	6.5	0.6	23.9	100.0
1965	63.2	0.0	6.0	6.1	0.4	24.7	100.0
1966	65.1	0.0	5.7	5.8	0.2	23.4	100.0
1967	66.5	0.0	5.6	6.0	0.2	21.9	100.0
1968	64.8	0.0	5.5	5.7	0.1	24.0	100.0
1969	61.8	0.0	5.4	5.4	0.0	27.4	100.0
1970	66.1	0.0	5.6	5.5	0.1	22.8	100.0
1971	65.5	0.0	5.5	5.5	0.1	23.5	100.0
1972	57.1	0.0	4.7	3.4	0.0	34.8	100.0
1973	56.8	0.0	5.6	4.0	0.0	33.6	100.0
1974	59.7	0.0	5.6	4.3	0.1	30.4	100.0
1975	55.9	0.0	5.1	4.5	0.1	34.5	100.0
1976	57.2	0.0	5.3	5.1	0.1	32.4	100.0
1977	58.7	0.0	5.8	5.3	0.1	30.2	100.0
1978	57.0	0.0	6.2	5.6	0.1	31.2	100.0
1979	55.1	1.7	6.4	6.5	0.1	30.3	100.0
1980	54.2	2.1	6.3	7.6	0.1	29.8	100.0
1981	51.5	2.7	5.8	8.9	0.1	31.1	100.0
1982	50.5	3.2	5.6	9.6	0.1	31.1	100.0
1983	49.7	3.6	5.3	9.7	0.2	31.7	100.0

point above. This trend has been especially noticeable since 1975, when large government bond issues began. We will see below that these are two aspects of the same phenomenon, namely, a gradual shift in the relative importance of the flow of funds through the Japanese financial system from indirect to direct financing.

4. The relative importance of equities and investment-trust-fund-type securities held by the personal sector peaked in the early 1960s and has been on the decline ever since. However, the relative importance of those instruments held by the nonfinancial corporate sector, having peaked in the early 1960s, recovered again somewhat in the 1970s demonstrating

that individuals' preference for equities was persistently on the decline after the stock market panic that followed the boom of the early 1960s. It also reflects the move toward stable shareholding by means of corporate crossholding of shares,—in other words, a relative shift of shareholding from individuals to nonfinancial corporations.

2. Changes in the Channels of the Flow of Funds through the Financial System

Changes in asset preferences described in sections I.2 and II.1 above were coincident with changes in the channels of the flow of funds through the financial system. These latter changes are shown in table 2.3

Indirect Financing. Since the second half of the 1970s, when the preference for money, especially demand deposits and fixed-term deposits offered by private banks, began to wane, the intermediation fraction of the private-sector banks has been on a constant downtrend, falling from nearly 70 percent in the past to around 40 percent recently. In contrast, among the same private-sector financial intermediaries, nonbank financial institutions such as the loan-trust sector of trust banks and insurance companies, which had shown a mild downtrend, bottomed in 1978 and began to pick up; this share is now just over 10 percent of the total. Also the channeling of funds from the postal system to the Trust Fund Bureau and into public financial intermediaries clearly increased in importance in the second half of the 1970s, rising from around 15 percent in the past to nearly 30 percent now.

Direct Financing. Funding through the securities market has been rising since the second half of the 1970s, increasing from just around 5 percent to over 10 percent. If investment-trust funds provided by securities companies are added, it comes to 15 percent of the total. Over the whole period, however, the relative importance of fund flows through the equities market has tended to decline from the peak in 1970. Thus the most significant element in the expansion of direct financing is the increased role of financial intermediation via the bond market, in particular via the government securities market. The share of corporate bonds, local government bonds, public corporation bonds, and public financial organization bonds in financial intermediation has not increased over the period.

III. Causes of Changes in the Financial System

In the late 1970s the private nonfinancial sector's accumulation of financial assets began to accelerate. Also, because the composition of these assets began to change, the Japanese financial system entered a

Table 2.3. Flow of Funds to Final Borrowers by Type of Lenders*

| Calendar Year | Private Financial Intermediaries (%) | Deposit Banks (%) | Trust Sector, Insurance Companies (%) | Public Financial Intermediaries (%) | Securities Market (%) | Domestic | | | Overseas (%) | Total (%) |
						Bonds (%)	Stocks (%)	Investment Trusts (%)		
1965	78.6	63.2	11.3	15.5	5.9	3.5	5.1	-3.0	0.3	100.0
1966	78.4	69.6	10.0	19.3	2.3	2.6	2.2	-1.7	-0.8	100.0
1967	77.4	66.1	12.0	16.2	6.4	3.1	1.0	-1.1	3.4	100.0
1968	72.5	58.3	13.0	18.4	9.1	2.5	2.7	0.2	3.7	100.0
1969	73.3	60.3	11.7	16.9	9.8	2.3	2.9	1.1	3.5	100.0
1970	71.0	60.3	12.8	16.7	12.3	3.0	4.8	0.6	3.9	100.0
1971	70.2	57.8	11.7	16.2	13.6	3.4	2.8	1.0	6.4	100.0
1972	77.5	66.2	10.5	16.1	6.4	1.3	2.0	1.4	1.7	100.0
1973	74.6	64.1	10.9	18.6	6.8	3.1	3.6	0.6	-0.5	100.0
1974	69.0	58.0	10.7	21.1	9.9	1.7	2.3	0.3	5.6	100.0
1975	69.8	58.8	10.4	23.3	6.9	3.5	2.0	1.6	-0.2	100.0
1976	67.4	56.0	10.2	23.7	8.9	3.9	1.8	1.0	2.2	100.0
1977	60.5	49.6	9.5	29.2	10.3	6.6	2.4	0.9	0.4	100.0
1978	62.4	54.2	6.7	25.4	12.2	6.4	1.4	0.7	3.7	100.0
1979	59.3	48.0	9.6	28.6	12.1	6.3	2.2	0.4	3.2	100.0
1980	54.9	41.9	11.6	31.2	13.9	7.6	1.6	-0.6	5.3	100.0
1981	61.4	49.8	9.9	25.5	13.1	7.3	2.4	1.9	1.5	100.0
1982	56.1	42.4	12.7	29.2	14.7	5.5	2.9	3.0	3.3	100.0
1983	54.5	41.6	10.0	26.6	18.9	8.5	1.2	5.8	3.4	100.0

*This table shows the channels through which funds were supplied by various types of lenders to final borrowers or users of funds inside the domestic financial system. The foreign lenders and users of funds are also included by type of source or use.

41

period of major evolution. As is already clear from the analysis above, these changes can be summarized in three points:

First, there has been a decline in the dominant position previously occupied by the private-sector banks. Second, public sector financial intermediaries (i.e., the Post Office system transferring funds to the Trust Fund Bureau, which in turn transfers the funds to other government financial institutions) and nonbank private-sector financial intermediaries have increased their share of the market. From the standpoint of channels of flow of funds, both sets of institutions now account for about 40 percent of total funding. Thus, they now rival the share of the private-sector banks. Third, short-, medium-, and long-term open markets, such as the gensaki market, the CD market, and medium- and long-term bond markets have developed to the point that the flow of funds raised by direct financing through these markets now accounts for 15 percent of the total flow of funds. These percentages are still low by comparison with those for the United States, but they represent a major change from the percentages prevailing in the Japanese financial system in the earlier period, when the share of direct financing remained around 5 percent of total fund-raising. For reasons I will give below, the future prospects are for the upward trend in the direct financing share to continue.

The first and second of the three changes represent changes in the relative importance of various institutions within the indirect financing sector, whereas the third represents a shift from indirect financing to direct financing. We now consider the reasons for each of these two types of changes in market share.

1. Variations in Market Shares within the Indirect Financing Sector

Many reasons can be given for variations in the share of indirect financing, but here we will concentrate on the four most fundamental causes.

1. With the economizing on money balances, the deposit banks, which were the main suppliers of transaction accounts, stood at a relative disadvantage in fund-raising compared with those financial institutions whose main role was the supply of investment accounts (the loan trust sector of trust banks, the long-term credit banks, life insurance companies, and the Post Office).

2. Also in parallel with the economizing on money balances and the faster buildup of financial assets, the demand for investment accounts has been increasing rapidly over the past ten years. Compared with financial intermediaries offering long-term assets (e.g., trust banks offering five-year loan trusts or the Post Office offering ten-year fixed-term deposits), the deposit banks were able to offer only fixed-term time deposits of two years and less, and were thus at a relative disadvantage in collection

of funds through investment accounts. This was (*a*) because interest rates on investment account assets offered by these financial intermediaries were either regulated or set by Ministry of Finance guidance so that the yield curve was always upward-sloping (i.e., the longer the term, the higher the rate of interest; see figure 1.4 in chapter 1), and, thus, in periods of monetary stringency long-term funds were more attractive and short-term funds less attractive; and, (*b*) because there was a strong tendency to use long-term asset accounts even for funds that might be converted to cash at short notice, as the fee charged for terminating a long-term asset contract before maturity was low, and as the yields on such broken long-term asset contracts were still higher than the yields on short-term assets. Needless to say, as long as people arbitrage rationally between long- and short-term rates, the yield on a long-term asset for a fixed term and the weighted average of the present yield and the future yield expected for short-term assets rolled over during the same term will be equalized. In this case, the expectation theory of the term structure teaches that, in a period of tight money, expectations that rates will eventually fall will cause the yield curve to be downward-sloping. In fact, as figure 1.4 in chapter 1 shows, even in Japan this proposition holds for the yield curve for free market interest rates.[4] However, the term structure of yields on controlled-rate financial assets offered by Japanese financial institutions always slopes upward; thus, people who arbitrage rationally between short and long rates will always tend to prefer longer-term assets. Under the Japanese system of determining regulated interest rates, even in tight money periods (e.g., March 1980, see figure 1.4 in chapter 1), the yield on fixed-sum deposits at the Post Office tends to be the highest, and in easy money periods (March 1979) the yield on bank debentures and loan trusts tends to be the highest. This is why in Table 2.1 the market share of the Post Office rises in periods of tight money and the market share of loan trust sector of trust banks and insurance companies rises in easy money periods.

3. Because the growth of income-elastic cumulative life insurance schemes is greater as income levels rise, and because the growth of old age pension schemes will increase as the population structure becomes older, the assets of the loan trust sector of trust banks, life insurance companies, and the Post Office, all of which accept pension funds and insurance funds, must increase in relative terms.

4. Postal savings deposits have an upper limit of ¥3 million per depositor in accounts on which interest is tax exempt; but because identification or name-registration is not perfect, there is a tendency for people to hold multiple accounts; thus, the total of interest-free deposit holdings

4. For a detailed analysis of the term structure of interest rates in the Japanese financial markets, see Kuroda and Ohkubo 1982.

per person in postal savings accounts exceeds the legal limit, with the advantage of interest income tax relief. Not surprisingly, growth of such deposits has been relatively high.[5]

2. Variations in Market Shares between Direct and Indirect Financing

Next, we consider the reason why the share of direct financing has grown relative to the share of indirect financing. As I explained earlier, the growth of direct financing has not been due to widespread fund-raising in the equity market but rather to the large issues of government securities on the bond market. However, the government bond issues themselves are not a sufficient condition for increased direct financing; if financial intermediaries purchase a large share of government bond issues, the direct/indirect financing ratio does not change. Hence the fundamental causes of increased direct financing must correspond to the reasons that the final lenders of funds prefer holding government bonds directly rather than acquiring assets offered by financial institutions.

Some types of bonds issued by the government of Japan—ten-year long-term bonds and five-year discount bonds—are underwritten by a syndicate of financial institutions. In addition, two- to four-year medium-term bonds are issued by tender or at a fixed rate at public offering. There are four possible reasons that people may prefer these latter two types of government bonds to assets offered by financial intermediaries.

1. As set out above, the yield curve of assets offered by financial intermediaries is upward-sloping to the right, but the yield to new sub-scribers on ten-year government bonds is furthest to the right and always higher. Thus, for the same reason that five-year loan trusts and five-year bank debentures are preferred to fixed-term time deposits (two years and under), long-term government bonds (ten years) are preferred to fixed-term time deposits, loan trusts, and bank debentures. Reflecting this, table 2.4 shows that securities brokers, who sell the two- to four-year medium-term bonds to their customers, take a much larger share of such bonds than do financial intermediaries.

However, only in times of monetary squeeze does the yield on fixed-sum postal savings deposits (which are in the same class of long-term assets) exceed the yield on long-term government bonds. Also, since the principal of government bonds may be at risk when they are sold before maturity, unless the original yield on government bonds exceeds by a certain margin the yields on fixed-term deposits and loan trusts (whose capital value on sales before maturity is not at risk), ordinary risk-averse investors will not prefer government bonds. In this sense, reasons 2, 3, and 4 below are more important ones for preferring government bonds.

5. There are a variety of other reasons for the systematic increase in postal savings accounts. For details, see Royama 1982, chapter 2.

Table 2.4. Composition of Government Bond Issues

Fiscal Year	Long-Term Government Bonds with Coupons (10 Years) and Government Discount Bonds (5 Years) Issued via the Underwriting Syndicate		Medium-Term Government Bonds with Coupons (2–4 Years) Issued by Tender or at Fixed Rates to the Public			Total
	Underwritten by Financial Intermediaries (%)	Underwritten by Securities Brokers (%)	Subscribed by Financial Intermediaries (%)	Subscribed by Securities Brokers (%)	Others*	Total
1975	93.2	6.8	0.0	0.0	0.0	100.0
1976	83.6	16.4	0.0	0.0	0.0	100.0
1977	73.6	26.4	0.0	0.0	0.0	100.0
1978	71.1	19.3	3.9	5.7	0.0	100.0
1979	78.3	12.1	5.9	3.7	0.0	100.0
1980	60.6	22.4	2.1	14.9	0.0	100.0
1981	47.6	14.4	3.3	24.6	10.1	100.0
1982	51.0	14.0	3.1	23.1	8.8	100.0
1983	36.8	11.0	8.8	26.7	16.7	100.0

*Direct placements at fixed rates to financial intermediaries of non-marketable long-term government bonds and medium-term government financial debentures.

2. After large-scale issues of government bonds began in the late 1970s, the secondary market in government bonds developed rapidly, but the yields in that market frequently far exceeded the yields on assets offered by financial intermediaries. Especially in tight money periods, the term structure of market interest rates conformed to theory by being downward-sloping (inverted), thus magnifying the discrepancy between yields in the short and medium maturities. Further, in such tight money periods, the predominant expectation that yields would eventually fall enhanced the probability of capital gains in the future. For these two reasons, the ultimate lenders in such periods were strongly tempted to shift their funds from assets offered by financial intermediaries to long-term government bonds in the secondary market. The main sellers of long-term government bonds in the secondary market were city banks and local banks, which together have a large share in the syndicate.

3. The tender-issue system for two- to four-year medium-term government bonds began in 1978. The yield in this market, as figure 1.1 in chapter 1 shows, was typically higher than the yields on comparable assets offered by financial intermediaries such as two-year fixed-term deposits, five-year loan trusts, and bank debentures. As a result the distribution of medium-term government bonds via the securities companies to the nonfinancial private sector was highly successful, as we see in table 2.4, and to that extent the preference for fixed-term time deposits, loan trusts, and bank debentures was undermined.

4. Because the yield on Japanese government Treasury bills (TBs) is controlled at a low rate, the TB market has not developed, and the open money market did not exist in the era of rapid economic growth. However, there was one financial innovation in the 1960s, the gensaki market, equivalent to the U.S. market in repurchases (RPs), which got under way thanks to the inventiveness of the private sector. Particularly in the late 1970s (as we discussed in section I.1) with the faster accumulation of financial assets by the nonfinancial corporate sector and with the corresponding expansion in the secondary market for government bonds, the gensaki market developed very rapidly. Also, after 1979 the issuance of negotiable CDs, with freely determined interest rates but subject to quantitative restrictions on the size of issue, was permitted. As a result of the development of the gensaki and CD markets, free open markets for short-term funds played a significant role for the first time in Japan's financial system. The interest rates in these markets are, as we see from figure 1.1 in chapter 1, substantially higher than the rates on corresponding fixed-term deposits. Thus nonfinancial corporations reduced their holdings of fixed-term deposits (table 2.2), replacing them with negotiable CDs and gensaki-type securities (negotiable securities, excluding equities), holdings of which rose proportionately. The shift to negotiable CDs does not

affect the proportion of direct financing, but the shift to the gensaki market raises the share of direct financing and reduces the share of indirect financing.

IV. Toward the New Financial System

The year 1985 marked an epoch in the Japanese financial system. In 1985 the first renewal of government borrowing in the form of ten-year long-term government bonds, large-scale issue of which started in 1975 and has continued since, commenced, marking a dramatic increase in gross issue volume. Also, at around the same time Nippon Telegraph and Telephone Public Corporation (NTT) began its Information Network System (INS) project, which is planned to spread out gradually across the country, bringing in the era of nationwide electronic banking.

In preparation for the major increase in the gross amount of government bond issues, the Ministry of Finance permitted retail sales by banks of newly issued ten-year bonds from April 1983, of newly issued two- to four-year government bonds from October 1983, and of secondary market government bonds from June 1984. The persistent trend toward less financial intermediation (from indirect to direct financing) mentioned above will accelerate more by the participation of financial institutions themselves. Also, as the maturity dates for large volumes of government bonds approach, an open money market approximating a TB market will take shape; thus, even without further expansion of the gensaki and CD markets, the increase in direct financing mentioned above will accelerate.

If under these circumstances controls and official guidance on interest rates on assets offered by financial intermediaries continue along the lines of the current tendency of keeping rates artificially low, the decline in the share of indirect financing will continue. On the other hand, if these controls and government guidance are abolished, or if they are made flexible enough to match equilibrium rates in the free market, there may be slowing of the downtrend in the share of indirect financing. If the irrational term structure of interest rates is also reformed, the reasons for the changes within the indirect financing sector may also cease to exist.

However, if the development by financial intermediaries of new instruments based on market interest rate criteria is permitted, it is not immediately clear how the shares of the direct financing and indirect financing sectors will move. Among financial innovations in investment accounts, the securities firms can already offer gensaki instruments, which are equivalent to RPs, and medium-term government bond funds, which are equivalent to money market mutual funds (MMMFs). On the other hand, financial intermediaries can offer only large CDs. One key to how the market shares will move will be whether financial intermediaries will be able to offer a new kind of market-interest–related investment account.[6]

For the deposit banks, another factor is the arrival of nationwide electronic banking. Their main financial innovations in transaction accounts have been the deposit combined account and automatic cash-dispensing/deposit machines. But, in the future, with transaction instructions for terminals linked to INS, home banking and firm banking, which have just started, will easily prevail. Another important point will be whether automatic transfers between transaction accounts and investment accounts with market interest rates (like sweep accounts) or transaction accounts bearing market interest rates (like Super-NOW accounts) will be permitted.

If the present controls on interest rates and official guidance are maintained, the change of financial system in the direction as analyzed in section III—that is, increased share of direct financing and decline of the banks' share within the indirect financing sector—will continue further. If these controls are abolished and financial innovations are further promoted, the financial system will shift in a new direction. Since there are to be changes regardless of what happens, it is desirable that these changes be in the direction of efficiency and fairness. Such a course would be gradually to reduce government controls and guidance and to permit financial innovations to continue. At the same time, these changes must not permit extreme bias, either between financial intermediaries and securities companies or between different types of financial intermediaries, and they must ensure against serious instability in the financial system as a whole.[7]

6. Some steps toward this were taken in 1985. They are deregulation of interest rates on time deposits with a minimum unit of 1 billion yen and introduction of MMCs (money market certificates) with a minimum unit of 50 million yen.

7. For further discussion, see Suzuki 1983b.

3

Financial Innovation
and Monetary Policy

I **Factors behind Financial Innovation**

Broadly speaking, six factors lie behind the recent worldwide trend toward financial innovation: (1) high, variable, and unpredictable inflation and interest rates, (2) the regulatory framework and revision thereof, (3) the existing structure of the financial industry, (4) changes in the international environment and increasing integration of domestic and international financial markets, (5) the increase in government deficits, and (6) the rapid development of technology in the financial sector.

In Japan, the most important element has been the large-scale issuance of government bonds (factor 5). However, this alone is not sufficient to account for all changes. Because of regulation of interest rates dating from the era of rapid economic growth (factor 2) and a financial system characterized by predominance of indirect financing supported by interest rate regulation (factor 3), a large portion of the bank portfolios came to be occupied by government bonds, which were issued in large quantities after 1975. As their funds position had tightened, banks were gradually allowed by the government to resell bonds, and, as a consequence, a secondary market for government bonds began to develop. At the beginning most financial innovations were made by securities companies and caused a declining market share for deposit banks. In response, authorities relaxed regulations concerning bank interest rates and the scope of bank business, which in turn induced financial innovation by the banks; now there is a good deal of competition between banks and securities companies. In addition, we should not neglect other factors: (*a*) the acceleration in the accumulation of financial assets and increasing sensitivity to interest rates among enterprises and individuals, (*b*) the

49

need for integration of domestic and foreign financial markets (factor 4), and (c) technological innovations in microelectronics and telecommunications (factor 6). In Japan, however, rates of inflation and interest showed disruptive fluctuations only in a short period around 1974; factor 1 was therefore not an essential in the financial system and financial innovation.

In the rest of this section, I shall refer to these six factors explicitly and explain the factors behind financial innovation and structural changes in the financial system of Japan.

As we saw in chapters 1 and 2, structural changes in the financial system in Japan began in 1974. The historical events behind the structural changes were the transition to slow economic growth after the first oil crisis and the increasing integration of the domestic and international financial markets accompanying the transition to the floating-rate system—factor 4 cited above.

As economic growth slowed, the public-sector deficit measured on a flow-of-funds basis, which had shown cyclical movements of 1 to 4 percent of GNP, rose to 8 percent (factor 5). On the other hand, the deficit of the corporate sector declined from 8 percent to 4 percent of GNP (see figure 1.3 in chapter 1). As a result, the ratio of government bonds outstanding to GNP rose rapidly, and by end-fiscal 1983 it had reached 39 percent. On the other hand, net financial assets (gross financial assets minus liabilities) held by the private nonfinancial sector, which grew during the high-growth era to only 31 percent of GNP at the end of 1973, rose rapidly after 1974 and reached 72 percent of GNP by the end of 1982.

If the private nonfinancial sector had held its rapidly accumulating financial assets predominantly in the form of bank deposits and had held its growing number of government bonds only indirectly through deposit banks, then the financial system would not have undergone any structural changes. However, in reality, as table 2.3 in chapter 2 suggests, in the portfolio of the private nonfinancial sector, the share of deposits declined, that of trusts and insurance schemes remained constant, and the shares of securities houses and the postal savings system rose. The causes may be summarized as follows.[1]

The supply of savings became more interest-sensitive, as the accumulation of financial assets accelerated and as business sales and wages stagnated. This increasing emphasis on interest rates, when combined with the following three institutional and structural conditions, led to a decline in bank deposits on investment account, as well as economizing on transactions accounts.

---

1. This chapter provides only a brief summary of the structural changes in the financial system since 1974 and their causes. For details, see chapter 2.

1. Interest Rate Regulations and
Institutional Features of the Financial System

The first reason for the structural change has to do with interest rate regulations (factor 2) and the structural characteristics of the financial system (factor 3). The private financial intermediaries of Japan may be classified into four categories according to their respective instruments of fund collection.

a. Institutions such as city banks, local banks, mutual loan and savings ("Soogo") banks, and credit associations ("Shinkin"), which can provide only demand deposits and time deposits of within two years. (In 1981, "maturity-designated time deposits" of three years, a new type of two-year time deposit, became available. See below.)

b. Institutions such as long-term credit banks, which, in addition to accepting deposits, also issue debentures of one- and five-year maturities.

c. Trust banks, which, in addition to accepting deposits, also provide trust accounts and loan-trust accounts of two and five years.

d. Insurance companies, which accept premiums.

Until 1983, institutions belonging to classes *a–d* were prohibited from using funds in the securities business, except to underwrite public debt. (From 1983, classes *a–c* were permitted to sell newly issued government bonds over-the-counter and from June 1984, dealing in already issued bonds was permitted. See below.) Apart from these exceptions, the underwriting, dealing, and brokerage of securities have been solely the business of securities companies. Thus, separation of banking and securities businesses has been a principle. On the other hand, public financial intermediaries provide saving accounts of up to ten years through the post office system.

Interest rates on the above financial assets (deposits, bank debentures, trust accounts, public financial intermediary deposits) and interest rates on newly issued securities (except for medium-term government bonds, to be discussed later) are either regulated, under administrative guidance, or determined in consultation with the government. (In what follows, these will be called "regulated interest rates.") Figure 1.4 in chapter 1 shows the yield curves of regulated interest rates and unregulated interest rates determined in the secondary market of long-term government bonds during a period of monetary ease (March 1979) and during a period of monetary stringency (March 1980). Two points are worth noting. First, the yield curves of regulated interest rates are always below those of unregulated interest rates; second, the yield curves of regulated interest rates, even in times of tight money, are always upward-sloping.

The low levels of regulated rates caused funds to shift from financial intermediaries to the secondary market for long-term government bonds.

This process was promoted by a financial innovation, repurchase contracts (gensaki), using long-term government bonds as collateral. (No TB market developed because rates on newly issued TBs were controlled at low levels.) The gensaki market had appeared in the 1960s, but it grew rapidly in the 1970s as the business sector shifted its growing surplus of funds out of three-month and six-month time deposits.

The different slopes of the two yield curves caused the second type of fund shift, that among the financial intermediaries. There has been a strong tendency in times of tight money for savings to shift from time deposits of within two years toward five-year trusts, loan trusts, and bank debentures, and further into ten-year postal savings and long-term government bonds. This shift from short-term to long-term assets is further promoted by the low transaction costs involved.

2. Developments in Deregulation

The second cause of structural changes in the financial sector is a consequence of the partial removal and revision of regulation of interest rates, and revision of regulation regarding the scope of business permitted to financial institutions.

a. Partial Deregulation of Interest Rates on Newly Issued Government Bonds. As the volume of government bonds issued grew, the method of issue through the underwriting syndicate at below-market rates could no longer work smoothly. As shown in figures 1.1 and 1.4 in chapter 1, a gap existed between yields in the primary and secondary markets; negotiations on interest rates between the government and the syndicate often failed, forcing the government to raise funds by other means. From 1978, public offering of two- to four-year medium-term government bonds was introduced; public offering at fixed rates followed in 1982. In short, interest rates have been liberalized, and they are determined in the market. As these interest rates are higher than regulated rates on assets with similar maturities, funds have flowed out of financial intermediaries and into the bond market.

This shift of funds was promoted by yet another financial innovation by the securities companies, the medium-term government bond fund—a form of short-term investment trust similar to the MMMF of the United States. Because this investment has the advantages that (1) it can be converted to cash after one month, and (2) its interest rate is higher than similar term bank deposits, funds from both the personal and corporate sectors have been flowing in rapidly. In addition, securities companies also began to offer new investment trusts such as the "Rikin fund," a short-term investment that uses interest on bonds, and medium- (two–five years) and long-term (seven years) high-yield government bond funds that incorporate outstanding long-term government bonds. The share of investment trusts in the flow of funds grew rapidly in 1981 and 1982, though in absolute terms it remained low.

In 1982, medium-term government bonds subscribed by securities companies and sold to the nonfinancial private sector directly or through investment trusts reached 23 percent of the total amount of government bonds issued. In addition, securities companies took 14 percent of the long-term government bonds issued via the underwriting syndicate. The remaining 63 percent was absorbed by financial intermediaries, mainly banks, and part of it became net excess sale in the gensaki market and the secondary market for government bonds. As far as government bonds are concerned, the role of the indirect financing sector is clearly declining.

b. The Partial Deregulation of Banking. As the market share of deposit banks declined, regulations imposed on banks were partly relaxed. From 1979 on, banks were permitted to issue negotiable certificates of deposit, with ¥500 million as the minimum unit, subject to a quantity ceiling that total issue did not exceed 10 percent of broadly defined net worth. The minimum unit was lowered to ¥300 million in January 1984, and the quantitative ceiling ratio was gradually raised to 75 percent. Thus, although banks are still subject to a quantity ceiling, it is possible for them to offer large-lot deposits to enterprises at unregulated interest rates. Although interest rates on time deposits are still regulated, since 1981 banks have been allowed to offer fixed-term time deposits of up to three years. At the same time, trust banks have been permitted to offer loan trusts of up to five years called "Bigs," and long-term credit banks can offer bank debentures of five years called "Wides."

All these instruments offer higher yields through compound interest and can easily be converted to cash before maturity. Furthermore, since 1983, banks have been allowed to sell newly issued long-term government bonds and newly issued medium-term government bonds over-the-counter. Deposit banks and trust banks have taken this opportunity to offer new accounts in which such newly issued bonds are deposited by customers with banks and the interest on the bonds is automatically transferred to a fixed-term time deposit or trust account at the bank; this procedure yields higher interest. Furthermore, from June 1984, such banks were permitted to sell secondary-market government bonds over-the-counter. If similar accounts are offered using these bonds, the yields will reflect unregulated interest rates in the secondary bond market. The implications of these financial innovations are comparable to those of money-market accounts in the United States. (See note on p. 75)

c. Deregulation of International Financial Business. Since the transition to the floating-rate system in 1973 , the domestic and international financial markets have become more and more integrated. This required liberalization of domestic interest rates and financial transactions, as was then taking place abroad. In 1974 came the liberalization of interest rates on foreign-currency deposits, which marked the first step in the deregulation of deposit interest rates in Japan. At that time, ownership of foreign-currency accounts by residents required a license, but from 1978, accounts of up to ¥3 million were made freely available; in 1980 this ceiling was totally removed. Borrowing in foreign currencies (impact loans) by residents from markets abroad directly or through Japanese banks was completely liberalized in 1980. Furthermore, the revised Banking Law of 1981 states explicitly the principle that no regulations are to be imposed on foreign banks besides those imposed on Japanese banks.

Over the same period, the holding of foreign securities by residents as well as investment in domestic securities by nonresidents was liberalized, except for a few transactions by the nonfinancial sector (investment by residents in foreign CDs, commercial paper [CPs]), and investment above a certain limit by nonresidents in the stock of eleven specified companies.

Such international financial transactions, as well as unregulated financial transactions in the domestic securities markets, encouraged the deregulation of domestic financial intermediaries.

3. The Impact of Technological Progress

The third reason for financial structure changes is related to innovations in microelectronics and telecommunications, that lower the information and management costs of financial transactions. As a result of technological change, financial innovation has occurred in transactions accounts, and progress has been made in the economizing of currency and demand deposits. This contributes to the declining share of banks in financial intermediation.

The economizing of currency has been facilitated by the spread of several practices that existed on a small scale before the first oil crisis: payment by personal credit cards, automatic deposit of monthly salaries through account transfers (1969), and automatic transfer payments of public utility charges (1955). Spread of these settlement practices was made possible by computerization within banks. Formation of nationwide, on-line systems among banks began in 1975.

Moreover, the economizing of demand deposits is very much the result of the establishment of the "deposit combined account" (*soogoo kooza*) in 1972. When the balance in the demand deposit account is not enough for a certain payment, this account automatically allows overdraft with time deposit or loan trust as collateral. In fact, this allows investment accounts to perform a transaction function. Again, computerization was critical in lowering costs so that banks could offer these services.

II. Major Changes in the Banking System and Financial Markets

1. Changes in Assets and Liabilities of Banks

a. Liability Management. Financial innovation and deregulation of interest rates has proceeded only gradually in Japan, so that interest rates on deposits, which make up the bulk of liabilities of financial institutions, remain largely regulated; the exceptions are interest rates on foreign currency deposits and CDs, the latter of which are subject to quantity ceilings. In fact, the ratio of liabilities with unregulated interest rates to total liabilities of financial institutions at the end of 1982 was only 15.2 percent (see table 3.1). From the supplier's viewpoint, CD and foreign currency deposits together made up only 4.8 percent of the total financial assets held by the nonfinancial corporate sector. The same ratio for the personal sector was below one percent. Also for the personal sector, the shares of fixed-term time deposits, Bigs, Wides, and government bonds have been increasing; by the end of 1982, altogether they amounted to 12.5 percent of total financial asset holdings for the personal sector.

Given the continued high proportion of regulated-rate liabilities, however, complications in liability management arising from interest rate fluctuations will become a problem only in the future. At present, the most urgent problems in liability management are in the areas of the handling of payment transfer, settlement, overdraft, interest payment, maturity management, and termination before maturity. Since liabilities offering sophisticated facilities can expand only with financial innovation, efficiency in use of computers and transmission of information among terminals is the most critical problem.

b. Variable-Rate Lending and Shortening of Debt Maturity. In Japan, no precise statistics on variable-rate lending exist. Ordinary lending, for terms shorter than one year, can be considered to be a kind of variable-rate lending, since interest rates can be changed as commercial bills mature (usually after three or six months). And even lending for terms longer than one year, with the exception of long-term credit banks, may be considered variable-rate lending, since rates may be changed at each interest payment (usually every three or six months). Table 3.2 shows the composition of loans by terms and types of banks over time. The share of long-term lending by long-term credit banks at fixed interest rates (centering on five-year loans) has declined since 1978, to 9.5 percent of total lending at the end of 1982 (24 percent of lending with term longer than one year). Furthermore, the share of variable-rate lending is growing, and the proportion of such lending with terms longer than one year (centering on three- to four-year loans) is also increasing. Interest rates on housing loans, a special kind of long-term lending, came to be fixed at different rates among different categories of banks, in view of differentials in costs of raising funds. But in 1983, when twenty-five- to thirty-

Table 3.1. Composition of Funds Raised by the Private Banking Sector

As at End of Year	Instruments with Regulated Rates Broadly Defined Total (A) (%)	Deposits (%)	Bank Debentures (%)	Borrowing from BOJ (%)	Instruments with Unregulated Rates Total (B) (%)	Call Money, Bills Sold (%)	CDs (%)	Gensaki (%)	Foreign Currency Deposits, Nonresident Yen Deposits (%)	Debentures in Foreign Currency (%)	Short-Term Foreign Liabilities (%)	Total Funds Raised (A + B) (%)
1965	96.0	83.4	8.9	3.7	4.0	3.1	0	0	0.9	0	—	100.0
1966	96.9	84.0	9.2	3.8	3.1	2.4	0	0	0.7	0	—	100.0
1967	96.6	84.4	9.4	2.9	3.4	2.8	0	0	0.6	0	—	100.0
1968	97.3	85.0	9.4	2.9	2.7	2.2	0	0	0.6	0	—	100.0
1969	96.9	84.9	9.0	3.0	3.1	2.6	0	0	0.5	0	—	100.0
1970	93.8	82.1	8.6	3.1	6.2	2.9	0	0	0.5	0	2.8	100.0
1971	93.8	84.5	8.6	0.7	6.2	2.2	0	0	1.2	0	2.7	100.0
1972	93.3	82.8	8.5	1.9	6.7	2.6	0	0	1.8	0	2.3	100.0
1973	91.1	80.9	8.4	1.7	8.9	4.4	0	0	1.7	0	2.9	100.0
1974	88.3	78.7	8.5	1.1	11.7	5.3	0	0	1.6	0	4.9	100.0
1975	89.7	79.8	8.9	1.0	10.3	4.1	0	0	1.6	0	4.6	100.0
1976	90.2	80.2	9.0	1.0	9.8	4.0	0	0	1.5	0.1	4.2	100.0
1977	91.0	80.8	9.2	1.0	9.0	4.1	0	0.2	1.7	0.1	3.0	100.0
1978	90.9	80.7	9.1	1.0	9.1	3.7	0	0.3	2.0	0.1	2.9	100.0
1979	88.9	79.3	8.8	0.7	11.1	3.8	0.6	0.4	1.7	0.1	4.4	100.0
1980	87.0	77.6	8.6	0.7	13.0	3.8	0.8	0.4	2.7	0.1	5.3	100.0
1981	85.8	76.9	8.4	0.4	14.2	3.5	1.0	0.3	2.9	0	6.6	100.0
1982	84.8	75.7	8.6	0.5	15.2	4.2	1.1	0.3	3.1	0	6.5	100.0
1983	83.8	74.0	8.9	0.9	16.2	4.7	1.4	0.2	3.7	0	6.3	100.0

Table 3.2. Term Composition of Bank Lending and Deposits (as percentage of total lending or total deposits)

| | Lending | | | Deposits | | | | | |
| | Under 1 Year | Over 1 Year | Long-Term Credit Banks | Demand Deposits | With Regulated Rates | | | | With Unregulated Rates† |
					Time Deposits	3-Month	6-Month	1 Year, 1 Year & 6 Months, 2 Years, Maturity-Designated, Installment Time Deposit	
65 Mar.-end	80.7	19.3	10.5	50.3	49.7	3.6	5.4	40.7	n.a.
66 "	79.7	20.3	10.8	49.5	50.5	3.5	5.2	41.8	n.a.
67 "	79.8	20.2	10.8	47.3	52.7	3.5	5.1	44.1	n.a.
68 "	78.9	21.1	11.2	45.8	54.2	3.6	4.8	45.8	n.a.
69 "	77.6	22.4	11.2	45.6	54.4	3.5	4.7	46.1	n.a.
70 "	75.9	24.1	11.2	45.9	54.1	3.6	4.8	45.8	n.a.
71 "	74.9	25.1	11.2	45.9	54.1	3.3	4.1	46.6	n.a.
72 "	70.3	29.7	11.6	44.2	53.3	3.0	5.7	44.6	2.4
73 "	67.4	32.6	11.2	44.0	52.0	3.3	5.0	43.7	4.0
74 "	64.9	35.1	11.2	43.5	52.2	2.6	5.5	44.0	4.4
75 "	63.8	36.2	11.3	41.8	52.8	2.2	6.0	44.6	5.4
76 "	61.8	38.2	11.4	41.4	52.9	2.1	4.7	46.2	5.6
77 "	61.8	38.2	11.3	40.6	54.0	2.0	4.1	47.9	5.4
78 "	62.0	38.0	10.6	38.8	55.4	2.1	4.5	48.8	5.8
79 "	59.9	40.1	10.1	37.9	55.1	2.3	4.7	48.2	6.9
80 "	58.9	41.1	10.4	36.7	55.1	2.4	4.0	48.7	8.3
81 "	59.2	40.8	10.2	33.1	57.3	1.7	3.1	52.5	9.6
82 "	58.9	41.1	9.9	29.7	56.8	1.7	3.0	52.1	13.6
83 "	60.7	39.3	9.5	30.5	56.6	1.7	3.0	51.8	12.9

*Maturity-designated time deposit (term less than three years) was established in June 1981.
†Share of deposits with unregulated rates as sum of share of CDs, foreign currency deposits, and nonresident yen deposits.

57

s

year loans that require repayment by children in case of the borrower's death were introduced, variable interest rates were also introduced. Thus, variable-rate lending has been increasing gradually, but the average maturity has not been shortening as in some foreign countries.

Next consider the deposit side. Reflecting financial innovations, the share of demand deposits has been declining whereas that of time deposits and deposits with unregulated interest rates (CDs, foreign-currency deposits, and nonresident yen deposits) have been rising. Within time deposits, the share of longer-term (one- and two-year) deposits has been rising, but the shares of three- and six-month deposits have been declining, as corporations shift toward deposits with unregulated interest rates and repurchases. Thus, the term structure of liabilities of Japanese banks fails to show a tendency toward shortening, in contrast with some foreign countries. There are two reasons why the term structures of assets and liabilities of Japanese banks have not shortened. First, since the yield curves of regulated interest rates including deposit interest rates are always upward-sloping, customers prefer longer-term assets; thus the shortening of deposit terms does not occur. The need to match asset and liability maturity structures thus requires the banks to lend long as well. The second reason is stable domestic prices, especially since 1977. Unpredictable, random fluctuations in interest rates have been rare, and therefore the incentive to shorten the term of both assets and liabilities as a means of risk aversion is weak, for both financial institutions and other corporations. The increased share of variable-rate lending is more due to interest rate deregulation and increasingly frequent revision of regulated rates.

2. Changes in Financial Services

a. Development of New Financial Markets. Among the new financial instruments born in the period of financial innovation, repurchases and CDs have developed markets of their own. An interbank money market has long existed, but instead of competing with or eroding the interbank market, the repurchase and CD markets developed into a previously nonexistent *open* money market.

A comparison is given in table 3.3. At the end of 1982, repurchases and CDs together represented 46.6 percent of the money market as a whole. These two markets have raised the share of direct finance in the Japanese financial system and have added two channels through which the effects of monetary policy are transmitted, as we shall see below.

Since, in the Japanese case, volatile and unpredictable fluctuations in interest rates are rare, there is no urgent need for the establishment of financial futures markets.

b. Development of Retail Banking Services. Retail banking innova-

Table 3.3. Trends in Money Market Transactions

(in billions of yen)

	Call money market	Share (%)	Commercial bill discount market	Share (%)	Gensaki market	Share (%)	CD market	Share (%)	Total	Share (%)
1965	1,809	100.0							10,809	100.0
1966	747	100.0							747	100.0
1967	1,012	86.9			1,152	13.1			1,164	100.0
1968	985	77.2			291	22.8			1,276	100.0
1969	1,546	79.1			408	20.9			1,954	100.0
1970	1,817	74.6			619	25.4			2,436	100.0
1971	1,472	54.1	369	13.5	882	32.4			2,723	100.0
1972	1,048	25.8	1,792	44.1	1,224	30.1			4,065	100.0
1973	1,227	17.4	4,089	58.0	1,738	24.6			7,053	100.0
1974	2,160	23.9	5,207	57.6	1,673	18.5			9,039	100.0
1975	2,332	27.2	4,403	51.4	1,835	21.4			8,570	100.0
1976	2,567	26.3	5,091	52.3	2,089	21.4			9,742	100.0
1977	2,616	22.7	6,084	51.4	3,136	26.5			11,837	100.0
1978	2,326	17.7	6,590	50.2	4,207	32.1			13,123	100.0
1979	3,473	22.3	6,327	40.6	3,960	25.4	1,820	11.7	15,580	100.0
1980	4,133	24.7	5,738	34.3	4,507	26.9	2,358	14.1	16,736	100.0
1981	4,699	28.5	4,016	24.3	4,481	27.2	3,291	20.0	16,486	100.0
1982	4,494	24.2	5,413	29.2	4,304	23.2	4,342	23.4	18,551	100.0
1983	4,456	21.0	6,763	31.9	4,288	20.3	5,665	26.8	21,172	100.0

tions include those that economize cash and those that economize deposits.

First, consider cash-economizing services. On the individuals' income side, direct deposit of salaries started in 1969. According to a survey conducted in June 1981, 42.6 percent of total payrolls or client enterprises of city banks were remitted directly to individual deposit accounts. On the payment side, the system of direct deduction of bills for telephone, electricity, and water as well as social security contributions and taxes began in 1955, and expanded substantially in the last decade. Credit cards are also popular now. According to 1981 statistics, 8.6 percent of the final consumption expenditure of the household sector uses sales credit such as credit cards. Also, the drawing and depositing of cash through machines diffused rapidly after the introduction of cash dispensers in 1969 and automated teller machines in 1979. Diffusion of these machines as of September 1982 is shown in table 3.4. The number of such machines installed reached 26,000 and their diffusion rate among city banks came close to 100 percent. Furthermore, since 1980, various financial institutions have linked their on-line systems to those of others, so forming interbank systems for drawing cash from deposits of other institutions. At present there are several such systems (member financial institutions number 610) and customers are free to draw cash from cash dispensers and automatic teller machines of other institutions belonging to the same

Table 3.4. Installation of Automatic Teller Machines and Cash Dispensers by Banks

	Number of CDs and ATMs Installed	ATMS	Number of Offices with CDs or ATMs Installed (A)	Total Number of Domestic Offices (B)	Diffusion Rate (A/B) (%)
All banks	22,466	10,360	9,072	9,659	93.9
City banks	11,264	6,251	2,943	2,952	99.7
Regional banks	10,713	3,763	5,779	6,298	91.8
Trust banks	489	346	350	350	100.0
Long-term credit banks	0	0	0	59	0.0
Soogoo banks	5,155	1,317	3,663	4,227	86.7
Shinkin banks	6,486	3,149	5,276	6,509	81.1
Credit cooperatives	329	77	298	2,750	10.8
Agricultural cooperatives	1,588	548	1,552	15,658	9.9
Others	144	42	144	2,799	5.1
Total	36,168	15,493	20,005	41,602	48.1

system. Plans to join all into one nationwide cash dispensing system are progressing.

The Nippon Telegraph and Telephone Public Corporation has planned and started the construction of an Information Network System (INS) that can link economic agents such as enterprises and households together through a system of optical fiber cables. In 1984 it provided services in one region on an experimental basis, and extension began from 1985. Through the nationwide INS, on-line systems (or terminals) of banks and customers will be linked. This will promote "firm banking" and eventually even "home banking."

The economizing of demand deposits has been facilitated by the establishment of deposit combined accounts in 1972, as discussed in section II. Theoretically, with deposit combined accounts, settlement can now be made with zero balance in demand deposit accounts. The interest rate on the overdraft is 0.25 percent higher than the interest rates of time deposits and loan trusts that act as collateral. In March 1983, 15 percent of total time deposits were available as collateral for deposit combined accounts.

With the development of the retail banking services depicted above, one can theoretically live without cash or demand deposit balances, and, in fact, as seen in section IV below, the velocity of M1 has been increasing. However, it will remain troublesome to draw cash from cash dispensers or automatic teller machines every time payment by credit cards is not accepted. So long as transaction costs exist, a world with zero money balances will remain a dream.

   c. Supply of Various Financial Services. In Japan, as elsewhere, the distinction between banks and securities companies is fading, and fringe industries are expanding into financial businesses.

First, let us consider banks. Banks were permitted to sell newly issued medium-term and long-term government bonds over-the-counter from 1983 and outstanding government bonds from 1984. At least as related to government bonds, there remains no difference between the financial services provided by banks and securities companies. Also, up to now, as banks have not been allowed to enter the credit card business, they have set up independent credit card companies jointly with their nonbank affiliates to escape such regulation. However, credit card operation was approved as part of the banking business in the revision of the Banking Law in 1982, so banks are now going to provide credit card services of their own. By combining the cash withdrawal function and the credit card function in a single card issued to each depositor, banks can with one card provide a variety of services, such as drawing and depositing, settlement of consumer credits, and loans. In this way, they can compete with consumer credit companies and small consumer finance companies ("Sarakin") and improve their services in the field of consumer finance.

Next let us consider securities companies. The establishment of medium-term government bond funds (described in section I.2.a) means that securities companies in fact offer a type of demand deposit, in the sense that customers are free to draw funds in small amounts from their accounts after one month on deposit. In addition, some securities companies plan to add a transaction function to these funds via coordination with a foreign bank or a credit association offering demand deposits. Also, investment trusts that include government bonds from the primary as well as the secondary market have essentially the same properties as time deposits, with the exception that principal is not guaranteed if contracts are terminated before maturity. In addition, securities firms can lend within limits on a case-by-case basis with government bonds as collateral; they requested the authority to establish general credit lines on similar terms with success. At a time when banks are planning to establish deposit combined accounts secured by government bonds, and when credit companies and large retailers are expanding into consumer finance (to be discussed next), it is impossible to maintain forever the strict regulation of loans secured by government bonds by securities companies to individuals. Furthermore, securities companies recently began to provide clients (investors) with on-line information on stocks and bonds. At present, although limited to provision of information, such systems are expected to be linked with the on-line systematization of investment transactions.

Fringe industries have moved vigorously to provide financial services. In the last few years, consumer credit companies, small consumer finance companies, and large retailers have been expanding into small-amount consumer finance. Such rapid expansion is supported on one hand by the installation of cash machines and the on-line systematization of credit information made possible by technological innovations, and on the other hand by the only weakly regulated environment of fringe industries. Office locations and interest rates are either only loosely regulated or totally free of control, in contrast to those of traditional financial institutions. In 1983–84, the business of small consumer finance companies expanded rapidly in terms of both the number of offices and the amounts of loans outstanding.

II. Implications for Monetary Policy

1. Definitions of Money and Measurement of Money Demand

a. Definitions. In Japan, M1 is defined as cash currency plus demand deposits, M2 as M1 plus time deposits, and M3 as M2 plus trust accounts, loan trusts, and postal savings. Innovation in transaction accounts with high interest rates gives rise to the problem of whether to include them in M1 or M2—a problem never faced before. Innovation in investment accounts gives rise to the problem of whether to include such accounts in the definition of money at all.

In practice, time deposits, trust accounts, and loan trusts are included, but investment trusts and bonds are not. That is, CDs are taken as a form of time deposits, and the aggregates M2 + CDs or M3 + CDs are used. Foreign currency deposits, another kind of unregulated interest rate deposit, are also considered quasi-money and therefore are included in M2, along with maturity-designated time deposits, designed to generate high yields. Loan trusts ("Bigs") are included in M3. The time deposit component of "government-bond time deposit accounts" is included in M2, whereas the trust account component of "government bond trust account" is included in M3. Government bonds held on deposit at institutions are excluded from all definitions of money. Other new instruments such as gensaki bonds, medium-term government bonds, bank debentures with compound interest rates ("Wides"), medium-term government bond funds and various government bond funds are also excluded, in line with the traditional exclusion of bonds and investment trusts from all definitions of money.

b. Changes in Money Velocity. Given these definitions, it is interesting to note that the money demand function has clearly shifted along with financial innovation. Figure 3.1 shows the velocities of M1 and M2 + CDs; from this we note that the trends in these velocities changed in 1974, the year that marked the beginning of structural changes and financial innovation. That is, the velocity of M1 declined until 1973, but began to rise in 1974. On the other hand, the velocity of M2 + CDs has declined consistently.

The rising velocity of M1 is the result of money-economizing financial innovations. The natural question to ask is why the trend in the velocity of M2 + CDs, which has M1 as a component, fails to show signs of reversal. In order to answer this question, "Divisia" monetary aggregates are estimated. This is done by first decomposing simple-sum monetary aggregates such as M1 and M2, and then reforming them as weighted averages of components, with the degree of moneyness of each component as the corresponding weight.[2]

The velocities of estimated Divisia M1 and M2 + CDs are also shown in Figure 3.1. Note that the trends in the velocities of simple-sum M1 and Divisia M1 have shown the same pattern. However, the velocity of Divisia M2 + CDs rose above that of simple sum M2 + CDs in 1977 and

---

2. See chapter 4 for a typology of assets. For studies of Divisia monetary aggregates, see Barnett 1980 and 1983, Barnett and Spindt 1982, and Cockerline and Murray 1981. Here, M1 and M2 + CDs are decomposed into five and six categories, respectively. The opportunity cost of holding each category of deposits is taken to correspond to its utility as money and is used as an index to measure the degree of moneyness.

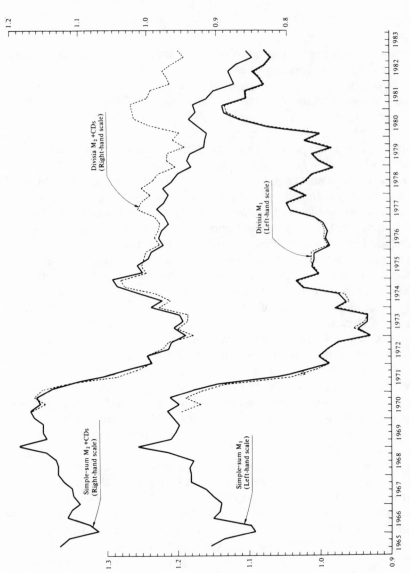

Figure 3.1. Trends in the Velocities of M1 and M2+CDs

has remained roughly constant since. Therefore, the velocity of simplesum M2 + CDs has fallen not because people hold more money for transactions purposes but rather because of expansion of components with high interest rates and low degrees of moneyness, reflecting financial innovation in investment accounts.

c. Shifts in the Money Demand Function. As we discussed above, innovation in transaction accounts has affected the demand for M1 while innovation in investment accounts has affected demand for M2. Therefore, the money demand function has clearly shown structural shifts since 1974. Let us consider the following specification for the money demand function, and estimate it for periods 1965/III–1973/IV and 1974/I–1983/I, and for the subperiods 1974/I–1980/I and 1980/II–1983/I:

$$\log (M/P)_t = \beta_0 + \beta_1 \log GNP(R)_t + \beta_2 \log RCALL_t + \beta_3 \log RTD_t + \alpha \log (M/P)_{t-1} + U_t$$

Here *M*: M1 or M2 + CDs, *P*:*GNP* deflator, *GNP* (*R*): real *GNP*, *RCALL*: (weighted average of) call money rates and market rates for commercial bills, *RTD*: interest rates on time deposit (one-year) and *U*: disturbance term. *M, RCALL, RTD* are quarterly averages of monthly data. Except for interest rates, all data are seasonally adjusted.

Results of estimations are shown in table 3.5.[3] Stability of these money demand functions is examined with *F*-statistics, and results are shown in table 3.6. As we can see from the results, the hypothesis of shifts in the money demand function between the period before 1973 and the period after 1974 for M1 and M2 + CDs can be accepted. On the contrary, when the same equation is estimated for the two subperiods since 1974, with 1980/I and 1980/II as the dividing lines, the hypothesis of structural shift is rejected. Therefore, we conclude that the money demand function shifted around 1973–74 along with structural changes in the financial system and financial innovation, but that no further shifts have occurred since.

Why did the money demand function shift in 1974? The parameters in the money demand functions before 1973 and after 1974 compare as follows. In the demand function for M1, income elasticity has clearly declined, with long-run elasticity $(\beta_1/1 - \alpha)$ falling from 1.24 to 0.65. This probably results from transaction-account–economizing financial innovations. On the other hand, the significance of the call money rate, representative of market interest rates, has declined (*t*-value 3.2 to 0.9). The time deposit rate, which had the wrong sign in the earlier period, has the correct sign in the later period, and its significance also has improved from 0.1 to 0.7, and to 1.6 for the period after 1980/II. For M2 + CDs, an estimation that corrects for serial correlation (the last row, table 3.5)

---

3. Empirical studies on the money demand function include Goldfeld 1976 and Heller and Khan 1979 for the United States, and Hamada and Hayashi 1983 for Japan.

Table 3.5. Estimation Results of the Money Demand Function

Dependent Variables	Sample Period	α	Explanatory Variables				ρ	R^2	S.E.	Durbin's h	$\frac{\beta_1}{1-\alpha}$	$\frac{\beta_2}{1-\alpha}$
			β_0	β_1	β_2	β_3						
M1		.8055 (12.70)	−.1873 (.827)	.2418 (3.23)	−.0826 (3.19)	.0114 (.0910)	—	.9969	.0177	1.267	1.243	−.4247
M2 + CDs	65/3–73/4	.7851 (19.80)	.1824 (1.96)	.2469 (5.41)	−.0784 (6.25)	.0265 (.446)	—	.9991	.0090	.6504	1.149	−.3648
M1		.7051 (7.25)	1.6484 (3.11)	.1926 (2.64)	−.0176 (.879)	−.0310 (.747)	—	.9781	.0149	.7484	.653	−.0597
M2 + CDs	74/1–83/1	.7474 (9.64)	−.9561 (3.40)	.3760 (3.41)	−.0296 (2.30)	−.0382 (1.50)	—	.9974	.0095	2.726†	1.489	−.1172
M1		.6129 (4.13)	.4375 (.622)	.3870 (2.49)	−.0118 (.581)	.0113 (.258)	—	.9766	.0143	1.134	1.000	−.0305
M2 + CDs	74/1–80/1	.6338 (6.17)	−1.8982 (3.98)	.5833 (4.11)	−.0261 (2.01)	.0639 (2.28)	—	.9954	.0091	2.285†	1.251	−.0713
M1		.4944 (2.29)	8.5370 (1.69)	.1154 (.284)	.0339 (.435)	−.2764 (1.55)	—	.9283	.0130	−1.099	.228	.0670
M2 + CDs	80/2–83/1	.7227 (4.55)	1.4024 (.488)	.2266 (.687)	−.0194 (.536)	−.0713 (.747)	—	.9905	.0075	−1.601	.817	−.0700
M2 + CDs*	74/1–83/1	.7251 (8.36)	−.9501 (2.68)	.4038 (3.28)	−.0196 (1.15)	.0138 (.411)	.440	.9999	.0086	.3762	1.469	−.0713

*Autoregressive (corrected for 1st order serial correlation).
†Serial correlation is not rejected at 1% level of significance.

66

Table 3.6. Tests of Structural Change in the Money Demand Function

Test Periods	Degrees of Freedom	F-value	
		M1	M2 + CDs
Structural change between 65/III–73/IV and 74/I–83/I	F (5,61)	3.464*	5.818†
	level of significance	.805 %	.019 %
Structural change between 74/I–80/I and 80/II–83/I	F (5,27)	1.158	1.868
	level of significance	35.5 %	13.3 %

*Significant at the 1% level.
†Significant at the 0.1% level.

is used for comparison between pre–1973 and post–1974 periods, as serial correlation is detected in the original estimation using post–1974 data (*DW*: 1.18). Although the income elasticity does not change significantly (long-run elasticity rises from 1.15 to 1.47), the market interest elasticity has clearly declined (long-run elasticity −0.365 to −0.071) and its significance also has fallen (*t*-value 6.3 to 1.2). This decline is probably caused by the higher responsiveness of interest rates on most assets included in M2 + CDs with respect to market rates. The time deposit rate is not significant in either period, probably due to multi-collinearity.

As depicted above, declining income elasticity for M1 and declining responsiveness to interest rate changes for M2 + CDs are the results of financial innovation. This is confirmed in figures 3.2 and 3.3. When the pre–1973 M1 demand function is extrapolated after 1974, predicted values tend to fluctuate around actual values, suggesting that, although income elasticity has remained about the same, interest elasticity has changed.

Finally, on the money supply side, because the Bank of Japan uses the market interest rate in the interbank market as the operating variable, instead of base money or reserve indicators, changes in the money multiplier accompanying structural shifts in the money demand function pose no particular problem for monetary control. (See section III.3 below.)

2. Levels and Flexibility of Interest Rates

Levels of major interest rates over the last twenty-four years are shown in figure 3.4. The difference between the pre–1973 era of rapid economic growth and the years that followed is immediately clear. Fluctuations in all interest rates, except the call money rate, were small before 1973 but became large thereafter.

There are three reasons why the amplitude of fluctuations was small during the earlier era. First, government policy stabilized interest rates

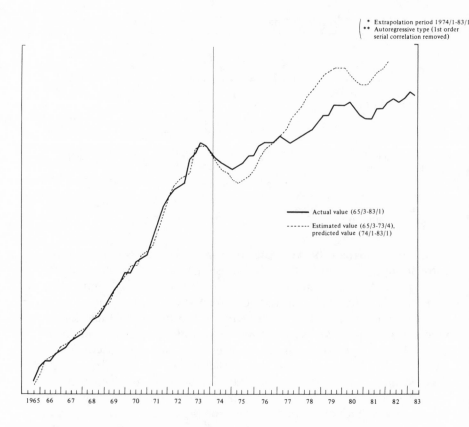

Figure 3.2. Extrapolation* Results of the M1 Demand Function**

at low levels, as we see from the flatness of the official discount rate. As a result, regulated rates including deposit rates were low and rigid. Second, low inflation made artificially low interest rates feasible; the average inflation rate from 1960 to 1972 was 4.9 percent in terms of the GDP deflator. Third, institutional factors generating segmentation of financial markets helped maintain rigidity of interest rates. Among such factors were the predominance of indirect financing and constraints on international capital movement due to foreign exchange controls. Under the indirect financing system, the call market was highly developed and the call money rate fluctuated flexibly; however, money markets and bond markets remained underdeveloped, and arbitrage between the call money rate and open market rates was weak. Furthermore, since arbitrage between the open markets and loan markets was also imperfect, the lending rate remained rigid and credit rationing predominated. Foreign-exchange controls tended to prevent international financial transactions from weak-

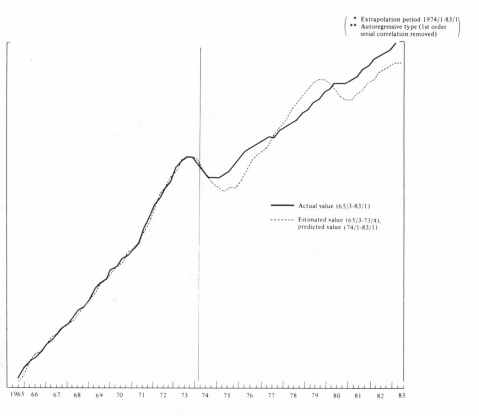

Figure 3.3. Extrapolation* Results of the M2 + CDs Demand Function**

ening either segmentations or the low and rigid interest rate system. When discussing interest rate behavior since 1973, it is appropriate to consider two subperiods separately. The first is from 1973 to 1978, which covers the occurrence and recovery from hyperinflation following the yen re- valuation of 1971 and the first oil crisis. The CPI inflation rate peaked at 26.2 percent in October 1974, and the WPI rate at 33.8 percent in February 1974. In response to this, the official discount rate and other regulated rates were raised sharply and the call market rates rose ac- cordingly. The interbank rate increases were so large, however, that even the relatively sticky open market rates and lending rates also rose. It took a long time before inflation calmed; even then, however, interest rates did not return to their former levels until 1976–77.

In the second subperiod, since 1979, conditions have been opposite to those prevailing before 1972. First, the artificially low interest rate policy has been abandoned, and a policy of adjusting interest rates flexibly has

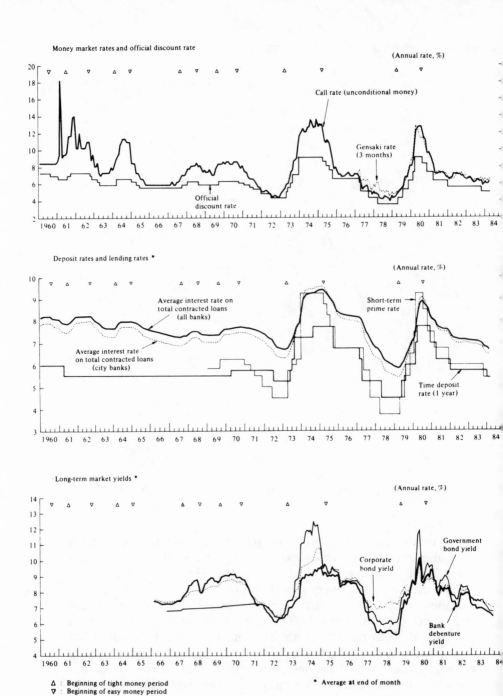

Money market rates and official discount rate

(Annual rate, %)

Call rate (unconditional money)

Gensaki rate
(3 months)

Official
discount rate

Deposit rates and lending rates *

(Annual rate, %)

Average interest rate on
total contracted loans
(all banks)

Short-term
prime rate

Average interest rate
on total contracted loans
(city banks)

Time deposit
rate (1 year)

Long-term market yields *

(Annual rate, %)

Government
bond yield

Corporate
bond yield

Bank
debenture
yield

Δ : Beginning of tight money period   * Average at end of month
▽ : Beginning of easy money period

Figure 3.4. Trends in Major Interest Rates

been adopted. After the second oil crisis, the official discount rate and regulated rates including the deposit rates were promptly raised to levels comparable to those at the last peak of the first crisis; they were then lowered quickly as inflation subsided (see figure 3.4). And this occurred despite the fact that peak inflation rates in this period, 9.0 percent for CPI (September 1980) and 18.4 percent for WPI (May 1980), were relatively low when compared with those of the previous inflation period. Second, competition rose and segmentation diminished, due to changes in the financial system such as declining private borrowing, development of open markets, advances in financial innovation, and increasing integration of domestic and foreign financial markets. The result has been more flexible interest rates, especially long-term ones. Secondary bond market yields have changed frequently, and reflecting this, longer-term regulated rates such as rates on newly issued government bonds underwritten by the syndicate, trust accounts, and loan trusts have been adjusted with increasing frequency. Moreover, the share of variable-rate lending in total long-term loans has been increasing.

The volatility of long-term market interest rates can be explained by four factors related to expectations theory.[4] First, as interest rates in the United States became volatile, so did expectations of short-term interest rates in Japan. The mechanism is this: as interest rates in the United States rise, the market believes that the Bank of Japan will prevent the interest rate spread from widening due to fear of yen depreciation; as a result, the market bids short-term interest rates up. The opposite occurs when interest rates in the United States decline. Second, when the government deficit in Japan is larger than expected, long-term interest rates rise, as in May 1982. This resulted from expectations of a higher path of short-term interest rates due to expected crowding-out. Third, government policy changes have combined with arbitrage to move long rates. Between April and October 1982, for example, the Bank of Japan's policy to prevent depreciation of the yen raised interbank rates; through arbitrage, this induced the increase in interest rates in open markets such as gensaki and CDs, which in turn affected current long-term interest rates, though to a smaller extent. Fourth, exchange-rate volatility has generated large-scale inflows and outflows of international capital, which, when used to purchase or sell domestic assets, has induced movements in interest rates.

3. The Transmission Mechanism

The transmission mechanism of monetary policy has also been affected by changes in financial structure and by innovations.

In the pre–1973 period, when the interest rate in the interbank market

4. On the term structure of interest rates of Japan, see Kuroda and Ohkubo 1981b and 1982, and Akio Kuroda 1983.

rose substantially above the official discount rate in response to the pressure from the Bank of Japan, banks and other private financial intermediaries reduced activity in fixed-rate markets such as those for loans or corporate bonds, and raised activity (either increased loans or decreased borrowings) in the interbank market. As a result, the availability of credit to the private nonfinancial sector was reduced. This process was supplemented by the Bank of Japan's window guidance on growth of bank lending, which accelerated the adjustment in the bank portfolios.[5] Since 1974, open markets have developed; the interest rates in these markets move flexibly, and they reflect arbitrage with the interbank market rate, which is directly affected by monetary policy. These developments have provided two new channels through which monetary policy operates. The first is financial disintermediation. Because the yield curve of market interest rates slopes negatively in periods of tight money but that of regulated interest rates is always positive, the differential between market and regulated rates always enlarges in such periods. As a result, funds flow out of financial intermediaries, and this reduces credit supply by private financial intermediaries. The second new channel is the direct effect of interest rates on private spending. Given the opportunities to hold financial assets at market rates, increases in these rates mean a higher opportunity cost of investment and consumption. During the monetary restraint of the second and third quarters of 1980, the private sector responded to higher interest rates by cutting spending; some banks were unable to lend the entire amount of their credit ceilings under window guidance. That is, the transmission mechanism based on interest elasticity has become more important than that based on credit rationing.

Evolution has not stopped, however, for either old mechanisms or new.[6] First, the traditional mechanism relies on the rigidity of lending rates and of interest rates on newly issued bonds. As these rates become more flexible, the credit rationing mechanism will vanish. Similarly, disintermediation depends on the rigidity of regulated interest rates. Therefore, if these rates are adjusted more frequently or completely liberalized, this mechanism vanishes as well. Thus, as financial innovation and interest rate deregulation advance, only the effect of interest rates on private spending will remain. However, this does not mean that the effectiveness of monetary policy will decline. As all interest rates will fluctuate more, the financial cost of spending to economic units who are both borrowers and investors will fluctuate more.

Elasticity pessimists may remain skeptical, but for Japan, a strong effect

5. For a discussion of the instruments of monetary policy and their transmission channels, see Suzuki 1980, parts II, III, and IV.

6. On the relation between financial innovation and the transmission mechanism, see Suzuki 1983a for detailed discussion.

of real interest rates on real expenditure has been confirmed by various statistical tests. A recent study applies a multivariate time series model and uses the method of relative power contribution to test the causality between real expenditure, the real interest rate, the nominal interest rate, and M2 + CDs. The results show that it is the real interest rate that has the largest effect on real expenditure, although real expenditure also has some feedback effect on the real interest rate, so that causality is not unidirectional.[7]

Yet another transmission effect works through the exchange rate: say a decline in the real interest rate brings about yen depreciation beyond purchasing power parity. This acts on the domestic economy as a real shock, causing higher prices and lower real income, though there is also a stimulus to exports. So long as the increase in exports fails to offset the real income loss due to the real shock, then a lower real interest rate has a net contractionary effect on the economy from the foreign side. This effect is opposite to the stimulative direct effect of lower interest rates on domestic economic activity, so the net effect is uncertain. But effects on the exchange rate and prices are certain—and undesirable. This was precisely the situation in Japan in 1982–83, and it explains why the Bank of Japan was unable to lower domestic interest rates to stimulate domestic activity. Finally, the combination of interest elasticity of real expenditure and high interest elasticity of money demand increases the importance of the crowding-out effect of large government deficits. Conversely, reducing the deficit will become more effective in lowering interest rates and improving the supply side of the macroeconomy in the long run; on the other hand, its deflationary effect in the short run will be small. This link between monetary and fiscal sides explains why reducing the deficit is one of the most desirable policy options available and why it is a matter of highest priority.

4. Monetary Control and Policy Options

Financial innovation has brought challenges to monetary policy implementation, but it has not caused disruption. Definitions of money have not been affected, and it has been relatively easy to detect structural shifts of money demand, including the decline in interest elasticity since 1974. Continued use of interbank rates as the operating target appears warranted, as statistical evidence is strong that causality runs primarily from interbank rates to M2 + CDs.[8] A wide variety of tests also confirm that causality runs from M2 + CDs to prices and nominal income, and that the feedbacks from the latter to M2 + CDs are weak. Thus, M2 + CDs has a

7. On relative power contribution and details of the empirical study, see Ohkubo 1983.
8. See Ohkubo 1983.

higher degree of exogeneity than the nominal and real interest rates, and is therefore the most appropriate indicator to use as the intermediate target.[9]

However, intermediate financial variables, such as bank credit, interest rates, and the exchange rate, retain some importance. An eclectic attitude toward policy implementation, paying full attention to intermediate financial variables in addition to money, is necessary because many factors including unpredictable expectations can disrupt the transmission channels.

In addition, short-run control of M2 + CDs is not needed. The effect of changes in M2 + CDs on nominal expenditure and prices spreads over two years; to stabilize current nominal expenditure and prices, it is sufficient to stabilize a weighted average of M2 + CDs over a two-year period. Attempts to stabilize short-run monetary growth are counterproductive, since the resultant fluctuations in interest rates and the exchange rate will raise uncertainty.

5. Financial Stability and Regulation

Japanese financial institutions are not threatened by interest rate fluctuations, because Japanese domestic interest rates do not fluctuate as violently as those in the Eurodollar or U.S. domestic market. But there is one major potential problem on the horizon. As deregulation progresses, financial institutions whose business is based on regulated interest rates will face serious interest rate competition, and the contraction of profit margins may force them into difficulty. This is the main worry of the 71 mutual loan and savings banks, the 456 credit associations, and the 468 credit cooperatives.[10] But safeguards remain. The Bank of Japan inspects financial institutions every two to three years, checks their soundness and stability, and ensures that difficulties in one institution will not cause systemic instability. And deregulation is implemented at a slow but deliberate pace to make sure that management will have enough time for adaptation. The Bank of Japan is also researching the problems of systemic risk posed by advancement of electronic funds transfer, and the potential for accidents, crime, and misuse.

Other problems are posed by quantity-based regulation on financial institutions' balance sheets, for instance, reserve requirements, CD issue limits, and so forth. When some instruments are regulated, there is always a temptation for institutions to use unregulated instruments to evade the intent of regulation. The dangerous period is the transition period. Regulations still exist, but the expanding degree of freedom affords ever-

---

9. See Kuroda, Namba, and Oritani 1980, Oritani 1979a, and Ohkubo 1983.
10. The Japanese names are "Soogo," "Shinkin," and "Shinso," respectively.

increasing opportunity for evasion; it becomes difficult for authorities to predict what will occur next. Once deregulation is complete, however, stability of the financial system will be restored.

Though the future is of course uncertain, it is clear that anachronistic regulations should be abolished. The old regulatory framework must be superseded by a framework compatible with new economic conditions, and with efficiency and fairness.

Note to I.2.b, The Partial Deregulation of Banking.

In March-April 1985, MMCs (money market certificates) with the minimum unit of 50 million and with the quantitative ceiling ratio to net worth of 75 percent were newly introduced.

Further in October 1985, interest rates on time deposits with the minimum unit of 1 billion were deregulated, the minimum unit of CDs was lowered to 100 million, the quantitative ceiling ratio of CDs was raised to 150 percent, and that of MMCs to the same percent.

Deregulation of interest rates on deposits is proceeding faster in the second half of the 1980s.

4

Interest Rate Decontrol
and the Effectiveness
of Monetary Policy

This chapter examines the problems of interest rate decontrol, the form of future financial innovations, and the effectiveness of monetary policy within the framework likely to emerge over the next several years. Such an examination requires consideration of three factors: interest rate determination (market rates or controlled rates), financial structure, and transmission channels of monetary policy.

I. Financial Structure and Transmission Channels of Policy

1. Types of Financial Assets

To discuss interest rate decontrol, financial innovation, and monetary policy, we must first examine what assets interpose themselves in the transmission channels of monetary policy and how interest rate decontrol and financial innovations will change these assets. Table 4.1 shows a classification of six types of assets, labeled (A) to (F). (A class of assets is hereafter always enclosed in parentheses, as distinguished from a specific asset that might be denoted by the same letter. For example, "(B)" is an asset of type (B) while "B" may denote bonds.) The classification is by function (transactions account assets or investment account assets), predictability of return (safe assets versus risky assets), interest determination mechanism (controlled rate or market rate), mode of issue (indirect securities or direct securities), and mode of transaction (market or bilateral). We will describe each type in some detail before proceeding.

In any financial system, the existing assets may be classified by function, that is, the motivation for their being held by people. The two major types of assets here are transactions-account assets and investment-account assets.

Table 4.1. Types of Financial Assets

Function	Transactions			Investment		
Predictability	Safe			Risky		
Interest Rate Mechanism	Controlled Rate			Free Rate		
Mode of Issue	Indirect Securities					Primary Securities
Mode of Transactions	Market	Bilateral		Market	Bilateral	Market
Type	(A) Currency, High Powered Money (Base Money)	(B) Deposit Money (Demand Deposits)	(C) Quasi Money (Time & Postal Deposits, Loan Trusts)	(D) CDs, Financial Debentures, Bills sold by banks	(E) Loans, Borrowings	(F) Public Bonds, Corporate Debentures, Equities, Commercial Papers, BAs, TBs

The most important function of transactions accounts is as means of settlement (means of payment or means of exchange) for transactions. In contrast, the most important role of investment accounts is as store of value. Hence, transactions accounts have higher liquidity than investment accounts, but the profitability of investment accounts is higher than that of transactions accounts.

In a world of nominal values (or a world of fixed prices), transactions-account assets have low profitability, but the variance of expected return is zero: in this sense they are safe assets. And because they are safe, transactions-account assets simultaneously serve as units of account. In contrast, investment-account assets have high returns, but their variance of expected return is positive, and in this sense they are risky. These attributes reflect the differences of motivation that people have for holding assets.

This discussion will proceed with a single distinction about holding motivation for assets. Assets are held either for transactions motives or for investment motives.[1] Choices of assets based on transactions motives

1. Keynes distinguished three motives for holding money—the transactions motive, the precautionary motive, and the speculative motive. But there is some ambiguity in making the precautionary motive separate when there is certainty about the time of expenditure or investment. Hence, we include the case of uncertain time of transactions with investment here, and distinguish only two motives for money holding, the transactions motive and a

of Baumol-Tobin[2] are usually thought to take place between a safe transactions asset and a safe investment asset. It is possible to conceive of a
risky investment-account asset held for transactions purposes, but considering the usually high transactions costs of risky assets (e.g., the fees
and trouble of securities transactions), such assets would not be in general
use.

On the other hand, among assets held for investment purposes, choice
is made between safe assets and risky assets; among safe assets, however,
safe investment assets with high returns dominate transactions assets with
low returns, so safe transactions assets will not be used for investment
motives. The choice of investment assets will be between safe investment
assets and risky ones.

Indeed, in a financial system where safe investment assets do not exist
(e.g., in the world of a "direct finance system" discussed below), the
choice between assets held for transactions motives and those held for
investment motives is made between safe transactions assets and risky
investment ones.

In the traditional financial system before recent financial innovation,
the interest rates on safe assets were fixed at controlled levels. But the
interest rates (rates of return) on risky assets fluctuated freely in the
market according to demand and supply conditions.

Let us continue our classification of assets by looking at the modes of
issue of assets within the financial system. Following the tradition of
financial theory of Gurley and Shaw 1960, we call the financial assets
supplied as liabilities of investment-surplus (funds-deficit) sectors "primary securities," and those supplied as the liabilities of financial intermediaries "indirect securities."

Safe transactions-account assets and safe investment-account assets are
necessarily indirect securities. Hence the issuers of indirect transactions-
account securities are "monetary financial intermediaries" (i.e., banks),
and those that issue indirect investment account securities are "nonmon-
etary" or "nonbank" financial intermediaries. This class would include
trust banks, trust departments of securities firms, thrift institutions, and
insurance companies.

In contrast, risky investment-account assets would include the indirect
securities issued by financial intermediaries (e.g., financial debentures)
and the primary securities issued by investment-surplus agents.

Finally, let us consider the mode of transactions. We call assets that

more general investment motive. On the ambiguity of the precautionary motive, see Tachi
and Hamada 1972.

2. For an explanation of the transactions motive of the Baumol-Tobin type, in which
transactions demand for money is a function of the interest rate, see Baumol 1952 and
Tobin 1956.

Table 4.2.   Flow-of-Funds Table for the Direct Finance Model

		Central Bank	Corporations	Households	Total
(A)	Currency	$-M$		M_h	0
(F)	Bonds	B	$-B_c$	B_h	0
	Real Assets		PK_c		PK_c
	Total	0	0	$NW = M_h + B_h$	$PK_c = NW$

Note: Minus sign denotes liability.
Notation: M: Currency B : Bonds (nominal) K: Real assets (real)
         P: Price level NW: Net worth = total savings (nominal)

are generated from bilateral loan agreements and that are not resellable "bilateral assets," and assets that are freely resellable (i.e., negotiable) "market assets." Among indirect transaction assets, currency is a market asset, and deposits are a bilateral asset. Among safe, indirect investment assets, time deposits, savings accounts, loan trust accounts (Japanese trust bank accounts), and other forms of quasi-money are bilateral assets. On the other hand, risky, indirect investment assets such as CDs, financial debentures, and bills sold by banks are market assets. Risky, primary investment account assets include bilateral assets such as loans, and market assets are public bonds, corporate bonds, equities, commercial paper, banker's acceptances, and treasury bills.

Using this classification system, we will now examine the relationships among the channels of transmission of policy effects and the financial system. Finally, we will consider the meaning and effects of financial innovation.

2. The World of Direct Finance: The IS-LM Model

First let us consider a world with only direct finance. In any financial system, a transactions asset (i.e., currency) is necessary, and such an asset can be issued only as the indirect liability of banks. Hence, let us bring the bare minimum of necessary indirect assets into the model, with a "central bank" that issues "currency." No other indirect assets exist. Thus, no private financial intermediaries exist, and so the indirect securities and bilateral assets they would issue do not exist either. All that exist are firms (investment-surplus agents) that issue "primary securities" and "households" (savings-surplus agents) that buy these primary securities directly. Currency is supplied by primary securities purchase operations of the central bank. Table 4.2 shows the flow-of-funds table (listed in stock form) of this world.

According to the classification of table 4.1, the two types of assets here are of type (A), a marketable, indirect, controlled-rate (at zero), safe, transactions-account asset, and type (F), a marketable, primary, free-rate, risky, investment-account asset. The crucial points about this world of direct finance are that both assets are marketable and that no bilateral assets exist. Moreover, except for marketability, these two assets differ in all their attributes. That is, because of the existence of the contrast that transactions assets are safe and investment assets are risky, all of people's asset-holding motives may be fulfilled. And because of the existence of one controlled interest rate, the general equilibrium system may be solved, and the free interest rate is uniquely determined (more on this below).

The model now has three assets: currency, M; securities, B; and real assets, K. The price level,[3] P (the price of real assets, equivalent to the price of commodities), is given. The rate of interest on currency is set at zero, and is a type of controlled rate. Thus, endogenous variables are the free rate of interest on securities, r, and the level of real income, y. In a general equilibrium framework with three assets in demand/supply equilibrium, one equation is not independent due to Walras's Law; we drop the equilibrium equation for the securities market, and so the following two equations give full equilibrium.

$$\frac{\overline{M}}{P} = L\ (r,y) : \text{currency market equilibrium} \tag{1}$$

$$I\ (r,y) + \overline{K}_{-1} = S(r,y) + \frac{\overline{W}_{-1}}{P} : \text{real asset market equilibrium} \tag{2}$$

where I is investment, S savings, $\overline{K}_{-1}$ the existing stock of real assets, and $\overline{W}_{-1}$ is accumulated savings (net worth).

---

3. In this model, real assets are nothing but the stock of real goods, so the two are identical commodities. Hence the price level is the same for both. In the general equilibrium asset selection model of Tobin 1969, "real assets" are called "real capital," and the variable q, which is the relative price ratio of the price of existing capital (equity) and newly produced capital, determines the level of investment. However, this construction describes the Anglo-American system, in which the price of equity correctly reflects the value of assets, with takeover bids and sales of firms, and with capital increases as the chief means of raising funds. It is unrealistic for Japan, where investment is funded through bank loans, bond issue, and own-capital (mostly a form of open market assets), and so it is sufficient to think of the choice being between real assets and financial ones. It is not necessary to go to the trouble of introducing the somewhat ambiguous concept of real capital and its price relative to goods in general. I cannot agree with Tachi that "it is unrealistic not to distinguish the price of goods from the price of existing capital." The "price of existing capital," that is, equity, does not move in a meaningful way so far as the Japanese investment decision mechanism is concerned. Indeed, the crucial factor is precisely the relationship of the rise in the price of existing assets, in this case goods, and the interest rate. For estimates of q for Japan, see Nihon Shooken Keizai Kenkyuu Sho 1980 and Suzuki and Otaki 1984.

With the above definitions, we can say $P\overline{K}_{-1} = \overline{W}_{-1}$,[4] so that equation (2) becomes

$$I(r,y) = S(r,y) : \text{goods market equilibrium} \tag{2'}$$

Equations (1) and (2') are nothing but Keynes's IS-LM model.

The transmissions channels for monetary policy in this world of direct finance are as follows. Let us consider a monetary tightening. The central bank sells securities, and absorbs currency. As a result the price of securities falls, that is, the rate of return rises. Seeing this, investors reduce their investments, and savers increase their savings (i.e., reduce consumption). Expenditure is reduced from both the investment and consumption sides, and so real income falls. The adjustment is completed when the reduction in currency demand accompanying the fall in real income has just balanced with the reduction in supply. A monetary expansion reverses the process, starting with a securities purchase.

This model can be solved because, among the financial assets, there was one asset, currency, with interest rate fixed at zero. Even in an enlarged model with more types of assets, unless one asset has a controlled interest rate at a fixed level, the model will be unsolvable. In this sense, we get the seeming paradox that the effectiveness of monetary policy through the fluctuation of interest rates is underpinned by the existence of one controlled interest rate (in this case that of currency, controlled at zero). If all assets had free interest rates, the level of interest rates could not be determined endogenously in the model, and hence we could not determine the effects of monetary policy through interest-rate fluctuations. This will be important when we consider the effects of financial innovation upon policy effectiveness.

3. The World of Indirect Finance: High-Growth Japan

To clarify just what the problem is, let us consider a world of indirect finance, one exactly opposite to that given above.

a. The High-Growth Financial System. Both Royama 1969 and Suzuki 1974[5] have pointed out that the direct finance world of the IS-LM model is inappropriate for analysis of Japan's high economic growth period.

In the high-growth period, particularly before the start of long-term

---

4. When the price level, P, moves, the value of existing goods, $PK(-1)$, changes. If we say that the capital gains and losses thereby generated also change the value of existing net worth $W(-1)$, then the relationship $PK(-1) = W(-1)$ will hold continuously.

5. See Royama 1969, pp. 2–6, and Suzuki 1974, pp. 75–82.

government bond issue in 1966, open markets[6] for both long- and short-term assets were severely underdeveloped. The only market in which private agents other than financial intermediaries could participate was the equity market. And even after 1966, since the subscribers' yield to bond buyers was held at a disequilibrium rate below market through the artificially low interest rate policy, and since the quantity of long-term government bonds circulating in the market was small, neither long- nor short-term securities markets could develop.[7] The rapid growth of the long- and short-term open markets came as a result of the repurchase (gensaki) and secondary government bond markets during the period of excess liquidity of 1971–73; it was furthered by the post-1974 large-scale issues of government bonds due to lower growth and the reduction in overborrowing[8] by the corporate sector and consequent increase in that sector's liquidity.

Hence, in building a theoretical model to discuss monetary policy effects in the high-growth era, we abstract from direct financial paths of open markets; the appropriate financial system is one simplified to include only indirect finance. In terms of the classification of assets in table 4.1, (F)-type primary, risky, market, free-rate, investment assets do not exist. We must construct a model in which these attributes (riskiness, marketability, free rate determination, and investment-orientation) are included in indirect securities.

b. A Model with Only Indirect Finance. This author presented such a model in 1966.[9] Table 4.3 gives the flow-of-funds table for the model, again interpreted as stocks.

In contrast to the model presented above in table 4.2, this model introduces banks (separated into city banks and local banks, linked by an interbank market) as economic agents, thus adding issuers of indirect securities. Among the assets of type (A) and type (F) available previously, only those of type (A) remain. But the attributes of (F)-type assets such as marketability, primariness, free rates, risk, and investment-orientation are inherited by assets of types (B), (C), (D), and (E), whereas (F)-type

6. An open market has the following characteristics: (*a*) agents other than financial intermediaries may participate; (*b*) the general public may trade in the market through brokers. Hence, interbank transactions, in which only financial institutions participate, and bilateral transactions in loans and deposits by intermediaries and their customers are not transactions in open markets. The archetypal short-term open markets are those in short-term government securities, CDs, and commercial paper; the archetypal long-term open market is that in government bonds. In Japan, the short-term money market was spontaneously generated with the development of the repurchase (gensaki) market in the mid-1960s.

7. For a description of the underdeveloped state of open markets until the mid-1960s and the reasons for this, see Suzuki 1974 and Teranishi 1982.

8. See Suzuki 1974.

9. See Suzuki 1966. The model in Suzuki 1974 is the same.

Table 4.3. Flow-of-Funds Table for the Indirect Finance Model

| | Bank of Japan | Commercial Banks | | Corporations | Households | Total |
		City	Local			
(A) Currency	$-M$	M_{cb}	M_{lb}	0	M_h	0
Direct Credit	C	$-C_{cb}$	0	0	0	0
(D) Call Loans	0	$-CL_{cb}$	CL_{lb}	0	0	0
(E) Loans	0	L_{cb}	L_{lb}	$-L_c$	0	0
(B), (C) Deposits	0	$-D_{cb}$	$-D_{lb}$	D_c	D_h	0
Real Assets	0	0	0	PK_c	0	PK_c
Total	0	0	0	0	NW $(= M_h + D_h)$	$PK_c = NW$

See notes to table 4.2. "Currency" here includes deposits of banks at the Bank of Japan.
New notation: CL: Call Loans
$\qquad\qquad\ \ L$: Loans
$\qquad\qquad\ \ D$: Deposits

83

assets themselves disappear. For households, the investment assets are deposits, type (*B*), and quasi-money, type (*C*). For banks, the investment assets are risky, free-rate, bilateral, primary assets (*E*) such as loans. Currency is supplied by the central bank through "direct credit," that is, through central bank loans.

This indirect-finance model has five of the types of assets listed in table 4.1, that is, (*A*)-, (*B*)-, (*C*)-, (*D*)-, and (*E*)-type assets. Of these (*A*)-, (*B*)-, and (*C*)-type usually have controlled interest rates, but (*D*)- and (*E*)-type usually have free rates. But in high-growth Japan, the "prime rate" on loans and the official discount rate were tied by a mechanical formula and were controlled at low levels under the artificially low interest rate policy. Hence, even loans not subject to the prime rate, which are usually free, had a tendency to be sticky. It is more realistic for this model to treat (*E*)-type assets as having controlled rates.

The channels of transmission of effects of monetary policy in this model are as follows.[10] When the Bank of Japan lowers the level of direct credit to banks (in this model, to city banks), the call market tightens and the call rate rises. But since the interest rate on loans to customers of the banks is sticky under the artificially low interest rate framework, the banks look at the high call rates and reduce lending to customers in favor of sending money to the call market (or repaying call loans in the case of city banks). As a result, there is a quantitative reduction in lending to customers, and hence in the money supply: through this the tightening effects permeate to expenditure activities on the real side. For a monetary easing, the path is: Rise in Bank of Japan lending—Fall of the call rate—Rise of lending to bank customers.[11]

Where, then, are the qualitative differences in channels of transmission of the direct model's policy effects and those of the indirect model? First, the original impact of a change in central bank credit is felt in the interbank market's free rate in the latter but in the open market free rate in the former. But both models have the common point that the impact is felt on marketable, free-rate, risky, investment assets. The difference is that these are (*D*)-type indirect securities in the indirect model, and (*F*)-type primary securities in the direct model.

Second, the transmission channels are different. For the indirect model, movements of the interbank rate affect banks' asset selection and change the quantity of credit provided, and hence the money supply. Through this, the expenditure decisions of economic agents are indirectly

10. For a detailed description of the monetary policy transmission channels in this model, see Suzuki 1974, particularly chapter 14.

11. Among the studies to examine and develop the model in Suzuki 1966 are Rooyama 1969, Moriguchi 1970, Tachi and Hamada 1972, Suzuki 1974, Hamada and Iwata 1980, and Horiuchi 1980. I owe a great deal to these research results.

affected. In contrast, in the direct-finance model, the change of the open market rates directly affects the expenditure decisions of agents. Thus, the third difference is that the indirect-finance model does not limit effects on agents to those through interest-rate movements, but rather the model generates quantitative reductions of credit or money, such as "credit crunches." In the direct-finance model, agents are affected primarily through interest rate changes.

These differences are important when we come to discuss the effects of financial innovations on policy influence.

4. A Mixed Direct and Indirect Finance World:
The Contemporary Japanese System

Open markets have been developing gradually in Japan since the last half of the 1960s. The basic background for this development is the structural change in flow of funds, internationalization of finance, and the liberalization of interest rates that has accompanied these trends. With the decline of indirect finance in the last half of the 1970s, the development of direct finance is accelerating.

The outlook is for the money market (i.e., the open market in short-term assets)—comprising repurchase, treasury bill, and CD markets—to develop further. Even the open markets in long-term bonds are expected to develop further, as the quantity and diversity of long-term bonds grows, and as rollover operations become standard occurrences.

It is only natural under the circumstances for the inconsistencies between the open market rates and the controlled rates in the indirect assets (e.g., deposit rates, financial debenture rates, expected yields on loan trusts, the prime rate on loans) to grow; these growing inconsistencies will become the impetus to further decontrol.

For a financial system that is a mix of a direct finance system and an indirect one, discussion of the channels of transmission of monetary policy effects requires integration of the direct and indirect models given above. To do this, we add the (F)-type assets, which were excluded when we moved from the direct system to the indirect one. The (F)-type assets that did not exist in the indirect finance system are marketable, free-rate, risky, investment assets, and their addition brings open markets into the model.

These (F)-type assets (here represented by securities) are held by the central bank, corporations, banks, and individuals, that is, by all sectors. They were the liabilities of the corporate sector. To avoid overcomplication of the model, we omit the public sector; but the securities issued by the public sector are central to the existence of the securities market, so a realistic model would have to include them. The flow-of-funds table for this model is given in table 4.4.

In this model, the balance sheets of the Bank of Japan and of the public sector are taken as policy variables, and hence are exogenous. Of the six assets, the interest rate on high-powered money is set at zero, so there are six endogenous variables, namely five interest rates and real income, y. With prices assumed given, equilibrium in the six asset markets and in the single goods market (equation (2') above) gives seven equations; six of these are independent and determine the six endogenous variables.[12]

Let us start in a period of monetary ease, with controlled rates at equilibrium levels and hence with the system in overall equilibrium. The Bank of Japan decides on a monetary tightening; it recalls direct loans, raises the official discount rate, and sells bills (all these operations in indirect assets), and also sells securities (in open markets), thus reducing high-powered money. The system would move to a new equilibrium if all interest rates were free rates, or if controlled rates moved immediately to new equilibrium levels. But in reality there are the following constraints. First, the deposit interest rate, r_D, is determined at an upper ceiling by guidelines. Second, the market rate on loans r_L, is difficult to move quickly due to the de facto link of the prime rate to the official discount rate and due to the long-term relationships with customers that lie behind bilateral assets such as loans. Hence, the loan rate is sticky and takes a great deal of time to adjust to its equilibrium level. (The discount rate can be thought of as going quickly to its equilibrium rate, since it is supposed to be a shadow penal rate including the Bank of Japan's attitude toward rationing of central bank credit at its discount window.)

Thus, the various measures of monetary tightening force the market into disequilibrium, and real income, y, is affected both through the routes of the direct-finance model and those of the indirect-finance model.

First, the indirect asset operations by the Bank of Japan—for example, recalling loans, raising the shadow penal rate, r, and selling bills—raise the interbank market rate, r_C. The direct asset operations—sales of securities—invite a rise of the open market rate, r_B. Moreover, since there is close arbitrage between these two markets, even if the Bank of Japan restricted credit in only one of them, both markets' interest rates, r_C and r_B, would rise.

Increases in these two interest rates will affect banks' and firms' behavior in the following ways. (*1*) For the banks, as seen in the indirect-finance model, the sticky loan rate will cause restraint in lending, and so corporate activity and hence real income, y, will receive an "indirect" restraining effect from the funds "quantity" side. (*2*) On the other hand,

12. We may conceive of this model as similar to the IS-LM model in table 4.2, but with the number of financial asset equilibrium conditions expanded from one to five.

Table 4.4. Flow-of-Funds Table for the Mixed Direct/Indirect Model

	Financial Assets		Bank of Japan	Comm. Banks		Corpo-rations	House-holds	Govern-ments	Total
Type	Description	Interest Rate		City	Local				
(A)	High-powered money	0	−	+	+	+	+	0	0
	Direct credit	r	+	−	0	0	0	0	0
(B),(C)	Deposits	r_D	0	−	−	+	+	0	0
(D)	Bills sold by banks and call loans	r_C	+	−	+	0	0	0	0
(E)	Commercial loans	r_L	0	+	+	−	0	0	0
(F)	Securities	r_B	+	+	+	±	+	−	0
	Real Assets/Wealth					+	−	+	0

Note: + indicates assets, − liabilities. For real wealth row, + indicates real assets and −, wealth.

as seen in the direct-finance model, the rise of interest rate r_B will directly affect firms and households, and thus restrain income, y. The rise of r_B is not only a rise in the cost of funds for deficit agents but also a rise in the opportunity cost of expenditure for surplus agents. Hence, expenditure will be reduced.

In the mixed direct/indirect–finance model, in addition to the above two channels, there is another channel of transmission: (3). As a result of the rise in the market rate, r_B, while the deposit rate, r_D, remains fixed, both households and firms will strengthen their preference for securities over deposits, and deposits will not flow into banks as previously. Hence, banks will face a shortage of funds and restrain lending, so that firms' investment activities and hence income, y, will be restrained from the quantity side. This reduction in the financial intermediation by banks is called "disintermediation."

These are the three channels of transmission of policy effects in the mixed financial model. There is one interest rate effect, channel (2), and two quantity effects, channels (1) and (3). Of these two types of transmission channel effects, the latter two quantity channel effects rely on the deposit and loan rates being controlled or sticky. That is, the stronger controls are, the stronger effects (1) and (3) are, whereas the strength of effect (2) weakens. However, if controls are weak or if interest rates are decontrolled, effect (2) strengthens, but effects (1) and (3) disappear. Hence, the viewpoint that emphasizes importance of quantity channels of transmission implies that relaxation of interest controls and interest rate decontrol will harm the effectiveness of monetary policy. But the viewpoint that emphasizes the interest rate channel says that interest rate decontrol will promote the effectiveness of monetary policy.

In what follows, we will dig deeper and examine these two points of view and their implications.

The quantity effects (1) and (3) change money stock from the supply side even before they affect transactions, whereas the interest rate effect (2) changes simultaneously money stock from the demand side and transactions. This will be an important point when we consider financial innovations in Section III below.

II. Prices or Controls?

1. Control-Based Monetary Policy

a. The Disintermediation Mechanism. The proposition that tight money policy functions effectively through disintermediation, and more generally through quantity reductions in bank credit, or more extremely through credit crunches, is clearly a minority view in the American academic world. But among economists who are close to practitioners, this viewpoint is held.[13] For Japan around 1965, both Tachi and Patrick have held that reductions of bank credit based on quantity controls such as "window guidance" (controls on lending growth) have mainly supported the effectiveness of monetary policy.[14] I myself have emphasized that the main reason for reductions of bank credit is not window guidance, but rather the rise in the call rate given the controlled interest rate structure.[15] (This is equivalent to the quantity effect (*1*) mentioned above.) But no matter which viewpoint one takes, there is no doubt that until about 1965 monetary tightening in Japan showed its effectiveness through quantitative pressure on bank credit. The debate was over what mechanism caused the quantitative pressure.

There are in general three types of controls that can cause financial disintermediation—or, more extremely, credit crunches.

The first is controls on interest rates of (*B*)-, (*C*)-, and (*E*)-type bilateral assets of financial intermediaries. For the case of (*B*)- and (*C*)-type assets, there are upper limits on deposit rates, such as the Regulation Q rates of the United States. (But according to the Depositary Institutions Deregulation and Monetary Control Act of 1980, deposit rates in the United States are to be totally deregulated, with the phased abolition of controls through March 1986.) Japan has always had upper limits on deposit rates controlled by guidelines, and actual deposit rates have actually been at these upper limits.

With controls on the upper limits of (*B*)- and (*C*)-type assets, a movement toward monetary tightening will raise the free rates on (*F*)-type market assets; deposits will become hard to collect, as funds are absorbed in the open money markets and the open bond markets. As a result, financial intermediaries will face a shortage of funds, and will be forced to restrain lending. This is disintermediation (transmission channel (*3*) mentioned above).

In Japan after 1975, decontrol of interest rates has progressed, and the open markets such as repurchase, CD, and secondary bond markets have expanded. The result has been disintermediation.

But before that, through the decade to 1975, the interest rate on (*E*)-type assets such as loans was inflexible due to the existence of controlled rates such as the prime rate; hence, when the interest rates on (*D*)-type assets such as call loans rose sharply, banks reduced lending and put funds into the call market. This put pressure on credit (transmission channel (*1*) from above).

13. See Wojnilower 1980.
14. See Tachi 1965 and Patrick 1962.
15. See Suzuki 1966, especially the introduction and chapter 4, section 5.

To summarize the above mechanism: Due to the controls on (B)-, (C)-, and (E)-type bilateral assets of financial intermediaries, changing the interest rates on (D)- and (F)-type free-rate market assets would generate disintermediation.

The second type of control is existence of reserve requirements on (B)- and (C)-type assets. When no interest is paid on reserves (as in Japan, the United States, and many developed nations), the cost of supplying (B)- and (C)-type liabilities subject to reserve requirements rises; a competitive disadvantage arises for these assets versus (F)-type securities, so that banks cannot offer attractive interest rates to depositors. Thus, deposits become hard to collect and disintermediation occurs (similar to transmission channel (3) above. But even if interest were paid on reserves, a rise in interbank rates (as in transmission channel (1) above) would still restrain bank credit.

A third type of control is direct quantitative control on bank credit. "Window guidance" in Japan is a classic form of this.

b. The Bank Credit School and Elasticity Pessimism. The proposition that monetary policy cannot be effective without quantitative pressure generated by disintermediation implicitly relies on one or both of the following assumptions.

First is the assumption that, when bank credit is quantitatively restrained, other means of raising funds are unavailable, so agents have no choice but to reduce investment. But disintermediation means that the flow of funds from savings-surplus agents to deficit agents shifts from the indirect deposit route to the direct securities route; hence the deficit agents should be able to obtain funds. Moreover, even deficit agents have some investments in the open markets, and will be able to fund real goods investment by redeeming these investments.

Hence, in order to say that disintermediation causes credit pressure, it is necessary to restrict ourselves to the case that virtually all deficit agents are unable to raise funds through the direct securities on the open market, and that the quantity of own-capital is small. This is the "overdraft economy" of Hicks 1974. Until the mid-1960s, Japan was relatively close to this world.

The second implicit assumption is that investment activity is inelastic with respect to interest rates. In this case, the effect of interest rates on activity is small, so that only quantitative controls on credit can make monetary policy effective.

The proposition that the effectiveness of monetary policy is basically due to credit pressure generated from reliance on controls rests on the two assumptions of the "credit paradigm of an overdraft economy" and "elasticity pessimism" about the interest elasticity of investment. If these two assumptions hold, the easing of controls or decontrol will certainly lower the effectiveness of monetary policy.

2. Monetary Policy and the Interest Rate Mechanism

a. The Asset School and Elasticity Optimism.   But are these two assumptions plausible? In the U.S. financial system and in the Japanese since 1975, the methods for corporate fund raising have been diverse. In the United States, in addition to bond issue and equity issue, funds can be raised by issue of commercial paper and bankers' acceptances. That is, (*F*)-type assets have been developing rapidly. Moreover, with internationalization of financial markets, both American and Japanese firms can raise funds in foreign markets easily. Moreover, for many years in the United States and since 1975 in Japan, corporations have managed large amounts of own-capital in open markets. In Hicks's terminology, both nations show many elements of the "auto-economy." Hence, disintermediation will not result in immediate quantitative difficulty for corporate fund-raising or in investment reduction. If such effects do occur, they are limited to housing loans and consumer credit or to the small group of people with little savings.

Moreover, elasticity pessimism about investment is most likely a leftover from the 1930s. According to the econometric studies that have developed so rapidly in the postwar period, interest elasticity of investment is high enough.

In Japan, since monetary policy in the period through the mid-1970s worked through quantitative pressure on credit, the interest elasticity of investment could not be ascertained. But in the first monetary tightening of the late 1970s, in 1979–80, investment was clearly restrained as "interest rates worked." At the time the open market rates (opportunity cost of investment) in the repurchase and CD markets rose to 13 to 14 percent, corporations refrained from redeeming funds from the market and instead reduced investment. As a result, even when the monetary tightening hit its peak in the second and third quarters of 1980, banks still could not fill their window guidance quotas. At the time some people spoke of "tightness without quantity pressure," that is, interest rates worked to restrain investment before quantitative constraints became binding, so that the window guidance quotas went unfilled.[16]

Econometric support for the importance of interest rates in determining investment has been provided by Suzuki and Otaki 1984, who use a two-step procedure. In their model, investment is determined inter alia by changes in the ratio of anticipated return on capital to the expected interest rate on financial assets, that is, the marginal Tobin's *q*. (Table 4.5 presents their regression supporting this part of the hypothesis.) The second step is to establish the independent importance of the interest rate

16. See Suzuki 1981, chapter 2, section 1, for a detailed explanation of the effects of the monetary tightening of 1979–80.

in influencing Tobin's q. This is done by using spectral methods to examine the relationship between the components; it is found that this relationship is characterized by high exogeneity of the interest rate versus the anticipated rate of return on capital, with very little feedback in the opposite direction. By extension, the interest rate is thus the prime mover behind changes in Tobin's q and hence in investment demand. And given the importance of interest rates, the conditions for effectiveness of free market monetary policy in an auto-economy are fulfilled.

Table 4.5. Estimation of the Fixed-Investment Function in the Manufacturing Sector

	Coefficients	t-statistic (in parentheses)
Constant	0.0281	(1.0)
Marginal q	0.0649	(12.0)
Real cost of capital goods	− 0.0694	(2.5)
Real cost of energy	− 0.0092	(4.5)
$\bar{R}^2$ / D.W.	0.830	0.53

Source: K. Suzuki and M. Otaki (1984).

As seen above, the United States for many years and Japan since 1975 have been very much auto-economies, in the sense that firms have had enough own-capital, and that fund-raising methods other than reliance on domestic credit have developed. Hence, it is a mistake to think monetary policy powerless unless there is credit pressure due to disintermediation. We must replace the policy paradigm of the bank credit school and elasticity pessimism with a new paradigm of the asset school and elasticity optimism.

Even if disintermediation were to occur due to controls, an economy with ample financial assets would not see quantitative credit pressure. However, even without causing quantitative credit pressure, monetary tightening effects will permeate the economy if interest rates are flexible.

Thus, even if controls are abolished, and even if disintermediation increases, the effectiveness of monetary policy need not decline. On the contrary, since abolition of controls will make interest rates more flexible, the effectiveness of monetary policy working through the interest rate mechanism will rise.

b. Demerits of Disintermediation. As we have seen above, from the point of view of maintaining the effectiveness of monetary policy it is meaningless to say monetary policy must be control-based. But monetary policy is not the only question. Continuation of controls also has demerits from the viewpoint of optimal allocation of funds and fair distribution of income. With these questions in mind, let us consider deposit-rate limits, reserve requirements, and window guidance—the three types of controls said to have underpinned effectiveness of monetary policy.

First, upper limits on deposit rates imply controls only on the interest rates paid by financial intermediaries for the funds they gather; they ignore the interest rates on the funds they lend (in loans or securities purchase). Hence, at times of credit pressure when there is disintermediation, the rates of return on intermediaries' lendings far exceed those on their deposits, giving rise to excess profits, either latent[17] or actual. This is a sign of unfair income distribution. Moreover, at times of disintermediation, the channels of fund flows from savings agents to investing agents change, and the share of intermediation falls for artificial reasons. This is a sign of inefficient funds allocation.

Required reserves act exactly as a tax, but only on the types of assets against which they must be held. This artificially lowers the market share of financial intermediaries that supply these liabilities, which is a sign of inefficient funds allocation. On the other hand, agents who supply similar but nonreservable liabilities reap excess profits, a situation that shows unfair income distribution.

These paragraphs show that the various controls that underpin monetary policy effectiveness all cause the institutions that are subject to control to lose market share, but they also cause excess profits somewhere in the financial system. These effects bring inefficient resource allocation and unfair income distribution to the nation's economy.

III. Financial Innovation and Monetary Policy Effectiveness

1. Progress of Financial Innovation

a. Causes of Financial Innovation. Financial innovation has been touched off by the loss of market share of institutions subject to various controls and by the excess profits existing in parts of the financial system. That is, there are movements among the financial institutions losing share to devise ways around controls and develop new financial instruments that somehow avoid controls. Moreover, individual firms in areas in which there are excess profits will often sacrifice a portion of those profits in the form of developing new financial instruments and thereby reap new profits and a larger market share. And in parts of the industry that are not enjoying excess profits there will be attempts at entry through devising new instruments that threaten the areas where excess profits exist. The process eliminates excess profits, and promotes efficiency and fairness in the sense of equalizing opportunity to trade.

17. "Excess profits" are those generated by existence of controls or oligopoly. These may be only latent in the sense that they are eaten away by X-inefficiencies such as insufficient reduction of costs or artificially low interest rates on government bonds.

The U.S. experience of the 1970s suggests two other factors. First is a rise in inflation. As inflation rose in the United States, open market free interest rates soared, and the deviations of free rates from the controlled rates reached unprecedented levels. The result was accelerated loss of share for financial institutions, as well as expanded excess profits in some parts of the financial system. In short, the incentive to innovate in the financial industry rose dramatically. Moreover, since customers raced to find inflation hedges, the demand for advantageous new assets was very strong and brought tremendous profits to founders.

But it is wrong to be blinded by inflation and consider financial innovation to be a special phenomenon generated only by inflation. Even had inflation not risen, financial innovation would have been unavoidable to the extent that the aforementioned controls existed and that the technological change (described below) progressed. But inflation did make the changes sudden. In this sense, inflation was a catalyst behind innovation but not a necessary ingredient. Indeed, in Japan, financial innovation has been proceeding even though inflation has been much lower than in the United States.

The second factor was the remarkable decline in transactions costs due to the microcomputer revolution. The transactions costs for financial intermediation and the costs of deposit, withdrawal, and transfer of funds declined both through the efficient management of fund acquisition and allocation through on-line systems and through data telecommunications systems with customers using telephone lines. Attractive financial instruments developed as a result. This technological revolution occurred very rapidly in Japan, and, as in the United States, it will only increase in importance as the technological impetus to financial innovation strengthens.

Thus, financial innovation was induced by loss of share of financial institutions restrained by regulation, by excess profits in some sections of the financial system, and by technological improvements that reduced transactions costs. The goals of financial innovations were avoidance of controls and expansion of market shares. These goals were achieved through sacrifice of excess profits and reduction of costs through technological improvement. The result has been rates of return hitherto not available on financial instruments. In what follows, we will look at the detailed structure of financial innovations, based on motives for holding financial assets.

b. Economization of Transaction Assets. Transactions account assets of (A)- and (B)-types have controlled interest rates, with currency and sight deposit rates at zero and demand deposit rates very low. Hence, there always exists an incentive for a bank wishing to raise its market share to circumvent the interest rate controls and attach a higher interest rate to a transaction-account asset.

As we saw above, asset selection based on transaction motives takes place between transactions assets and investment assets. Hence, if the "round trip" transactions cost between transactions and investment accounts is less than the interest income from holding assets in the investment account just until the day of payment, then investment assets will be held; if not, then transactions assets will be held.[18] Thus, with sacrifice of excess profits and fall of transactions costs causing fall in the transfer fee between transactions and investment accounts, people will economize on transactions assets and increase holding of investment assets. Looked at from another angle, this means paying interest on transactions accounts in excess of the controlled rate. If a bank performs these innovations, then (A)- and (B)-type assets will be economized and all funds will gather in (C)-type quasi-money assets. Moreover, for the part of transactions assets held in risky (F)-type assets, if the transactions cost differential between (F)-type and (C)-type assets is higher than the interest-rate differential less the risk premium, then there will be a shift to (C)-type assets from (F)-type assets. Thus many banks, which are losing market share due to control on (A)- and (B)-type asset interest rates at zero or low levels, recover to an extent. The specific innovations that have brought economization of currency and deposits include checks and credit cards, automatic paycheck deposit, automatic fee transfers (e.g., utility payments), and automatic teller machines. Those innovations that have caused economization of deposits and shift into quasi-money include NOW accounts, automatic transfer systems (ATS), and telephone transfers.

In Japan this type of innovation is proceeding in the form of changing ordinary deposit accounts into general accounts, that is, accounts with overdraft privileges using quasi-money accounts (time deposits and loan trusts) as collateral.

c. Advent of Safe Investment Assets with Market Rates.   Let us consider financial innovations relating to the investment motive for holding assets. As we saw above, the asset selection relevant to the investment motive is between safe investment accounts and risky investment accounts. In the traditional financial system, the safe investment asset is (C)-type quasi-money, with a controlled interest rate. But because of controls, the banks have the incentive to attempt to recover market share by avoiding interest rate controls, sacrificing excess profits, and offering advantageous, safe, investment-account assets. In this case, the competition is from (D)- and (F)-type risky, free-rate, marketable investment assets. Hence, when (C)-type assets are given market rates, they are more attractive since their expected return becomes the same as that of the competing assets, and the principal-guarantee of safe assets exists. Possible innovations with this in mind include six-month fixed deposits with interest rates tied to the subscribers' yield on six-month Treasury bills, and 2-1/2 year fixed deposits with interest rate tied to the average yield on 2-1/2 year Treasury notes.

18. See Baumol 1952 and Tobin 1956.

Japan had not seen the advent of such accounts until 1985 when MMCs with interest rates tied to those on CDs were introduced, and interest rates on time deposits with units above 1 billion were deregulated.

With banks sacrificing some of their excess profits in order to offer more attractive new instruments and thus raise their market shares, the securities industry will start innovations in order to compete. In fact, to be accurate, the securities-industry innovations mentioned below actually came first (threatening banks' excess profits by entry), and bank innovations mentioned above were actually responses.

The assets traditionally handled by the securities industry are (F)-type assets such as government securities, corporate bonds, and equities. These assets have high yields but have the drawbacks of high risk, large units, and high transactions costs. Moreover, the securities industry cannot combine these with (B)-type assets and give them a transactions aspect. Hence, if the yields on banks' (C)-type assets equalize with those of (F)-type assets such as money market certificates and small savers certificates, then the (F)-type assets lose their competitiveness. However, the securities industry has already developed innovations such as repurchase agreements and money market mutual funds (MMMFs). The latter is an "investment trust" that invests the funds it gathers in (F)- and (D)-type assets of the short-term money market (i.e., CDs, commercial paper, bankers acceptances, and Treasury bills). In the sense that the fear of capital loss is low, these assets are close to being safe assets, and they also have small unit transactions ($500 to $1,000), are freely convertible, and have no time limits. Moreover, one can also open a demand deposit account at a bank with a hookup to the securities firm, and when there is a shortage of funds, have funds automatically transferred from the MMMF, thus giving the latter a transactions facility. In Japan the asset similar to MMMFs is the medium-term government bond fund. The motivation for securities firms to offer such an asset is to acquire the excess profits of banks.

d. Avoidance of Reserve Requirements and Window Guidance. The previous sections considered innovations by banks to avoid interest rate controls and those by securities firms in reaction to those of the banks. However, the banks' NOW accounts, though de jure (C)-type savings accounts, are de facto (B)-type demand deposit accounts. And the securities firms' MMMFs are formally investment trusts formed by (F)-type assets, but in fact function as (C)-type quasi-money. Both function as (B)- and (C)-type assets, that is, as deposits. Thus, both these assets help circumvent reserve requirements.

In response to this fact, there are those in the United States who hold that NOW accounts should be required to be backed by the high reserves required for demand deposits, and that MMMFs should be included among reservable assets and thus be backed by the same levels of reserves as required for savings deposits. But this would only lead to repeated rounds of innovation and expansion of reservable assets. As long as controls exist, attempts to avoid them will continue. For example, a bank can have a subsidiary float commercial paper or raise funds abroad in Euromarkets, and thus acquire de facto deposits without incurring liabilities. There is an infinite variety of schemes to avoid incurring reservable liabilities and avoid interest rate controls through issue of what are formally (D)-, (E)-, and (F)-type assets but are actually (C)-type ones.

One way to erase the incentive to avoid reserve requirements is to pay market rates of interest on reserve deposits. As long as the transactions costs of gathering reservable deposits are not higher than those of gathering other ones, reservable assets will thus be made at least no less attractive. But if such interest is paid, effectiveness of the cost effect lying behind the reserve requirement system will disappear, and only the liquidity effect will remain; to this extent, the effectiveness of monetary policy will decline.[19]

Innovations to avoid window guidance controls are not a topic of discussion now, but such innovations are possible. One possibility is repurchase agreements based on loan securities. Another is acquisition of customers by local banks outside the strictest window guidance controls. Another is introduction of impact loans from abroad through the good offices of the bank. In this sense, window guidance is at the very most an emergency measure for tight money periods, and only acts as supplementary means of speeding up the adjustment process. It should not be continued in periods of easy credit.

2. The Financial System of the Future

Innovation will continue so long as there are controls; but as we saw above, the continuation of controls is not a necessary condition for effectiveness of monetary policy. Thus, it is desirable to ease controls at a pace that is deliberate but will not cause confusion in the financial system, and to eliminate as many controls as possible.

Once controls have been abolished, excess profits have been eliminated, and innovation has furthered the efficiency and fairness of the financial system, what sort of system will exist? We will not reach such a system for some time, but it is meaningful to compare the current state and the most extreme vision of the future, to investigate the problems of the transition period.

a. Currency: Economization and Continuation. How thorough will be the economization of (A)-type currency in the financial system of the future? It can be conceived that every person will have a bank identifi-

19. For an explanation of the cost effect and liquidity effect of the reserve requirements system, see Suzuki 1974, chapter 12.

cation card with a password, with which to order payments for transactions from computer terminals placed in homes or stores or places of business. (This is also known as "home banking" or "firm banking.") But no matter how much technology advances, the transactions costs of using telecommunications systems will not go to zero. Thus, the cost of economizing on cash use will always be positive. As long as that cost exceeds the benefit of economization of cash, the use of cash will continue. In fact, for small transactions, the convenience of cash is quite high. And, though this is a factor of a different magnitude, the underground economy will also exist in any world, and it will use cash.

From the viewpoint of monetary policy, the extinction of currency will cause difficulty. Even in a world in which all interest rates are free to fluctuate, the rate of return on currency is fixed, at zero. It is due to the existence of this controlled rate that the general equilibrium system is uniquely solvable, so that the levels of other interest rates are determined. The use by the populace of central bank liabilities in the form of currency with zero interest rate is the foundation of monetary policy effectiveness.

Since the use of currency is a necessary condition for maintaining the effectiveness of monetary policy, one might conceive of the idea that, in order to force the use of currency, reserve requirements should be imposed on all other financial assets. But no matter how much electronic information systems develop, it would still be too complex to keep track of all financial assets (the lending and borrowing of all economic agents) and impose reserve requirements on all of them. If this is the case, then allowing even a few exceptions to the rule would create new financial instruments that avoid the reserve requirements, and again start an endless fight between controls and innovations. Hence, the realistic response is not to broaden reserve requirements but rather to pay market interest rates on reservable deposits. This proposal does have the defect that the cost factor making reserve requirements effective is eliminated. But in either case, coming to a conclusion is premature, since we do not know how future electronic information and telecommunications systems will develop.

b. Potential for Elimination of Deposit Money.   Even if (A)-type currency continues to exist, what will happen to (B)-type deposit money? It is likely that zero or low interest rate accounts will continue to play a role on a flow basis as transactions accounts, but will disappear on a stock basis, as most are transferred into investment accounts. Recently in the United States the advent of sweep accounts has shown the shape of this part of the future. In this type of account, a given limit for demand deposits is established; when the balance exceeds that amount, the excess is automatically transferred into an MMMF, and if there is a shortfall this is made up by transfer from the MMMF. The term "sweep" is used because the transactions account is continually "swept clean" at a given level.

What will happen when sweep accounts disseminate widely? The level of (B)-type assets will be equal to the sum of sweep account contract levels, and will be at this fixed level regardless of transactions needs. If the economization of cash has also proceeded greatly, then the narrow money supply M1 comprising (A)- and (B)-type assets will lose its relation to economic activity, and cease to move at all. This will be a world in which transactions balances are almost stationary. Moreover, there is the possibility that competition will drive the deposit balance of sweep accounts to zero. In this case, transactions accounts will be active during business hours, but will disappear from the world at night, and become (C)-type investment accounts with payments facility. In fact, in the United States transactions accounts with market interest rates (such as money market deposit accounts and Super-NOW accounts) were approved as of December 1982.

From the point of view of the motivation for holding money, it is only natural that the level of (A)- and (B)-type assets that compose M1 should shrink with the progress of financial innovation. Transactions motive money is held only because the "round trip" transactions cost of transfer from the high rate investment account asset exceeds the interest earned on the investment asset. And money held for investment motives is held because of the existence of interest income uncertainty of risky investment assets. That is, the holding of money is underpinned by the existence of transactions costs (a market imperfection) and uncertainty about the future (risk aversion). But financial innovations have reduced transactions costs, and have developed safe investment account assets. Indeed, the essence of financial innovation is reduction of transactions costs and reductions of uncertainty about investment account income. Hence, the progress of financial innovation necessarily reduces demand for pure money such as M1.

c. *The Future of Investment Accounts.* Finally, let us consider the future of investment accounts. Probably all (C)-type safe, bilateral, investment assets will come to reflect market interest rates, as do money market certificates and MMMFs. As a result, the expected yield differential between these assets and (D)- and (F)-type risky, marketable assets will be equal to the management costs and profits of banks and securities companies, and the management costs are expected to be very small given the microcomputer revolution. Since most people are risk-averse, it is likely that, in choosing a point on their indifference curves, they will prefer new but safe (C)-type assets to old but risky (D)- and (F)-type assets.

Moreover, the choice between investment assets of (C)-type assets on one hand and (D)- and (F)-type assets on the other probably will not be influenced greatly by movements of market interest rates. This is because the interest rates on the two types of assets will fluctuate together, maintaining a fixed spread. Thus, interest rate fluctuation will no longer be able to cause disintermediation (monetary policy transmission channel (*3*) seen above). But this also means that even if market rates change, the level of (*C*)-type assets cannot be controlled from the supply side.

We have seen that the level of M1, with (*A*)- and (*B*)-type assets, will be low and virtually fixed, while the level of M2 or M3, which includes (*C*)-type assets, will be virtually unaffected by market interest rate fluctuations.

How then will M2 and M3 be influenced by interest rates? It is likely that future (*C*)-type asset accounts will be divided into those that have facility for quick transfer into (*B*)-type accounts and/or payments facility and those that are pure investment accounts. This is because the transfer and transactions costs of (*B*)-type assets will never go to zero despite the computer revolution. In other words, there will be a return differential between (*C*)-type assets with payments facility and pure (*C*)-type assets, and this differential will affect composition of M2 and M3.

In summary, the investment accounts that people in the future will hold will be of three varieties: (*C*)-type assets with payments facility, pure (*C*)-type assets, and risky (*D*)- and (*F*)-type assets. The interest rates on these assets will fluctuate together, with fixed differentials due to trans-actions costs and risk.

Among these three assets, the (*C*)-type assets with payments facility will be the ones that reflect the level of transactions in the economy. Hence a newly constructed M2 or M3 that includes (*C*)-type assets with payments facility will certainly have a close correlation with total transac-tions. Hence, monetary transmission channel (*2*) from above will affect to-tal transactions through interest rate fluctuations, and will move M2 and M3 as well.

3. Financial Innovation and Monetary Policy

Using the view of the future given above, we can discuss the problems of financial innovation in the period of transition.

The first problem is the change in the nature of intermediate targets of monetary policy, the money supply indicators. The growth rate of M1 is falling on trend, and gradually reducing its level of variance; hence, it will continue losing its meaning as an indicator of the level of transactions. In the United States in 1981, the actual level of M1 continually undershot its target level. This was because the target levels overlooked the rise in M1 velocity due to the progress of financial innovation. In Japan, as well, velocity of M1 is rising on trend due to financial innovations.

The broader measures of money, M2 and M3, will increasingly become (*C*)-type assets reflecting market rates, so that their sensitivity to fluctu-ation of interest rates will fall (i.e., decline of interest elasticity of demand and elimination of monetary policy channel (*2*) above). From the viewpoint of investment asset selection, there will be expansion in attractive, high interest rate, safe assets such as MMMFs and money market certificates; because these are included in M2 and M3, there will be a trend increase in the growth of these aggregates (outward shift of the demand curve). In the United States in 1981, M2 was continually skirting the upper end of its target range. This was because the target range overlooked the decline in the interest sensitivity of M2 and the trend increase in growth.

As financial innovations progress, these changes in the character of money supply imply that M1 will gradually become inappropriate as an intermediate indicator. And efforts should be made immediately to create M2 and M3 series that include newly developed (C)-type assets. If possible, it would be desirable to create a time series that includes only (C)-type assets with transfer facility and with payments facility, and add these to M1 to make the new series for M2 and M3.

However, even with these efforts, new M2 and M3 will still differ from their predecessors in two ways. The first is that control of M2 and M3 from the supply side through the fluctuation of interest rates will become impossible. As we saw earlier, monetary policy transmission channels (1) and (3) based on controls will disappear with deregulation. Thus, M2 and M3 will move to reflect demand. That is, M2 and M3 will move along with total transactions, so that they cannot be expected to function as leading indicators for policy of nominal income or prices.

Here is where we hit the second problem for monetary policy. Does the fall in the controllability of the money supply imply a decline in the effectiveness of monetary policy? And will the money supply completely lose its meaning as an intermediate indicator?

The decline in the controllability of the money supply is due to the change of interest rates on (B)- and (C)-type safe, indirect, bilateral assets from controlled rates to free rates. As we saw above, the policy transmission channels (1) and (3), which depend on controls, will decline in importance, and channel (2), which relies on the interest rate mechanism, will strengthen. The implication of this for policy is, as we have seen, that monetary policy effects will strengthen overall, not weaken.

On the other hand, the loss of money's ability to be a leading indicator will certainly mean reduction of its role as an intermediate indicator. But it will have the qualities of an accurate, immediately available, and coincident indicator, and hence will not lose its importance as an essential indicator for monetary policy. To this extent, policy focusing on money supply will continue.

If we look back over time, the development of the financial system in Japan has been accompanied by changes in the operating target among the monetary aggregates, from bank notes to bank lending, from M1 to M2 or M3, and then to these plus CDs. It should be no surprise if the internal composition of the money supply continues to change as financial innovation progresses. The critical point is to be cautious enough not to allow this change to occur at an uncontrollable or unpredictable speed. As long as the speed is slow enough that changes in the character of money can be reflected in revisions of money supply data, and as long as money demand shifts can be understood as a type of special effect versus the same period of earlier years, there need not be any confusion in monetary policy. In the meantime, the effectiveness of monetary policy will be preserved by transmission channel (2), discussed above. This is because, in the process of improving the efficiency of the financial system, the interest rate mechanism will function better, and the effects of interest rates on the choice between financial assets and real assets will strengthen.

Because of the continued existence of many controlled interest rates in Japan, the degree of financial innovation achieved so far is relatively low compared to that in the United States. Interest rate regulations on deposits still remain, except for CDs, MMCs, and time deposits of large denominations, and interest rates on newly issued bonds and bank debentures are still strongly influenced by the guidance of the Ministry of Finance, except for tender issues of two- to four-year bonds.

However, a watershed came in 1985, making further deregulation inevitable. Since the large-scale issue of ten-year government bonds began in 1975, in 1985 a large-scale refunding started, and gross government bond issues increased tremendously. Also in the secondary bond market there came to be a great number of government bonds with maturities of less than two years. These bonds have become very competitive with bank time deposits that have regulated interest rates. And since over-the-counter sales of secondary market bonds have begun, the competition is likely to intensify.

Without deregulating interest rates on newly issued ten-year bonds, the government will not be able to continue their issue. Needless to say, a differential between market rates and guided rates is essentially a tax on syndicate members, and they will not be able to withstand such a large de facto tax. Also, without deregulation of interest rates on deposits, funds would shift from bank deposits to government bonds with short maturities in the secondary market. Banks would not be able to tolerate such a decline in market share.

Another development in 1985 was the start of an Information Network System sponsored by Nippon Telephone and Telegraph (the Japanese counterpart of AT&T). With this, it will be possible for computers at banks and securities firms to be linked with those at their customer companies, and with terminals at business offices and homes; in other words, office banking and home banking will start with a further decline in the cost of financial transactions due to INS.

Thus, the 1980s will push innovation and decontrol in Japanese financial markets further, with the Japanese financial system and transmissions channels of monetary policy developing along the lines described in this chapter.

II

MONEY AND MACROECONOMIC PERFORMANCE

5

Japan in the Worldwide Inflation

$\mathbf{A}$fter recovery from World War II, the industrial countries made remarkable progress, both economic and social, through the 1960s. Unemployment declined steadily, and inflation remained at 3 to 5 percent. With opportunities for employment and with social security permeating society, these countries achieved a high and stable standard of living.

But, having passed through the 1970s and entered the 1980s, what can be said about life today? Indeed, the average rate of inflation in terms of consumer price index during the nine years from 1973 to 1981 in OECD member states was 10.1 percent. It declined from 12.8 percent in 1980 to 5.5 percent in 1983 due to the concerted disinflationary policy in major industrial countries, but as a result, the average rate of unemployment in OECD member states rose from 6.1 percent in 1980 to 9.0 percent in 1983. This is definitely abnormal for peacetime. Standards of living were threatened by this extraordinary economic unrest.

We must ask why the industrial countries strayed from the economic prosperity of the 1960s to the stagflation of the 1980s. The change was not sudden; indeed, the seeds were sown in the 1960s. The synchronized escalation of inflation in the advanced countries from the late 1960s was an inevitable result of the methods of economic management, and was an overture to the stagflation from 1973 to the present. Today's stagflation stems directly from the ideology of economic management in the 1960s, the intellectual structure of economic theory, and the policy recommendations derived therefrom.

Economists and policymakers alike emphasized economic growth and employment, neglected resultant tightening of the labor market, and ig-

Table 5.1. CPI Inflation in OECD Countries

	Period of Adjustable Peg			Period of Floating Rates		
	1961–64	1965–68	1969–72	1973–76	1977–81	1982–84
OECD average	2.5	3.1	5.3	10.3	9.8	5.9
United States	1.2	2.9	4.7	8.0	9.4	4.3
Europe	3.8	3.7	5.1	11.4	11.6	7.9
West Germany	2.7	2.8	4.0	6.1	4.3	3.6
Japan	6.1	5.3	5.8	14.2	5.8	2.3
Memorandum item: Unemployment rate (OECD average)	3.2	2.9	3.5	4.6	5.9	8.6

Note: Figures for 1984 are estimated values.

Source: OECD, Economic Outlook, December 1984.

nored price stability and the monetary restraint necessary to achieve it. These preferences originated with those who interpreted Keynes's *General Theory* (1936) to be applicable to all times and places.

This chapter will start with a discussion of the causes of worldwide inflation since the 1960s, and then describe how the Japanese economy has responded to this international environment.

II. Causes of Inflation

In examining worldwide inflation from the 1960s to the 1980s, it is appropriate to divide the period into two parts. The first is the period of the adjustable peg system (postwar years before 1973), and the second the age of floating exchange rates (1973 to present). The reason for this demarcation is that the foreign exchange rate system played an important part in the transmission of inflation among countries, and affected the independence of anti-inflationary measures.

1. Creeping Inflation before 1973

Inflation in the first period was characterized by three things: (*a*) it was creeping inflation; (*b*) it accelerated gradually; and (*c*) inflation rates were gradually synchronized among countries. These characteristics are seen distinctly when this period is divided further into subperiods of 1960–64, 1965–68, and 1969–72 as in table 5.1. The average rate of inflation in OECD countries in the first period ranged from 2 to 5 percent, remaining within the limits of creeping inflation. The rate, however, accelerated from 2.5 percent to 3.1 percent, and then to 5.3 percent as the period progressed. Moreover, the table shows how inflation became synchronized. Between the first two subperiods, the inflation rate rose in some regions but fell in others. Synchronization was conspicuous in 1969–72, however, as inflation rates rose in all regions.

The fundamental reason for acceleration and synchronization of inflation was that higher inflation in the United States aggravated the U.S. international payments position. Under the fixed-parity system, the resultant dollar glut induced simultaneous monetary expansion in other countries. Policymakers acquiesced to this expansion because of the influence of economists who believed in the stability of a downward-sloping Phillips curve, that is, that unemployment would fall if inflation were allowed to rise.

This inflation in the first period seriously endangered the Bretton Woods Agreement. Acceleration of inflation in various countries and the widening gap in the rates of inflation among the countries gradually increased the frequency and extent of parity adjustment. For example, the British pound was devalued in 1967, the French franc devalued in 1969, and the German mark revalued, also in 1969. Escalation of inflation and dollar drain from the United States undermined confidence in the dollar and led to suspension of the convertibility of the dollar to gold and to the eventual realignment of the exchange rates of major currencies at the Smithsonian Conference of 1971.

Nevertheless, the parity changes did not adjust international payments enough, and speculative movements of short-term funds seeking exchange profits were enormous. In February and March 1973, major countries let their exchange rates float, thereby ending the adjustable peg parity system.

Worldwide inflation also resulted in further deterioration of the terms of trade for primary products relative to industrial goods. The sense of growing crisis in primary product producer countries gradually paved the way for the outbreak of the oil crisis. Thus, in the autumn of 1973, the member countries of OPEC quadrupled the price of crude oil, and thereby ushered in a new era of global inflation.

2. Inflation and Unemployment after 1973

The years from 1973 to the present have been inflationary ones, during which the floating exchange rate system and intermittent increases of crude oil prices have been institutionalized. In this period, inflation stopped creeping and started galloping. This situation is confirmed in table 5.1 above, in which we see the average rate of inflation in OECD countries in 1973–76 and 1977–81 to have been close to or into double digits. Inflation in this period was also accompanied by increasing unemployment. In 1982–84, inflation finally subsided to some extent, at the cost of high unemployment. Also interesting is the fact that the synchronized transmission of inflation became less conspicuous. For example, the rate of inflation has been consistently lower in West Germany than in other countries, and that of Japan slowed substantially in 1977–81 and 1982–84 and declined to a level lower than that of the first period.

The fundamental reason why inflation in the second period has exhibited these characteristics is that the floating rate system has allowed countries to adopt economic policies independently. Hence there have emerged larger divergences in economic performance than in the first period. For example, it is still fresh in our memory that OECD countries were bipolarized in 1976–77. The stronger countries, such as the United States, Japan, and West Germany, had emerged from the trilemma of double-digit inflation, zero growth, and balance of payments deficit. The weaker countries such as the United Kingdom, France, and Italy continued to suffer partially or wholly from the trilemma, and proposed the "locomotive theory." A second polarization took place within the group of stronger countries after 1978. The United States took on the role of locomotive, stimulated gross national expenditure from both fiscal and monetary sides, and consequently entered a period of nearly double-digit inflation. Japan and West Germany held their inflation at only a 4 or 5 percent level. But, there is even a perceived difference in performance between Japan and West Germany, with the former outperforming the latter in terms of growth rate and current account balance in 1979–83.

Various reasons can be given for the large differences among the countries in the rates of inflation in the second period. The principal differences are in three areas—monetary control, wages, and productivity.

Success of monetary control has depended on how soon authorities ceased believing that a stable tradeoff exists between inflation and unemployment. Some policymakers accepted at an early stage the arguments of more recent economic theory that the relationship between inflation and unemployment is influenced by inflationary expectations, and that the tradeoff relation disappears in the long run. Such policymakers feel that only through stabilization of prices can efficiency be raised, growth encouraged, and unemployment lowered.

The sooner countries changed their economic policies in this direction, the better their performances became. Where such changes lagged, confidence in the will and ability of policymakers to control money supply and thereby to achieve price stability declined; such countries suffered from stagflation and volatile financial variables under persistent inflationary psychology. Examples are the United States and some European countries.

Wages and productivity behavior, the remaining two factors behind divergent performance, came to the fore every time supply shocks were felt, for example, in the form of oil price hikes. Such differences will always exist, and must be absorbed by fluctuations of exchange rates. The result is that inflation in countries of poor economic performance will be accelerated by depreciations of their exchange rates, and this acceleration will thereby aggravate worldwide inflation. Since this inflation erodes efficiency of the market economy, and since supply shocks intensify supply constraints, economic growth will slow, and stagflation worsen. We shall discuss this subject further in section III of this chapter.

II. The Inflation Debate in Japan: A Historical Survey

Given this background on the international inflationary environment, the next task is to reexamine the first thirty years of Japanese macro performance in the postwar period. To do so we will survey what Japanese economists have considered important problems and what arguments they have developed to deal with them. This will frame the economic history of postwar Japan and lead to a reexamination of the role of the economics profession in Japan. This section focuses mostly on inflation in postwar Japan, and the debate surrounding it.

1. Overview of Postwar Japanese Inflation

The evolution of the Japanese economy after World War II may be broadly divided into three periods. The first period was the postwar recovery period (1945–55), which was supported by American economic aid and special procurements for the Korean War. The second period was the high-growth period (1956–73), which was the last spurt of the post–Mieji era industrialization aimed at catching up with the West. The third period dates from 1974, which saw the collapse of the Bretton Woods system and changes caused by the oligopolistic increase in oil prices; it continues to the present.[1]

The history of postwar Japanese inflation for the most part corresponds to these three periods. The first, the postwar recovery period, was a period of typical demand-pull inflation. Productive capacity fell to 60–70 percent of its prewar peak because of the wartime expansion of munitions production, the lack of resource imports, and the destruction of plant and equipment by air raids. Meanwhile, aggregate demand increased sharply because of the expansion of public expenditures and the unleashing of consumer purchasing power. Inflation surged immediately following the war and continued throughout this first period; during the first half of the period it centered on wholesale prices and during the second half on consumer prices.

---

1. Details on this periodization are given in Suzuki 1981, introduction and part 1. It is quite commonly accepted; for example, see Kosai 1981.

It was clear to everyone that inflation in this period was due to the deficiency of supply capacity relative to demand. That is, the aggregate demand curve intersected the aggregate supply curve in the latter's vertical segment. In chapter 20 of the *General Theory* (1936), Keynes holds that such a situation occurs under full employment; he calls it "true inflation." However, Japan in the late 1940s suffered from "true inflation" because of deficiency of capital and raw materials even before full employment of the labor force was achieved.

Since the character of inflation in the first period was clear, the inflation debate during this period, rather than revolving around the cause of inflation, was centered on debate over policy—over what steps to take to restrain aggregate demand and what steps to increase aggregate supply. Out of this debate was born the "priority production system," and the Dodge Line was also implemented.[2]

It was in the second postwar period that the cause of inflation itself became the center of debate. One of the special features of this period was the stability of wholesale prices; however, even though wholesale prices remained stable, consumer prices began to rise at an annual rate of 5 to 6 percent from the beginning of 1960. Since assessments of the cause of inflation differed, it was only natural that anti-inflation policy proposals also differed. A policy debate ensued over dealing with inflation, centering around the pros and cons of tight money.[3] This second postwar period is of great interest from the viewpoint of history of economics because so many theories of inflation were advanced and debated.

From the end of this second period (1972) to the early part of the third period, the Great Inflation of the 1970s occurred, again due to three obvious causes: (1) excessive money supply, (2) excessive fiscal stimulus, and (3) the first oil crisis in late 1973.[4] Of these, the first and second were implemented to offset deflationary effects anticipated from the revaluation of the yen in the Smithsonian Conference of December 1971 and the rise of the yen after February 1973, when the international monetary system shifted to the floating exchange rate regime.

The Great Inflation shares a common feature with inflation of the first

2. For a detailed discussion about inflation in the first period and the measures taken to combat it, see Yoshino 1962, chapter 2 (written by M. Ishikawa).

3. In opposition to the Bank of Japan demand-pull school, which asserted that the basis of anti-inflation policy was aggregate demand management beginning with tight-money policy, other groups advocated their respective theories, and a lively debate was carried on. For example, the non-Marxian cost-push school advocated strict application of anti-monopoly laws and abolition of protectionist policies; Shimomura advocated rationalization of the service sector; and the imported inflation school advocated revaluation of the yen. These theories are introduced in detail in the text.

4. For a systematic analysis of inflation in this period, refer to Komiya and Suzuki 1977 and Komiya 1976.

period, in that its causes were plain to see. But there is a great theoretical interest in various implications that follow from a comparison of the two. The second oil crisis, which occurred in 1979, brought the same degree of imported cost-push inflation in Japan as the first oil crisis, but control of the money supply, among other factors, helped limit inflation to single-digit rates and to end inflation in little less than a year.[5] This provided an opportunity for the role of the money supply in inflation to be reexamined by many people.[6]

Inflation in this third postwar period raised various problems for explanations given by earlier economic theory for inflation in the second subperiod. It is interesting to note that, in order to explain the new phenomena, American economics too entered a new era of development.[7]

Next we shall survey the inflation debate in the second and third postwar subperiods, which are the most interesting from the viewpoint of the history of economics. We shall assess the debate in the second subperiod from the standpoint of economic theory newly developed in the third period.

2. Inflation Theory in the High-Growth Period

a. Disparate Growth of Wholesale and Consumer Prices. The distinguishing feature of inflation in the second postwar period was the disparity of wholesale and consumer price inflation. While wholesale prices showed a degree of stability almost unknown in other countries (WPI inflation of 0.5 percent in 1956–60, 0.4 percent in 1961–65, and 1.5 percent in 1966–72), consumer prices continued to rise persistently after 1960 (1.5 percent, 6.1 percent, and 5.4 percent for the three periods, respectively). Needless to say, this wide disparity between wholesale and consumer price inflation occurred because changes in relative prices were occurring quickly.

For a long time, postwar Japan continued, as in the prewar era, to be plagued by a labor surplus. A popular expression of the time, the "second and third son problem," refers to rural communities' chronic problem of excess population. Part of this group drifted to the cities looking for work and formed the core of disguised unemployed. The existence of this group was instrumental in depressing the wages of rural day laborers and people

5. For a comparative analysis of the Great Inflation following the first oil crisis and the inflation following the second oil crisis in terms of the difference in the money supply behavior, see Suzuki 1981, chapter 2.

6. The *Economic White Paper*, which the Economic Planning Agency publishes each summer, started to fully analyze the role of money in inflation for the first time in its 1981 edition, which, for this reason, is called the "Monetarism White Paper." See Economic Planning Agency (1981), part I, Chapter 3.

7. Saito 1981 has made an interesting sketch of the new movements of this kind of economics.

employed in small urban businesses far below the wages in large firms. This gave rise to the "dual structure of wages." However, the high growth of the second postwar period raised the demand for labor substantially. With 1960 as the dividing line, latent unemployment began to disappear, and the labor market tightened. As a result, the dual structure of wages headed toward dissolution, and the wages in farm communities and small business concerns began to approach those of big enterprises. Through this process, the rate of wage increase in the former continued to exceed that in the latter, and this narrowing discrepancy became a major factor in the increase of farm product prices, private service fees, retail margins, and relative prices of consumer goods produced by small enterprises, compared to prices of goods produced by large firms.

On the other hand, the industries that led the way in high growth were process industries located in coastal areas and characterized by intensive use of imported raw materials. Chiefly these consisted of materials industries (steel, textiles, oil refining, petrochemicals, paper and pulp) dominated by large firms. The differential in the rate of productivity change between these industries and the farm, service, retail, and small firm consumer goods industries was greatly enlarged. This differential became a primary factor in the fall of relative prices of products of large firms.

These two factors, dissolution of the dual structure of wages and enlargement of the productivity differential, brought relatively high increases in the prices of goods and services of the farming and small business industries relative to the products of big enterprises. Since the former were largely consumer prices and the latter largely wholesale prices, the change in this price structure is what produced the wide disparity between consumer and wholesale prices.

There was no major difference of opinion on this particular feature, especially after 1960. All theories of inflation recognized it.[8] There is little sense in arguing over which school of inflation theory was the first to point out the divergence. The Marxian cost-push school attracted attention because it used the expression "productivity differential inflation," but essays had appeared at an earlier time[9] about change in the

8. As described in the text, there are four representative theories of inflation in the second postwar period, namely, the Marxian cost-push school, the non-Marxian cost-push school, the demand-pull school, and the Shimomura theory. All state that the (1) dissolution of the dual structure of wages and (2) enlargement of the productivity differentials are what caused the disparity between consumer prices and wholesale prices.

9. Representative of the Marxian cost-push school are chapter 1 (October 1961) and chapter 2 (May 1962) of Takasuga 1972, but the proposition that the change in the price structure that accompanied high growth was the background for consumer price increases had already been pointed out, for example, in March 1961 by Bank of Japan Research Department 1961.

price structure due to the two factors mentioned above and the disparity between consumer and wholesale prices that reflected that change.

The point of contention in the inflation debate was not the disparity of the price indexes per se, but the question of why, when there are large-scale changes in relative prices, individual prices that should fall fail to do so. In other words, why does the aggregate price level, which averages many individual prices, rise, when rises in some nominal prices and declines in others would accomplish the needed change in relative prices? The theory about this question was largely divided into two camps. These were the cost-push school, which sought the cause in the downward rigidity of prices and nominal wages, and the demand-pull school, which sought the cause in demand/supply stringency.

The cost-push school can be further divided into the Marxian faction, which strongly advocated the thesis of administered prices, and the non-Marxian school of American-trained economists who had studied the theory of creeping inflation.

On the other side, the demand-pull theory was propounded by various people, though perhaps the purest exposition was given by research economists at the Bank of Japan.

Let us examine these three theories, two cost-push theories and one demand-pull theory, in order.

b. *The Marxian Cost–Push School.* The theory of productivity differential inflation put forth by Takasuga 1972 is representative of the Marxian cost-push school. According to Takasuga, the characteristic feature of a modern capitalist economy like that of Japan is that the oligopoly system that controls the basic segment of the economy enforces a monopolistic price policy so as to keep prices rigid, notwithstanding increases in productivity. As a result, monopolistic excess profits are generated and wholesale prices, which ought to drop, do not do so.

On the other hand, wages tend to rise in the oligopoly system, as workers seek a share of monopolistic excess profits. The demand and supply interactions of the labor market result in an overall increase in wages even in industries in which a productivity increase has not occurred. Because of higher wages, these industries increase prices to a level that restores the previous rates of profit, in turn inviting an increase of consumer prices. Consequently, "the evolutionary base of this mechanism is the productivity differential, and its developmental axis the leveling-up of wages" (Takasuga 1972, p. 60). Thus, when relative prices change, there is downward rigidity, and prices that ought to decline do not decline absolutely, and the overall level of nominal prices rises. This interpretation is essentially the same as that of the non-Marxian cost-push school, which is presented next.

c. *The Non-Marxian Cost-Push School.* Tachi, Komiya, and Niida

(1964) wrote an essay on "creeping inflation" that is representative of the non–Marxian or "modern economics" cost-push school. Their theory is precisely that proposed by the American Keynesians in the 1960s. Having returned from the United States, the authors seem to have been impassioned with a desire to expound the theory of creeping inflation to the Japanese.

According to Tachi, Komiya, and Niida, the reason prices that ought to decline do not do so is "downward price rigidity," which is of course an essential presupposition of Keynesian economics. This rigidity was said to have two causes: (1) the existence of many large, oligopolistic manufacturing firms, and (2) protectionism.

As for the controversy over cost-push versus demand-pull, they essentially sided with the cost-push explanation of inflation by making the following two points. First, they said that in the case of the Japanese economy in the early 1960s, it did not seem that aggregate demand exceeded aggregate supply to create an inflationary gap; they did not believe the Japanese economy had fallen into the condition Keynes called "true inflation."

Second, although at a glance it may have appeared as if prices rose because wages rose during labor market tightening or because of higher demand based on higher money supply, these authors argued that such appearances were misleading. Wage increases originated in oligopolistic, large enterprises when profits increased, and then spilled over into other enterprises, raising wages in all other sectors, just as Takasuga had seen. In this sense, the wage increase was not "induced" by a tightening of the labor market, but, they asserted, was an "aggressive wage increase" originating in downward price rigidity in the oligopolistic firm sector.

On the other hand, increases in the money supply and in aggregate demand did not, they held, come about "autonomously" but originated in downward price rigidity in oligopolistic firms, for two reasons. First, as profits increased due to downward price rigidity, aggregate demand expanded. Second, in order to avoid a decline in capacity utilization and an increase in unemployment that might result from aggressive wage increases left unopposed, increases in the money supply and hence in aggregate demand were implemented to support employment.

Thus, the initial cause of inflation was said to be downward price rigidity. Increases in wages, in aggregate demand, and in the money supply were all regarded as deriving from such rigidity, and nothing more. Conversely, even if the money supply and aggregate demand were brought under control, "in all probability prices will not decline that much; rather, we believe, this will result in increases in idle capacity and in latent unemployment, a curtailment of earnings of the lower-income class, and so forth" (Tachi, Komiya, and Niida 1964, p. 38).

This judgment is essentially an assertion that there exists a stable

Phillips curve with a moderate downward slope. In such a world, suppression of aggregate demand increases unemployment greatly and lowers inflation only slightly. This theoretical model holds under downward rigidity of wages and prices when the aggregate demand curve intersects the aggregate supply curve with a moderate upward slope (i.e., with idle capacity and involuntary unemployment).

First to come to grips with the Phillips curve hypothesis in explaining inflation in Japan by using econometric estimates was Tsunehiko Watanabe 1966, asserting that (1) the money supply in Japan at this time was passive, or supportive; (2) control of aggregate demand did not immediately lead to a fall in consumer prices; and (3) despite the apparent absence of an inflationary gap, consumer prices continued to rise. Watanabe concluded that inflation in this period was not of the demand-pull type but rather of the cost-push type, with creeping inflation following the downward-sloping Phillips curve based on downward wage and price rigidity from the southeast to the northwest direction.

The anti-inflation policy proposed by this school did not aim at control of the money supply or aggregate demand but rather at downward price rigidity. Tachi and his coauthors stressed in particular the strict application of antimonopoly policies and abolition of protectionism.[10]

d. The Bank of Japan Demand-Pull School. Next let us survey the inflation theory of the demand-pull school. Though a number of economists agreed with some demand-pull positions, many took an eclectic approach and combined this hypothesis with the cost-push one.[11] However, to clarify the distinctions among the schools, let us focus on the Bank of Japan group of Toshihiko Yoshino et al. (1962), who represent the demand-pull school. This group clearly defined the demand-pull line

10. Going to a logical conclusion, the Keynesian cost-push inflation theory advocates countermeasures aimed at downward price rigidity (strict application of antimonopoly laws, abolition of protectionist policies, etc.) and, along with them, countermeasures aimed at downward wage rigidity, namely, "incomes policy." This was, in fact, the case in the United States and Europe. Since Tachi, Komiya, and Niida 1964, too, said that the rise of wages in Japan was not due to tightening in the labor market but an "aggressive" increase, it would seem to be wanting in consistency as a policy proposal unless they promote an incomes policy. But for some reason Tachi et al. had doubts about the effectiveness of an incomes policy in Japan and were negative toward it. Not only these three but most of Japan's Keynesians as well were against an incomes policy. The few exceptions were the "Kumagai Report" on incomes policy (a September 1968 report of the price, wage, incomes, and productivity committee of the Economic Council chaired by Hisao Kumagai) and Hisao Kanamori's supportive statement.

11. Examples of the strong argument of the demand-pull school are Minobe 1967, Kumagai 1963 and 1966, and Nakamura 1962 and 1963. However, these works also cite the rigidity of oligopoly prices and the aggressive increase of big enterprise wages as important factors of inflation. In this regard, Yoshino 1962 is very distinctly of the demand-pull school.

of thinking at an early stage, did not borrow from other schools, and continued debate with the cost-push school.

The demand-pull hypothesis may be summarized as follows. Because aggregate demand exceeds aggregate supply, prices that decline relatively in the price system do not decline absolutely; as a result, the general price level, which is the average of all individual prices, tends to rise. This assertion sharply contrasts with those of the cost-push schools on two points.

First, the cost-push school asserted that, because Japan was not in the condition Keynes called true inflation, the inflation was not demand-pull. In contrast, the demand-pull school insisted that bottlenecks could occur in some sectors of the economy even short of full employment, thereby pushing the general price level upward. To be sure, from 1960 onward, bottlenecks occurred due to a shortage of capital stock and labor in the farm, service, distribution, and small business sectors, whose product prices increased.[12] Tachi, Komiya, and Niida (1964) maintained that bottlenecks in specific sectors such as these were not the inflationary gap at full employment, and therefore that there was no demand-pull inflation. However, as Kumugai (1963) pointed out, "it is of course impossible to draw a clear line between an inflationary gap and bottlenecks; an inflationary gap comes into being when bottlenecks have become quite common throughout the entire economy" (p. 18). Thus the real point of contention between the demand-pull school and the cost-push school hinges on a judgment as to whether "bottlenecks have become quite common." The demand-pull school said that "because they have become quite common, prices are increasing," whereas the cost-push school took the position that "they have not become common, but specific bottlenecks are causing prices as a whole to rise because prices that ought to fall are downward rigid, and do not fall."[13]

The second point of contention between the demand-pull school and the cost-push school concerns the cause of wage increases accompanying price increases. The cost-push school, as shown in Tachi, Komiya, and Niida 1964, maintained that wage increases were due to the downward rigidity of prices of oligopolistic big enterprises. In contrast, the demand-pull school held that wages were rising because the labor market was tight, since latent unemployment in the farm labor force and the urban lower classes was being eliminated and the overall labor shortage was intensifying.

Given the demand-pull school's explanation of the cause of inflation as stated above, its anti-inflation policy was, naturally, control of aggre-

---

12. The occurrence of bottlenecks in many sectors of the economy is analyzed in detail in Yoshino 1962, chapter 3 (written by Yoshio Suzuki).

13. This demand-pull hypothesis is also quoted in Tachi, Komiya, and Niida 1964.

gate demand; that is to say, elimination of bottlenecks and easing of labor-market stringency by tighter monetary and fiscal policy. This policy proposal contrasted sharply with that of the cost-push school, which favored the strict application of antimonopoly laws and the abolition of protectionism to fight inflation. The cost-push school opposed aggregate-demand control on the grounds that it required a large sacrifice, higher unemployment, for a small gain, lower inflation.

3. The New Phase of Inflation Theory

a. Money Supply Causes Inflation.   In the summer of 1963, Milton Friedman of the University of Chicago visited Japan and took the opportunity of a discussion with Saburo Okita[14] to point out a statistical fact that, in Japan as elsewhere, changes in the money supply lead changes in the consumer price level by two quarters or so, and to insist that his analysis and policy proposals[15] pertaining to the American economy were equally applicable to Japan.

Friedman's suggestions upset the factual assertions of the non-Marxian cost-push school. Both Tachi, Komiya, and Niida 1964 and Watanabe 1966 stated that the money supply changed not exogenously but rather supportively or passively in response to money demand. But how could supportive or passive money supply *lead* prices? The statistical fact that changes in money supply led changes in prices appeared to support the autonomous nature of the supply of money, which causes inflation to advance through demand-pull.

Touched off by Friedman's visit, the Bank of Japan Research Department (1963) undertook a study from this viewpoint, and published it in the fall of 1963, just after Friedman's return to the United States. The following year Suzuki published a study (1964) that further expanded this hypothesis.

These studies not only looked at lead-lag relationships of peaks and troughs by means of semilog graphs and rates of change diagrams as Friedman had done, but also utilized quarterly data from a ten-year period (1953/I to 1962/IV) to calculate various correlation coefficients. They showed that the rate of change in the money supply had strong correlation with the rates of change of price indexes (GNP deflator, wholesale prices, consumer prices, investment goods prices, and export prices) with a lag of one or two quarters, and of real economic activity indicators (industrial production index, real fixed business investment). The conclusion: "The statistical fact that the money supply is a leading indicator suggests that it is wrong to assert that the money supply merely reflects changes in

14. The discussions are in Friedman and Okita 1963.
15. For the lead-lag relationships between the money supply and prices in the United States and Friedman's assertions based on them, see Friedman and Schwartz 1963.

prices and in real economic activity. And this is not all. The fact that the rate of change in the quantity of money is strongly correlated ($\rho = 0.797$) with the rate of change of the GNP deflator two quarters later, suggests that the causal relationship runs from a change in the volume of money to a change in the general price level two quarters afterward" (Suzuki 1964, p. 5). Moreover, another statistical finding—that fluctuations in the aforementioned five price indexes follow the same wave pattern—"attests to the erroneousness of the view that recent consumer price increases are independent of changes in the general price level, which is determined by aggregate demand and aggregate supply, backed by the volume of money. Recent changes in consumer prices are covariant with changes in all other prices in the economy and reflect changes in the general price level" (Suzuki 1964, p. 6).

This assertion lent considerable support to the contention of the de-mand-pull school. No persuasive counterargument with substantial factual backing has since come from the non-Marxian cost-push school to attempt to revive their contention that downward price rigidity is the takeoff point for inflation and that money is merely supportive or passive.

Suzuki 1964, however, was not based on Friedman's hypothesis of a natural rate of unemployment, which appeared in well-defined form only in 1968, but rather on a Keynesian model formulated by Klein 1947.[16] In short, the level of nominal wages, which "is determined by collective bargaining of labor and management under varied conditions" that in-fluence wage negotiations, is treated as an exogenous variable. In con-trast, Friedman's natural-rate hypothesis refers to a world of classical equilibrium theory in which the labor market is cleared by the real wage rate and the nominal wage rate is determined endogenously.

Suzuki 1964 belonged to the Keynesian universe because its demand-pull theory existed on the stable, downward-sloping Phillips curve. But it differed from the cost-push school in the mechanism that moves the economy along the Phillips curve. This work asserted that the movement comes about through an increase in the money supply, whereas the cost-push school held that downward price rigidity is the primary cause. In order for either school to break away from the world of the stable, down-ward sloping Phillips curve, subsequent developments in economic the-ory, spurred by the Great Inflation, were needed.

   b. *The Outbreak of Imported Inflation.*   During the late 1960s, an entirely new type of inflation emerged in Japan. Until about 1965, the inflation debate in Japan, though strongly influenced by foreign economic

---

16. "The Mathematical Models of Keynesian Economics and the Classical School of Economics" in the Technical Appendix of Klein 1947 is the basis of Suzuki 1964, chapter 7, "I. The Aggregate Demand Function and the Aggregate Supply Function Determining the General Price Level."

Table 5.2. Indicators of Imported Inflation

		1956–60	1961–65	1966–70	1969	1970	1971	1972
Basic Balance (BOP)	$bln	—	−1.2	0.9	2.3	1.4	7.7	4.7
Export Price Change	%	−0.8	−0.8	1.7	2.6	4.8	0.6	−2.9
Import Price Change	%	−3.3	−0.1	1.4	2.3	3.5	−0.1	−4.3
Wholesale Price Change	%	0.5	0.4	2.2	2.1	3.6	−0.7	0.8
Consumer Price Change	%	1.5	6.1	5.4	5.2	7.7	6.1	4.5
Real Growth	%	8.5	10.0	11.6	10.6	10.9	5.2	9.5

thought, concentrated almost entirely on domestic factors. However, from the mid-1960s, inflation in Japan gradually began to take on an international character, and, accordingly, inflation theory and the price policy based on it became linked even more closely with the foreign debate.

Until 1967–68, Japan's postwar monetary policy was able to pursue simultaneously three policy goals—stable prices, full employment, and balance-of-payments equilibrium—because there were no tradeoffs among these goals. It may be that, of the three, balance-of-payments equilibrium was given the highest priority, only because the Bretton Woods system regarded the restoration of balance-of-payments equilibrium as the most urgent. There was no contradiction whatsoever between this and the other two goals.[17]

But in 1969 inflation began, even while Japan continued to maintain a large surplus in the balance of payments (see table 5.2 for related indicators). The rates of inflation in 1969 and 1970 were 2.1 percent and 3.5 percent respectively for wholesale prices and 5.2 percent and 7.7 percent for consumer prices. Going back a little and looking at the five-year period from 1966 to 1970, the annual average rate of inflation was 2.2 percent for wholesale prices and 5.4 percent for consumer prices. Consumer prices had not risen much compared to the rate of inflation in the early 1960s, but wholesale prices clearly began to show a change when compared to 0.5 percent for the period 1956–60 and 0.4 percent for 1961–65.

This increase in the rate of inflation centering on wholesale prices and persistent surpluses in the balance of payments clearly followed global economic changes in the balance of payments observed during this period. In the late 1960s, with the worsening of America's trade balance, the outflow of dollars increased, and international liquidity became excessive. From 1969 to the first half of 1971 in particular, the outflow of dollars

17. For a detailed study of policy goals of postwar Japanese monetary policy, see Suzuki 1974, part IV, chapter 13, "I. Ultimate Economic Objectives of Policy: Prices, Balance of Payments, and Effective Demand."

rose sharply, corresponding exactly to the expansion of Japan's basic balance in the same period (see table 5.2).

Further, the formation of this excessive international liquidity enabled national governments to implement expansionary policies aimed at growth and employment. Every country ran headlong toward expansionary policy, giving rise to simultaneous acceleration of inflation throughout the world in 1969–72. In the case of Japan, prosperity continued for five years, from 1966 to 1970, with the annual average growth rate of 11.6 percent, far above rates of the 1956–60 (8.5 percent) and 1961–65 (10.0 percent) periods. This was the peak of the high–growth period. And at the end of this period, that is, in 1969–70, the aforementioned acceleration of wholesale-price inflation occurred.

In the face of this acceleration of inflation, the Bank of Japan implemented a moderate tight-money policy extending over a one-year period from autumn of 1969 to autumn of 1970; in 1971, wholesale prices fell by 0.7 percent. On the other hand, expansion of balance of payments surpluses, shown in the table by the basic balance (current account balance plus net long-term capital flows), accelerated further. Faced for the first time in the postwar period by the tradeoff between price stability and balance of payments equilibrium, the Bank of Japan chose price stability.

c. The Imported Inflation Hypothesis and Sterilization Policy. Against this change of circumstances, non-Marxian economists advanced a hypothesis that the core of inflation from 1969 on was imported inflation, so that the appropriate countermeasure was not management of aggregate demand but rather revaluation of the yen. Yasuba 1970 and Shinkai 1971 maintained this thesis from a comparatively early time. Their assertion ultimately led to "A Proposal on a Crawling Peg for the Yen Exchange Rate" (Kawase Seisaku Kenkyuu Kai 1972), to which most non-Marxian economists subscribed. Yasuba and Shinkai's theory of imported inflation went as follows: the persistent inflation in the United States, the key currency nation, accompanied by balance of payments deficits, exported inflation to Japan by three routes.

First, American inflation allowed international prices to increase in sympathy, implying an increase in Japanese export and import prices. As shown in table 5.2, Japanese export and import prices, which had fallen from 1956 to 1965, rose from 1966 onward. This became an increase of 2–4 percent in 1969 and 1970 particularly. Through the cost-push of imported raw materials and the competition between export goods, import goods, and domestic goods in the domestic market, this caused an increase in domestic prices, especially wholesale prices.

Second, because America's deficits in the balance of payments brought an increase in Japanese exports and a reduction of Japanese imports, Japan's economic growth was stimulated. This was why the domestic goods markets tightened in Japan. In fact, as shown in table 5.2, the economic growth rate for 1966–70 was the highest of any of the periods, at 11.6 percent. The demand/supply gap in terms of GNP registered excess demand in 1968–70. There is no doubt that this lay behind the increase in wholesale prices in 1969–70.

Third, in contrast to the persistence of deficits in the U.S. balance of payments, Japan's balance of payments surpluses continued and followed an upward trend from 1969 on, as shown in table 5.2. Under the Bretton Woods system, unless offset by other policy measures, such surpluses would induce an increase in the money supply in Japan and cause domestic prices to rise. As a matter of fact, in 1969–70, monetary policy was tightened; funds released from the Foreign Exchange Special Account due to balance of payments surpluses were offset by open market sales and reductions of Bank of Japan credit. Thus, no excessive increase in the money supply occurred. Imported inflation from this route surfaced only in 1972.

The pressure of imported inflation along the above three routes was countered in Japan by tight money measures in 1969–70, and, as already stated, success was achieved in the form of low growth of wholesale prices. Inflation in this period was, as before, demand-pull inflation, accelerated by the demand-pull effect of imported inflation. Conversely, the cost-push effect of imported inflation (due to higher prices of imported raw materials) was still small.

But Japan's success in containing inflation by demand restraint resulted in differentials between domestic and foreign prices that eventually expanded balance of payments surpluses by a large margin. In this sense, tight monetary policy did not stamp out imported inflation, but only "sterilized" it, as Yasuba 1970 said. The imported inflation sterilized in the form of higher official holdings of foreign exchange eventually triggered the Nixon shock of 15 August 1971. In December of that year at the Smithsonian Conference the yen-dollar exchange rate was revalued by 17 percent, to ¥308/$.

On account of the revaluation of the yen, export and import prices fell by 3–4 percent in 1972; wholesale prices and consumer prices returned to the same sort of changes as observed in the early 1960s (0.8 percent and 4.5 percent respectively). And the revaluation of the yen had a much smaller deflationary effect than had been feared. The rate of real growth for 1972 reached 9.5 percent. However, the balance of payments surplus continued as large as before; in 1972, the surplus came to $4.7 billion.

Moreover, U.S. balance of payments deficits did not decrease in the least, and the world's central banks were finally forced to float the dollar against other principal currencies in February–March 1973. The Bretton Woods system collapsed completely. As a result, Japan's exchange rate strengthened further, and reached ¥254/$ (a 42 percent strengthening from the old Bretton Woods rate of ¥360/$). Consequently, as might be expected, Japan's balance of payments surplus finally began to shrink. Imported inflation, which had been sterilized and suppressed, did not occur because large revaluations of the yen lowered the yen price of raw materials. At the same time, Japanese inflation entered a new phase from 1973 onward. This was the start of the Great Inflation of 1973–74.

   d. The Great Inflation and the Shimomura Hypothesis.   The Great Inflation of 1973–74 began with the Shimomura-Suzuki debate (Nihon Keizai Shimbun Sha 1973) over whether then-current price increases were a true inflation. In this debate, carried on in the pages of the *Nihon Keizai Shimbun* (Japan Economic Journal) in June–July 1973, Shimomura said that the situation was not one of true inflation, while Suzuki asserted that it was the start of a true inflation. Let us survey Shimomura's unique theory of inflation, based on Shimomura 1963 and essays published in the former debate.

   According to Shimomura, inflation is a condition in which prices of "goods" continuously increase. However, he contended that, if there is a surplus on current account, the price level is below the equilibrium level, so that the increase in prices is merely an adjustment toward the equilibrium level and cannot be called true inflation. Conversely, when the current account is in deficit, Shimomura held, prices are in a latently inflationary condition, even if actual prices are stable.

   Based on this definition, Shimomura continued to assert that the increase in consumer prices from 1960 onward was not inflationary because wholesale prices, which are prices of goods, remained stable, and the current account was in equilibrium—a situation that is not inflationary according to Shimomura's definition. The increase in consumer prices was due chiefly to the increase in services prices. Wages were rising in all sectors, but productivity growth in the goods sector allowed prices to remain stable. Productivity growth in services was not nearly so fast; thus prices had to rise, to cover wage costs. Hence, price changes were due to differential productivity growth. To call this inflationary is wrong, Shimomura asserted.

   Based on this line of thought, Shimomura held that the appropriate countermeasure for consumer price increases was not to eliminate bottlenecks or to reduce growth in order to ease the shortage of labor, but, conversely, by means of stimulating growth, to promote "modernization, rationalization, and elevation" of lagging industries—namely farming, small business, distribution, and services. This suggested policy stance was diametrically opposed to that of the Bank of Japan demand-pull school, represented by Suzuki, which urged tight money as a disinflationary measure.

   The Shimomura-Suzuki debate occurred in mid-1973. The year before, from October 1972, wholesale prices had begun to rise at double-digit rates. Shimomura asserted that, because prices were increasing while there was a surplus in the current account, the price changes represented merely convergence toward an equilibrium price level, and not inflation. The Shimomura theory says, in effect, that when inflation rises abroad and Japan's balance on current account shows a surplus, no matter how much prices in Japan increase, the situation is not inflationary until the current account surplus is wiped out. Suzuki critized Shimomura's approach for two reasons.

First, the Shimomura theory takes the domestic price level compatible with external equilibrium as a gauge and defines inflation to be an increase in domestic prices that exceeds this level. Therefore, no matter how fast domestic prices may increase, there is no inflation so long as foreign prices are rising even faster. However, while prices continuously rise, even though at a comparatively lower speed than foreign inflation, the efficient allocation of resources and the equitable distribution of income are disturbed, and economic welfare is impeded. Therefore, continuous increases in prices should be defined as inflation, whatever the relative speeds of foreign and domestic price changes.

Second, the Shimomura policy implies that price increases must be tolerated as an adjustment toward the equilibrium price level until the current account surplus is eliminated. This is an "adjustment inflation theory" holding that current account equilibrium is achieved by means of an increase in domestic prices. In fact, however, prices in Japan are a means of welfare improvement for the Japanese people, and should not be a means of adjusting the Japanese economy to circumstances abroad. Trade and exchange rate policies ought to be used for external adjustment.

These were the two most important disagreements in the Shimomura-Suzuki debate. Shimomura's theory of inflation possessed a certain practical relevance to the high-growth period prior to 1968. In those days, since inflation abroad was still at the creeping stage, it was not too far removed from reality to define increases in domestic prices that did not exceed that rate as not inflationary. On the contrary, when price increases in Japan accelerated, Japan's balance of payments went quickly into the red; tight money policy had to be adopted for price stability in the deceleration of growth. Thus, even if Shimomura's definition of inflation had been applied, there was no danger that domestic prices would greatly increase.

However, for the period 1969–73, when (1) the outflow of dollars from the United States led to formation of excess international liquidity, and (2) inflation spread on a global scale, use of the Shimomura definition distorted reality. For, according to this definition, there would be no inflation even with double-digit price increases. Its policy implication was that the required adjustment to current account surplus was not revaluation of the exchange rate, but rather an increase in domestic prices.

e. Imported Inflation or Homemade Inflation?   Even as this debate, which at times resembled a theological controversy, continued, inflation of both wholesale and consumer prices accelerated to double-digit rates. And inflation was given its final jolt by the first oil crisis, in the autumn of 1973. The annual rate of inflation measured in February 1974 peaked at 40 percent for wholesale prices and 26 percent for consumer prices. Inflation rates of these indexes fell back to single-digit rates only in 1975 for wholesale prices and 1976 for consumer prices. Thus, double-digit inflation continued over a period of two to three years.

Since this Great Inflation followed the "sterilized" imported inflation of 1970–71, it was initially thought to be the same type of inflation, realized with a lag (see Shinkai 1973). To be sure, for some periods of 1971–72, we could find periods when the money supply increased greatly due to the balance-of-payments surplus, when cost–push was visible owing to a sharp jump in import prices, and when increased exports took the lead in the expansion of aggregate demand.

However, in contrast, an assertion was soon made that the core of the Great Inflation was homemade, that is, based on domestic factors. Proponents of the homemade-inflation hypothesis were Komiya and Suzuki 1977 and Komiya 1976. The former paper was presented in 1975 at a Brookings conference on inflation during the 1960s and early 1970s. The latter paper is a subsequent elaboration. These works are noteworthy because they were virtually the first to attribute the major portion of the Great Inflation of 1972–74 to homemade inflation. Today, this view is the majority view, but in 1975 the view emphasizing imported inflation was still predominant.

In their 1977 study, Komiya and Suzuki give several reasons why none of the three routes of imported inflation was the principal cause of the Great Inflation. First, expenditure items that led the expansion of aggregate demand in 1972–74 were neither an increase in exports nor a decrease in imports (i.e., current account surplus), but rather domestic demand. Further, with the advance of inflation, public expenditures, based on the super-expansionary budget generated by Prime Minister Tanaka's Archipelago Restructuring Plan, were actually curtailed. The expansion of aggregate demand was led for the most part by a big expansion of private expenditure.

Second, this increase in domestic private expenditure was caused by excessive money supply. But the only year in which higher money growth was due mainly to balance-of-payments surplus was 1971. The latter's contribution to money supply increase fell rapidly in 1972, and disappeared completely in 1973. Consequently, the excess money supply in 1972–73 was attributable to the fact that banks became too generous in granting credit as monetary policy was eased.

Third, the sharp jump in export and import prices, especially the cost-push of the increase in prices of imported raw materials, is certainly recognizable, but double-digit inflation did not depend on that factor alone. In particular, the revaluation of the yen in 1972–73 largely wiped out this cost-push. An inflation rate above 20 percent in consumer prices arose because unit labor costs and gross profits (i.e., the GNP deflator) rose at a rate above 20 percent. The expansion of nominal value added per unit of output was based on domestic factors.

Today, the third point of Komiya and Suzuki's assertions has become plain to everyone, partly due to experience in the second oil crisis. Table 5.3 demonstrates this. A comparison of 1973–74 and 1979–80 reveals that the rate of increase in import prices did not differ much between the periods, and hence the size of imported cost-push was nearly identical in both periods. Nevertheless, the rate of inflation of consumer prices reached 24 percent in the former case, but only 8 percent in the latter. The reason for the difference is that the GNP deflator rose by 20 percent in the former period, but by only 2 percent in the latter. (Recall, of course, that a final demand deflator, like consumer prices, is a weighted average of import prices and the GNP deflator.) In short, in the former period, as shown by the sharp increase in the GNP deflator, homemade inflation advanced, whereas in the latter period it was limited to imported inflation. And one of the important factors that produced this difference in the GNP deflator was the difference in the money supply.[18] Indeed, money growth exceeded 20 percent in the former period, but was restrained to between 9 and 11 percent in the latter.

f. Money Does Matter.   Today, having experienced the influence of the money supply on the Great Inflation of 1973–74 and the effect of restraint on the money supply on inflation in 1979–80, very few would deny the active role of money in the process of inflation. Even among those non-Marxian economists who once asserted the "supportive" or "passive" role of money in the age of creeping inflation, many have revised their opinions.[19]

However, most economists believed that "money does matter," because of its effect on aggregate demand. That is, money was regarded as

18. A detailed analysis of the inflation in 1972–74 surrounding the first oil crisis and that in 1979–80 following the second oil crisis, and of the difference between the two, is given in Suzuki 1981, chapter 2.

19. For example, Niida 1971, before the Great Inflation, came to view the money supply as an autonomous factor. At this point Niida appears to have switched to the demand-pull school of the same persuasion as Suzuki 1964. As stated in the text, Komiya, in Komiya and Suzuki 1977 and Komiya 1976, posits the money supply as the most fundamental autonomous factor of inflation. Since the mid-1960s Komiya has written in the field of international finance on the monetary approach to the balance of payments (e.g., Komiya 1969). In all probability his view of inflation has also greatly changed since the time that Tachi, Komiya, and Niida 1964 was written.

Table 5.3. Data on Money, Prices, GNP, and the Exchange Rate

		Percentage Change over the Previous Year				Average of Monthly Figures
	Money Stock (M2 + CD)	Consumer Prices CPI. All Japan General	Implicit Price Deflator for GNP	Price of Imported Goods	GNP at Constant Prices	Foreign Exchange Rate Yen per U.S. Dollar
1972	26.5	4.5	5.2	− 4.4	9.0	302.91
1973	22.7	11.7	11.9	21.4	8.8	271.14
1974	11.9	24.5	20.6	67.6	− 1.2	292.44
1975	13.1	11.8	7.8	7.4	2.4	297.25
1976	15.1	9.3	6.4	5.2	5.3	296.38
1977	11.4	8.1	5.7	− 4.5	5.3	266.93
1978	11.7	3.8	4.6	− 17.5	5.1	207.87
1979	11.9	3.6	2.6	28.7	5.2	221.37
1980	9.2	8.0	2.8	44.7	4.8	225.77
1981	8.9	4.9	2.7	1.6	4.0	221.46
1982	9.2	2.7	1.7	7.9	3.3	249.94
1983	7.4	1.9	0.7	− 7.8	3.0	237.80

exogenous, but with effects only on the demand side. Papers by the Bank of Japan Research Department (1963) and Suzuki (1964) are not exceptions to this, even though they were the first to assert in the inflation debate in Japan empirically that the money supply was an exogenous factor.

In contrast, a new theory has emerged from the experience of the 1972–74 inflation: money supply moves not only the aggregate demand curve but the aggregate supply curve as well. That is, "money does matter," and in two ways. Acceleration of inflation in this period was not due simply to a shift of the aggregate demand curve in the northeast direction; rather, rising inflationary expectations, which are affected by money growth, shifted the supply curve inward as well.

A pioneering econometric model based on the idea that the rate of inflation depends not only on the gap between demand and supply but also on the expected rate of inflation is the St. Louis monetarist model (e.g., Anderson and Carlson 1970). Suzuki (1973) introduced this St. Louis model to Japan in June 1973. Quoting results of Keran, who estimated this type of model for the Japanese economy for the first time, Suzuki maintained that inflation at the time could not be explained unless we followed the causal chain that runs from the money supply to inflationary expectations and on to increases in prices.

In 1975, the Bank of Japan Research Department published a research report; based on it, Suzuki presented a report titled "The Influence of Money Supply in Japan on Income and Prices" at the annual convention of the Japan Association of Economics and Econometrics in November 1975. He held that money supply, instead of acting through aggregate expenditure, directly affects prices through a shift of the aggregate supply curve due to inflationary expectations. This view has become more persuasive theoretically and econometrically since 1979 as Shirakawa (1979), Kato (1980), and others introduced the Lucas aggregate supply function based on the natural rate of unemployment hypothesis. (See Lucas 1972, 1973.) Shimpo (1979) and Seo and Takahashi (1982) have carried out empirical studies of Japan, based on Barro's studies of the United States (1976, 1977, 1978, and 1979), which combine the rational expectations hypothesis with the Lucas supply function.[20] This series of studies has started to advance theoretical and empirical explication of the mechanism by which the money supply causes the aggregate supply function to shift inward via inflationary expectations, and hence causes prices to rise. We shall discuss these studies further in chapter 6.

20. It is since 1972–73 that American economists began to use the Lucas-type aggregate supply function for theoretical and empirical purposes in showing the mechanism of inflationary expectations leading to shifts of the aggregate supply curve. It is from 1976 on that Barro began to conduct empirical work on the mechanism of the money supply leading to inflationary expectations.

In 1973–75 the Bank of Japan Research Department 1975 and Suzuki 1973 asserted that there was no doubt that the mechanism of the money supply leading to inflationary expectations that shift the aggregate supply curve was at work in Japan. In other words, the same problem was put forth at about the same time. However, it was not until 1979 that the Japanese discussion was linked to the American argument. It may be that this lag of three to six years resulted because proper attention was not paid by the Japanese economists to the natural rate of unemployment hypothesis and the macroeconomic rational expectations hypothesis.

The Japanese economy, after having 10-percent annual average growth from 1961–1965, had average growth of 10.6 percent in 1966–72. Judging from these figures, one cannot take the view that real GNP in 1972 was below the growth path that corresponded to the natural rate of unemployment. In fiscal 1972 the growth rate was 9.7 percent and the inflation rate of the GNP deflator was 6.2 percent. In fiscal 1973, the growth rate dropped to 5.3 percent and the inflation rate climbed to 14.9 percent. In the Lucas-type aggregate supply function, this pattern can be interpreted as a result of a rise in the expected rate of inflation in 1973, which shifted the aggregate supply curve upward.

III. Changes in Macroeconomic Performance since the Middle of the 1970s

1. Differences Between the First and Second Oil Crises

The performance of the Japanese economy after the second oil crisis was very different from that experienced after the first. A look at table 5.3 makes this clear. Inflation in terms of consumer prices reached a high of 24.4 percent in 1974, just after the first oil crisis; in 1980, following the second crisis, it peaked at only 8.0 percent. Economic growth in real terms, which had been running at just under 10 percent per year before the first crisis, shrank suddenly to near zero in 1974 and 1975. By contrast, economic growth has declined rather gradually during the years following the second oil crisis. After the first crisis, the current account stayed in the red for the three years 1973–75, while the foreign exchange rate lingered at nearly ¥300 to the U.S. dollar through 1976. On the other hand, after the second crisis, deficits in the current account were recorded in only two years, 1979 and 1980, and the depreciation of the yen in foreign exchange markets was smaller than in the years after the first crisis (except in 1982, when the yen depreciated mainly due to a wide differential of real interest rates between Japan and the United States).

The basic factor that brought about these differences is the fact that the inflation following the second crisis was mild and short-lived. Mild inflation meant a smaller reduction in real incomes, and a shorter duration for tight monetary and fiscal policies. Hence the ensuing business recession was less severe. Lower inflation also meant that goods lost less of their price competitiveness, and thus that deficits in the current account balance could be overcome earlier.

But we must ask why the second inflation was mild and short-lived. The Komiya-Suzuki (1977) approach forces us to ask why the rise in the GNP deflator was so much lower after the second oil crisis.

First, Japan had made great progress in the conservation of oil since the first oil crisis, so that the impact of oil price increases on domestic prices was less during the second oil crisis than during the first. Table 5.4 shows this clearly. If oil consumption per unit of GNP in real terms is indexed as 100 for 1973, the year of the first oil crisis, the figure for Japan drops to 66.4 in 1980, far lower than the 83.4 for the United States and the 73.7 for West Germany. This indicates that Japan achieved the greatest degree of oil conservation among the major industrialized nations.

Compared to oil consumption elsewhere in the world, that in Japan is marked by a comparatively high proportion of industrial use. It is in the industrial sector that reductions in oil consumption have been greatest. These reductions occurred partly because of positive capital investment in energy conservation and partly conversion to other sources of energy. Another contributing factor is the change in Japan's industrial structure

Table 5.4. Prices, Productivity, and Income in Japan, the United States, and West Germany (compared with previous year, in percent)

	Japan			United States			West Germany		
	78	79	80	78	79	80	78	79	80
Final consumption deflator	3.4	4.2	7.0	7.3	8.8	9.7	3.2	4.6	6.0
Import deflator	−14.9	26.1	33.3	4.2	14.6	18.2	−1.9	7.1	10.1
GNP deflator	4.6	2.5	3.1	7.3	8.5	9.0	3.9	3.8	5.1
Gross profits per unit product	7.0	2.3	1.6	6.8	7.8	8.2	5.2	5.3	4.3
Wage cost (E/D = C/A)	2.6	2.6	4.5	7.7	8.9	9.5	3.0	3.0	5.6
Labor productivity (D = A/B)	3.4	3.8	3.5	0.2	0.1	−0.1	2.4	2.1	1.2
Hourly wages (E = C/B)	6.1	6.6	8.1	7.8	9.1	9.4	5.5	5.2	7.2
Real GNP (A)	5.1	5.6	4.2	4.8	3.2	−0.2	3.6	4.5	1.8
Total working hours (B)	1.6	1.7	0.7	4.6	3.1	−0.1	1.2	2.3	0.6
Employees' income (C)	7.9	8.4	8.9	12.8	12.4	9.3	6.7	7.7	7.9
Oil consumption per unit of real GNP (1973 = 100)	78.7	77.2	66.4	95.1	90.5	83.4	87.2	85.6	73.7

Source: Bank of Japan

129

that is now in progress, with the energy-intensive materials industries becoming steadily less important relative to the fabricating and assembly industries, which consume less energy and generate higher value added.

2. Preventing Homemade Inflation

The second reason for short and mild CPI inflation after the second oil crisis is that the increases in the implicit price deflator for GNP were quite different in the two oil crisis periods, as is evident from table 5.3. Whereas the deflator grew by 11.8 percent in 1973 and 20.6 percent in 1974, it remained stable at 2.8 percent in 1980. This means that wages and profit per unit of product, which rose at double-digit annual rates during the first crisis period, hardly rose at all during the second.

During the first oil crisis, in short, increases in the price of imported goods not only caused imported inflation in the form of rising consumer prices but also triggered domestically created inflation in the form of advances in consumer prices due to the inflated wages and profit per unit of product. During the second oil crisis, however, even though prices of imported goods rose in a similar manner, these rises did not lead to inflation of wages and profit per unit of product. Hence, there was no domestically created inflation of consumer prices.

But why did wages and profit per unit of product fail to follow import prices in the aftermath of the second crisis? The answer lies in the different behavior of expectations between the first and second oil crises.

From the outbreak of the first oil crisis in the autumn of 1973 to the winter of the following year, expectation of inflation mounted among the Japanese people. Companies bought hastily and held back on sales, and consumers began hoarding. This speculative mood spread quickly and prices soared. Profit per unit of product also became inflated. "Price frenzy" was the name given at the time to the price spiral that developed, and real wages declined markedly. The proportion of income flowing to companies grew, but that flowing to workers dropped sharply.

Thus, during the annual collective bargaining talks in the spring of 1974, the thrust was in the direction of regaining the previous level of wages in real terms, and nominal wage increases averaged 33 percent. Part of this substantial rise in nominal wages came out of corporate profits, but part of it was also passed along into prices of goods. Both wages and profits per unit of product were inflated considerably, in a pattern of domestically generated inflation.

In the years following the second oil crisis, however, there was no spread of speculative activity fueled by expectations of inflation, due to three factors.

First, business conditions were different. When the first oil crisis occurred in the autumn of 1973, business was at its peak, and goods in the domestic market were already in short supply. The outbreak of the oil crisis compounded the supply problems by widespread expectations of greater shortages in the future due to the imposition of constraints on oil supplies and due to the cost increases caused by oil price hikes. All this led people to expect increasingly higher rates of inflation in the future. In contrast, when the second oil crisis occurred in 1979, the economy was at an early point in the cycle and the demand-supply situation in the domestic market was loose. This looseness weakened any impulse toward speculation.

Another reason for the lack of speculation after the second oil crisis is that lessons had been learned from the first one. Those companies that had carried out speculative stockpiling during the first crisis, by hasty purchasing of inputs and holding back of sales, sustained enormous losses on those stockpiles during the decline in prices that occurred in the ensuing two-year period (1974–75) of zero growth. Moreover, companies learned that, even when profits are increased temporarily by price hikes, the subsequent large wage increases and the resulting profit squeeze prevent any profit from inflation in the long run. Having learned these lessons, Japanese companies with very few exceptions refrained from speculative stockpiling after the second oil crisis.

Consumers, too, learned a lesson from their experience in the first oil crisis. Shortages of goods that they had hoarded did not occur after all. Thus there was no strong move to hoard during the second crisis. Another lesson learned was that, even if substantial wage increases are won, the resulting profit squeeze for companies undermines stability in employment. And if part of the wage increase is passed along in the form of higher prices for consumer goods, then there is no improvement in purchasing power in real terms. Hence wage demands remained moderate in the period following the second oil crisis.

This does not mean, however, that Japanese workers faced unreasonably small wage increases. A look at table 5.4 shows that the rates of growth of both employees' income and hourly wages were higher in Japan than in West Germany. Nevertheless, the rates of growth of the wage cost and GNP deflator were lower in Japan than in West Germany. This is because the rate of increase in labor productivity in Japan was higher.

On the other hand, the rises in employees' income and hourly wages in Japan were slightly lower than in the United States. In the United States, however, there has been no increase in labor productivity, and thus wage rises were translated directly into price rises. For this reason, there has been no increase in wages in real terms in the United States. In Japan, due to increases in labor productivity, the rise in prices has trailed the rise in wages, which means a steady increase in real wages. The rise in real wages in Japan, in fact, has been higher than that in both the United States and West Germany.

3. Success in Monetary Control

The third reason for the absence of speculation after the second oil crisis is that monetary policy adequately controlled monetary growth. As we see in figure 5.1, Japan's monetary growth was quite high in the three years immediately preceding the first oil crisis (1971–73). Thus, when the first crisis struck, there was excess liquidity in the economy that financed speculative accumulation through stockpiling. But monetary growth in 1977 and 1978, immediately before the second oil crisis, was controlled at comparatively low levels, and after the second oil crisis it was held to even lower levels. This served as a financing-side constraint on speculative stockpiling, making possible the control of domestically generated inflation.

Figure 5.2 shows the rate of inflation in terms of the GDP deflator for Japan, the United States, and West Germany. The trends in this graph are very similar to those in monetary growth in these three countries. This is a clear indication of the fact that Japan, which succeeded in controlling monetary growth through monetary policy, was the most successful of the three countries in the control of domestically generated inflation.

If domestic prices are maintained at stable levels by proper control of monetary growth, disturbances arising from the oil crisis can be held to a minimum. If disturbances are minimal, the active application of entrepreneurial initiative will continue to push productivity upward, creating a beneficial cycle between development and stability of the economy.

How to maintain this cycle is the future task of economic policy in Japan. As far as the monetary aspect of this task is concerned, the Bank of Japan will maintain the following three elements of monetary policy, which have been implemented over the last decade.

The first concerns policy priorities. Before the first oil crisis, a certain tradeoff between prices and output actually existed, so that it was possible to achieve higher production and employment if a higher inflation rate were allowed. In this respect, policy could pursue manifold objectives, namely, price stability, economic expansion, and so forth. However, after the first oil crisis, the situation changed. The high inflation and simultaneous deep recession generated a new consciousness, not only in the Bank of Japan, but also in the government and in the industrial sector. Society gradually accepted the view that neglect of inflation might temporarily bring higher production and employment, but in the medium and long run would erode the basis of stable economic expansion. The result was a national consensus for price stability as the top priority.

The Bank of Japan responded quickly to the second oil crisis; even though the cycle was far from overheating, rather strong precautionary restrictive measures were implemented, based on the judgment that no

(ratio to upper band limit)

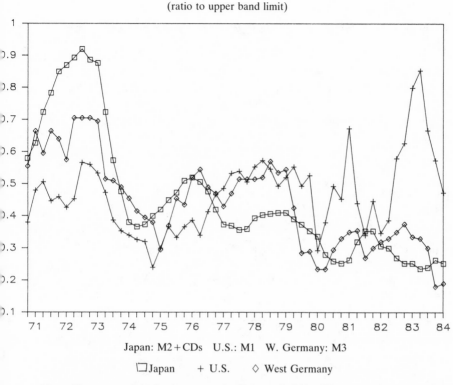

Japan: M2 + CDs   U.S.: M1   W. Germany: M3

☐ Japan   + U.S.   ◇ West Germany

NOTE: Money growth in the three countries fluctuated within different bands. This figure shows the growth rate in any one period relative to the upper limit of each country's band. The band limits were: Japan, 30 percent; U.S., 15 percent; W. Germany, 20 percent.

Figure 5.1. Money Growth in Japan, the United States, and West Germany

long-run tradeoff exists between prices and output, and that the choice of price stability as the top priority would lead the economy to stable expansion in the future. (The empirical basis for this judgment will be discussed in chapter 6.)

The second change in monetary policy is the introduction of stricter surveillance and control over the money stock as an intermediate target, in view of the bitter experience of the sharp increase in the money stock in 1972 and 1973 just before the first oil crisis. Since July 1978, the Bank of Japan has announced a quarterly "forecast" in the form of year-on-year percentage increases in the stock of M2 + CDs, averaged over the quarter concerned. Because the estimated "projection" is based upon the policy of the Bank of Japan itself, it is actually an indicator of the policy intention of the Bank of Japan, even though it is called a projection. The stable monetary growth since 1977 has owed very much to the change in

%   GDP Deflator Growth

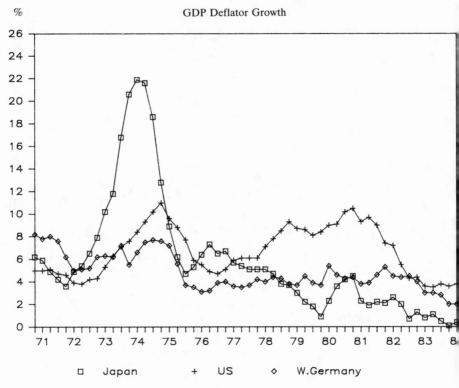

Figure 5.2. Inflation in Japan, the United States, and West Germany

monetary control. There will be further discussion of this subject in chapter 8.

The third change concerning monetary policy is the attempt to deregulate interest rates as far as feasible so as to enable the transmission of policy effects by means of freely fluctuating interest rates. This is a natural consequence of the use of the money stock as the intermediate target. We have already discussed this subject in detail in chapter 4.

6

Money, Prices, and Output

I. **Is Money Stock a Cause or an Effect of Expenditure?**

1. Neglect of Money in the High-Growth Period

a. Neglect of Money by Keynesians. Unfortunately, money supply has been the focus of general attention in postwar Japan only in times of great inflations. The first instance was the postwar reconstruction period after 1945, and the second was inflation of the 1973–74 period of excess liquidity.

In the postwar reconstruction period, monetary expansion was accompanied by a tremendous increase of government expenditure, and special demand due to the Korean War caused a rapid surge in exports. Since these factors were all intertwined, there was little debate about whether the excess demand that generated the inflation was induced by money supply or by exogenous or autonomous factors such as government expenditure or exports. The sense that a problem even existed in determining the importance of the role of money as a factor in aggregate demand did not gain general attention until the Great Inflation of the 1973–74 period.

Indeed, in the second period of postwar economic history, from 1956 to 1973, neglect of money supply as a contributor to aggregate demand was even more thorough. Many felt that money was not a cause of aggregate demand, but rather an effect of it. If this were the case, aggregate demand would be determined by government spending, corporate investment, and other such real side elements, with the price level determined by interaction of this aggregate demand with aggregate supply. Movements of observed money outstanding would only reflect money demand generated by real income, in turn determined by the real side

135

elements and the price level; observed money did not include any effects of discretionary money supply. The only way in which money could have an effect on real income and prices was through the channel of influencing investment through interest rates. And conversely, so long as interest rates did not change, no change of the money supply of any size could ever affect aggregate demand or prices.

The classic statement of this is given in Osamu Shimomura 1963.[1] Most notable is Shimomura's theoretical structure, in which declining interest rates caused by increasing money supply are an essential and immediate requirement for economic growth; moreover, as long as interest rates fail to decline, it is permissible to ignore the influence of money supply on aggregate expenditure and prices.

Shimomura's contentions of course are strongly influenced by Keynes's *General Theory* (1936), but they also inherit its problems, of which there are at least three.[2] The first is the existence of an area in which even large increases in money supply fail to lower interest rates (i.e., a liquidity trap) where the interest elasticity of money demand is close to infinity; the second is the existence of a region in which investment will not respond even if interest rates do fall (interest elasticity of investment close to zero). These assumptions of the liquidity trap and elasticity pessimism underlay Keynes's views that effects of money supply on aggregate demand are insignificant.

Reflecting Keynes's influence, the chief topic of postwar economics became antideflation measures. Major countries such as the United States and the United Kingdom kept interest rates as low as possible and raised their money supplies, but they soon faced surprising and unexpected inflation. As a result, in the last part of the 1940s and early 1950s, there was a revival of monetary policy in all these nations; money supply was restrained, interest rates raised, and success achieved in controlling price increases. The classic example of this was the "accord" between the U.S. Treasury and the Federal Reserve of March 1951, and the resultant restraint of inflation.[3] After this historical experience, the 1950s saw the tremendous expansion of econometric analysis and of macroeconometric models. Both the liquidity trap and the interest inelasticity of investment were rejected in many empirical analyses. It is surprising that Keynes's ideas, which were disproved by historical facts and empirical analysis in Western countries in the years 1945–55, were brought into Japan for the high-growth period of 1956–73. It is even more surprising that Shimomura

1. See Shimomura 1963.
2. I have pointed out problems with Shimomura 1963 in other work, e.g., Suzuki 1964. But at the time, my arguments were not found convincing.
3. For an account of the revival of monetary policy, see M. H. De Kock 1954, chapter 16. The accord between the Treasury and the Federal Reserve is also discussed there.

could make these contentions in 1963, completely ignoring the historical fact of the revival of monetary policy and the results of the econometric models of the 1950s.

b. Inflationary Consequences of Ignoring Money. In addition to disregarding historical facts and empirical results, Shimomura failed to pay attention to important theoretical developments, such as the correction of the Keynesian framework that had taken place by the mid-1950s. This is the second problem with his book. That is, there is an absence of consideration of wealth effects, such as pointed out by Pigou 1943 and Patinkin 1948.[4] Today, when using the Keynesian framework, it is usual to use a corrected version of the *General Theory*, which incorporates wealth effects at least in the consumption function.[5]

The theory of wealth effects points out that the outstanding level of net worth of individuals has a positive effect on consumption. Hence, to the extent that an increase in money supply is an increase in net worth, the rise in money should bring a rise in expenditure through a wealth effect. That is, the effect of money supply on nominal expenditure is not limited to the indirect effect passing through interest rates; there is also a direct effect through outstanding wealth. Thus, Shimomura commits a theoretical error when he contends that expansion of money supply, no matter how large, has no effect on expenditure so long as interest rates remain unchanged. The result of adopting policies based on his prescription would be inflation, through excessive expansion of nominal aggregate demand.

The third problem with Shimomura 1963 is that it commits another theoretical error concerning the transmission channel of interest rate effects. Shimomura contended that money supply should increase continuously so that interest rates remain low. Of all the cause and effect relationships between prices and interest rates, he considers only the liquidity effect, that is, "raising money supply lowers interest rates." But there are other relationships between money and interest rates. For example, higher money supply leads to higher aggregate expenditure and hence higher money demand; so interest rates can be pressured upward. This is an income effect. There is also the Fisher effect, whereby higher money leads to higher prices, and higher prices lead to higher expected inflation, which in turn raises interest rates.[6]

---

4. Pioneering criticisms of Keynes 1936 that point out wealth effects are Pigou 1943 and Patinkin 1948, written nearly twenty years before Shimomura 1963. The representative, and now classic, treatment of the problems in the Keynesian structure from the viewpoint of wealth effects is Patinkin 1965, which is based on the two earlier articles.

5. For an accessible account of a Keynesian framework corrected to include wealth effects and for an account of the debate about them, see Tachi 1982, chapters 6 and 7.

6. The name Fisher effect derives from Irving Fisher 1930, the first to study in detail

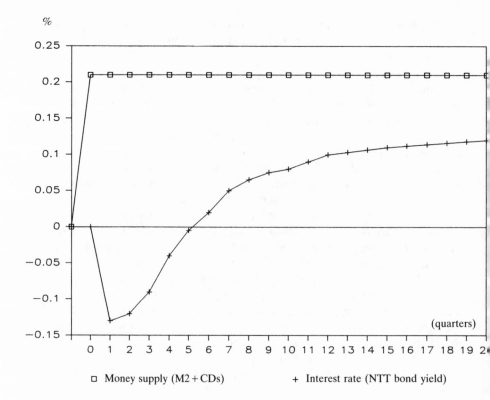

□ Money supply (M2 + CDs)   + Interest rate (NTT bond yield)

Figure 6.1. Money and Interest Rates in Japan

A time profile of the effects of money supply increase shows that at first the liquidity effect does lower interest rates, but soon the income effects accompanying expansion of aggregate expenditure and the Fisher effect accompanying inflation raise interest rates. Narukawa (1982) considers this time profile theoretically, and carries out empirical analysis. His results are given in figure 6.1. He uses quarterly data from 1966/II to 1980/I, and estimates a bivariate time series model with money supply (M2 + CDs, growth vs. previous year) and interest rates (secondary market yields on Nippon Telephone and Telegraph bonds). He then performs counterfactual simulations raising the growth rate of money supply by one percent per year and estimating the effects on the level of interest rates.[7] The rise in money would lower interest rates for the first year or

---

the relationship of inflationary expectations and interest rates. For examinations of the Fisher effect in Japan, see Oritani 1979b and Akio Kuroda 1982, chapter 7.

7. For details, see Narukawa 1982.

so, but after that it would actually raise interest rates. Similar results for Japan have been obtained by Sakakibara et al. 1980 and Cagan 1972.

Hence, for interest rates to be kept continuously low, as in Shimomura 1963, money supply would have to be continuously increased so that the liquidity effect of lowering interest rates would overcome the upward pressure of interest rates from the income and Fisher effects. This implies unlimited accommodation of price increases and aggregate demand increases by money supply. Shimomura's contention is typical of inflationists, and indeed is a classic statement of what is today known as the accelerationist[8] position.

But the idea of promoting growth through unlimited inflation or acceleration of money supply disintegrated in the 1970s, in the face of stagflation, that is, of simultaneous high inflation and low growth. The difficulty of defending inflationist or accelerationist positions on either empirical or theoretical grounds will be considered again in sections III, IV, and V.

2. Cause and Effect between Money and Expenditure

a. *Leads and Lags between Money and Expenditure.*   As we have seen above, it was conventional wisdom in high growth period Japan that money did not "cause" expenditure, but rather the reverse, and that money supply had no effect on expenditure so long as interest rates were constant. In this environment, a statement by Milton Friedman caused quite a stir from an empirical angle. As we saw in chapter 5, Friedman came to Japan in early summer of 1963 and pointed out that even in Japan movements of money supply led movements of prices and aggregate expenditure.[9] I visited Friedman at his lodgings at International House in Tokyo at the time, and obtained the evidence for the statement. Since he was traveling, and given that this was in the period before even desktop calculators, he showed semi-log graphs of money supply, nominal income, and consumer prices using quarterly data, and pointed out how money supply led the others.

Stimulated by this, the Bank of Japan Research Department 1963 in October of that year and Suzuki 1964 the next year published research results. These two studies used ten years of quarterly data from 1953/I to 1963/IV, and presented results comparing movements of money, prices (GNP deflators, consumer prices, wholesale prices, etc.), and real activity (industrial production). One method was comparing leads and lags of

8. An accelerationist is, in the world of the natural rate of unemployment, one who argues for accelerating increases in money growth in order to keep the real rate of growth high. For details, see Phelps 1970.

9. A record of Friedman's statement is included in a discussion between Friedman and Saburo Okita (1963).

peaks and troughs in growth rates; another was calculation of correlation coefficients of different series at different lags. The results showed that movements of money led movements of prices and real activity by one or two quarters. This finding implied a conflict between the facts and the then-current wisdom that money was an effect rather than a cause of aggregate demand.

Ten years later, in July 1975, the Bank of Japan Research Department published similar findings about chronological cross-relations. Data were broken into three periods (1958/II–1964/IV, 1965/I–1970/IV, and 1971/I–1974/IV), and correlations between money, prices (GNP deflator and WPI), nominal expenditure, and real expenditure were calculated. The following statistical facts emerged:

(1) Correlation between money (particularly M2) movements and price movements a few quarters later was strong. But the lag gradually lengthened from one or two quarters in the first period to four quarters in the last.

(2) The correlation between M2 and real or nominal expenditure was high in the first and last periods but zero or even negative in the middle period. The reason for the temporary disappearance of the correlation in the middle period is technical: expenditure growth in this period, both nominal and real, was extremely stable, so attributing variance to other factors is difficult.

These results showed the statistical fact that movements of money supply led prices and expenditure in Japan, and that this relationship was observable over long periods. That money was chronologically prior strongly suggests that it was a "cause" of income, and not at all an effect.

Let us next examine how this relationship has done recently. Figure 6.2 shows calculations of correlations of money (M1 and M2 + CDs) with nominal expenditure for the last ten-plus years, from 1970/I to 1983/III, in terms of percentage increase over the year. Both narrowly defined money (M1) and broadly defined money (M2 + CDs) clearly lead nominal expenditure. The leading relationship in the correlation coefficients is particularly strong in the case of broad money, because broad money represents the latent purchasing power to finance future expenditure, and hence has influence on economic agents' attitude toward current and future expenditure.

This graph suggests why the Bank of Japan's money-oriented monetary policy, as we will discuss in chapter 8, emphasizes M2 + CDs over all other quantitative monetary indicators.

b. The Sims Test of Causality. The chronological cross correlation analysis above suggests that, since the correlation between current money and nominal income a few quarters in the future is high, there is a causal relationship with current money determining future expenditure. But,

(correlation coefficients)

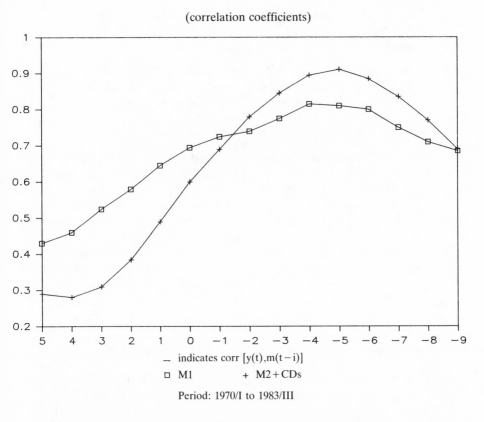

— indicates corr [y(t),m(t − i)]
□ M1   + M2 + CDs

Period: 1970/I to 1983/III

Figure 6.2. Chronological Cross Correlations of Money and Nominal Expenditure

taking things a step further, it has now become possible to investigate statistically whether causality exists.[10]

Sims 1972 presents a simple causality test for a bivariate time series model, as an application of time series methods. This test is now called

10. The term "causality" will be used below according to the definition of Granger 1969. When forecasting *Y*, if a forecast that is based on all information including past values of *X* performs better than a forecast based on all information except past values of *X*, then there is a causal relationship from *X* to *Y*. This type of causality is, as discussed by Oritani 1979c, a necessary condition for everyday notions of not only forecast power, but controlling power as well. But in a field like economics where experimental examination of control relationships is difficult, this confusion is unavoidable. However, we must admit the danger of mistaking chronological order for causality.

the Sims test. The point of the Sims test is to take two time series, X and Y, and to establish unidirectional causality from X to Y if the following two conditions are met.[11]

(*I*) In a regression of current Y onto future, current, and past values of X, current and past values of X must be significant (in an F-test), and the future values of X must be insignificant (in an F-test).

(*II*) In a regression of current X onto future, current, and past levels of Y, the future values of Y must be significant (in an F-test).

Sims (1972) uses this method to investigate causality between money supply and nominal expenditure. Calling X the money supply and Y nominal expenditure, he showed that both conditions (*I*) and (*II*) above held in the United States. That is, a unidirectional causality from money to nominal income existed in the United States. Goodhart (1976) carried out the same investigation for the United Kingdom, but the coefficients of determination for his regression were low (i.e., estimates were of low reliability), and so the same result could not be obtained for England.

Oritani (1979a) has applied this method to Japan.[12] Using data from 1962/I to 1976/III on M2 and nominal GNP (seasonally adjusted), he found that unidirectional causality from money to GNP did exist. That is, in the regression explaining GNP with M2, current and past values of M2 were significant in explaining current GNP (appropriate F-statistic was 2.404, significant at the 10 percent level), but future values of M2 did not help explain nominal GNP (F-statistic of 0.809). Hence condition (*I*) was fulfilled. Moreover, in the regression explaining M2 with future, current, and past values of nominal GNP, the future values of nominal GNP were significant (F- statistic 2.280, significant at the 10 percent level) in explaining M2, so condition (*II*) was fulfilled. Table 6.1 summarizes the results of Sims 1972, Goodhart 1976, and Oritani 1979a, giving the various F-statistics.

Sims and Oritani also carry out causality tests on government expenditure and nominal expenditure. The table also shows results of these tests. Examination of the table shows that in both the United States and Japan, no unidirectional causality from government spending to aggregate expenditure (both nominal) could be found. For the United States, future values of government expenditure are significant in explaining current aggregate expenditure, so condition (*I*) is rejected. For Japan, the current and past values of government spending are not significant in explaining current aggregate expenditure, and so again condition (*I*) is rejected. Moreover, future values of aggregate expenditure fail to explain signifi-

---

11. For descriptions of the Sims test, see Sims (1972), Oritani 1979a, or Goodhart et al. 1976.

12. For details of Oritani's study see Oritani 1979a.

Table 6.1. Sims Tests on Money, Nominal Expenditure, and Fiscal Expenditure

	$Y = f(M)$		$M = f(Y)$	
	Future M	Present and Past M	Future Y	Present and Past Y
Japan	0.809	2.404*	2.280*	0.793
U.S.	0.36	1.89*	4.29**	n.a.
U.K.	2.44*	0.34	0.97	0.40
	$Y = f(E)$		$E = f(Y)$	
	Future E	Present and Past E	Future Y	Present and Past Y
Japan	1.581	1.514	1.226	1.886
U.S.	4.60**	2.91**	3.40*	5.61**

Note: Figures represent F-statistics on the hypothesis that the variables in question do not belong in the relevant equation.

* indicates significance at the 10% level.
** indicates significance at the 5% level.

cantly the current value of government spending, so condition (*II*) is also rejected.

Thus, judging from the results of these Sims tests, at least as far as the United States and Japan are concerned, the monetarist hypothesis of unidirectional causality from money to aggregate expenditure is supported, and the Keynesian hypothesis of unidirectional causality from government spending to aggregate expenditure is not supported.

c. Power Spectrum Analysis of Causality.   The Sims tests given above are a simple method of investigating causality in a bivariate model, but a more precise method of investigating causality in a bi- or multi-variate system has been developed. This is "relative power contribution" (RPC) analysis, which may be briefly described as follows.[13]

For now, let us consider a bivariate system. Say the two time series variables X and Y have a "mutually interactive relationship." In this case, variations in Y can be separated into the "portion explained by variations in X," and the "portion not explained by variations in X." Variations in X can be similarly decomposed. The portion of each variable not explained by the other is referred to as the "noise" in each variable. Let us denote the noise of X by U_x and the noise of Y by U_y.

Let us also recall that a bivariate time series model is precisely one that uses past values of U_x and U_y to explain current values of X and Y.

The relative power contribution is a numerical expression in the fre-

13. Investigation of causality with power spectrum analysis is a rather sophisticated statistical procedure. A statistical treatment is given in Akaike and Nakagawa 1971. Description of its application to economics is given in Ohkubo 1983.

quency domain of the extent to which variations of X and Y are controlled by U_x and U_y. The variations of economic variables are considered to be amalgams of cycles of different periodicities (frequencies). When the influence of U_x on movements of Y at a given periodicity (power contribution of X to Y) is large, and the influence of U_y on X at that periodicity (power contribution of Y to X) is negligibly small, then we say that a unidirectional causality from X to Y exists at that periodicity.

A statement of this principle for money and aggregate expenditure would go as follows: if there exist periodicities at which movements of aggregate expenditure are strongly influenced by unexplained money-supply variations and at which money-supply movements are *not* influenced by unexplained aggregate-expenditure variations, then there exists unidirectional causality from money to aggregate expenditure at that periodicity.

Ohkubo 1983 has used power spectrum analysis to investigate causality between money supply and aggregate expenditure. In addition to tests based on the entire twenty-five years of data from 1956/II to 1981/IV, Ohkubo considered the possibility of a structural change in the Japanese economy after the first oil shock, and carried out tests on the subperiods ending in 1973/IV and, omitting 1974/I-III as outliers, starting in 1974/IV. The results show that, for the period as a whole, there existed unidirectional causality at long periods from money, defined either as M1 or M2 (or M2 + CDs, once CDs began to be issued), to aggregate expenditure. However, when the period is broken into subperiods, we see that the first subperiod shows a reverse causality from nominal expenditure to M2. This is probably due to inclusion of time deposits in M2; since nominal expenditure is equivalent to nominal income, and since income generates nominal savings, and since a large part of savings are held in time deposits, the causality appears to run from expenditure to M2. But this anomaly disappears after 1974; with development of the financial system, means of holding savings diversified away from time deposits and toward assets with higher returns such as loan trusts, postal deposits, government bonds, and life insurance funds.

Ohkubo also considered interest rates, which Keynes assumed to be the channel through which the effects of money on aggregate expenditure certainly flowed. Causality tests were conducted using power spectra between interest rates and expenditure. Among the rates that influence nonbanking sector expenditure decisions, Ohkubo chose the market yield on coupon-bearing Nippon Telephone and Telegraph bonds, which has fluctuated freely for many years. He analyzed its causal relations with both nominal and real expenditure.

Overall, the power contribution of the interest rate is lower than that of the money supply, and clear causality is not evident. If one were forced to draw a conclusion, it would be that, in the first subperiod, causality in short periods (high frequencies) ran from interest rates to expenditure and causality in long periods ran from expenditure to interest rates. As I explained earlier using the work of Narukawa (1982) this shows the dominance in the short run of the liquidity effect causing interest rates to fall, and the dominance in the long run of the income effect causing interest rates to rise. In the subperiod starting in 1974/IV, a causal relation between interest rates and real expenditure may be seen. But the analysis here does not include a relation between the real interest rate and expenditure, so judging the interest elasticity of expenditure from this result alone is a bit risky. More recent work by Ohkubo (1983) shows causality from real interest rates to real expenditure and to prices.

II. The Keynesian-Monetarist Controversy and Aggregate Expenditure

1. Income Multiplier or Money Multiplier?

The various results presented above show that there exists unidirectional causality from money supply to nominal aggregate expenditure; but there are factors other than money supply that display unidirectional causality versus nominal expenditure. Keynes (1936) and his followers have emphasized the role of autonomous expenditure, such as government spending, as is well known. This is the theory that an increase in government spending raises aggregate expenditure through the income multiplier (inverse of the marginal propensity to save). Moreover, Keynes and the Keynesians are skeptical of the influence of money supply on aggregate expenditure, based on their elasticity pessimism. And even if they admit the existence of effects of money, they contend that these effects are small relative to those of government spending.

In response to this, Milton Friedman contended, based on results of analysis of fifty years of time series data from the United States, that the income multiplier (effect of a rise of government spending on aggregate expenditure) was less stable than the "money multiplier" (effect of a rise in money supply on aggregate expenditure).[14] That is, the unidirectional causality from the money supply to expenditure not only exists but is stable, whereas the effect of government spending, when not accompanied by supportive monetary policy, is small.

As the theoretical underpinning for his viewpoint, many economists point to the crowding-out effect, and use the following argument. Even

---

14. Here the term "money multiplier" expresses the number of times the level of the money supply is multiplied to obtain the level of nominal income. But the same term is also used to indicate the ratio of the money supply to base money. The latter definition is the one most used today, with the term "velocity" usually applied to the former. The original terminology is used in the text, despite the possibility of confusion.

if a rise in expenditure is realized through the income multiplier based on government spending, there will be a rise in money demand for transactions, based on the higher income. When money supply is fixed in such a situation, interest rates will rise and private sector expenditures will fall. The result is downward pressure on income equal to this expenditure fall times the income multiplier. (This is the crowding-out effect.) The early rise in expenditure and the later fall in expenditure tend to cancel each other, so the final level of expenditure is uncertain. But the final income multiplier will not be large. Thus, in the absence of supportive monetary policy, it is uncertain the extent to which total expenditure will rise after a rise in government spending.

In contrast, the effect of the money supply on aggregate expenditure is independent; it does not depend on a supportive role from any other factor. Hence, monetarists' view goes, the money multiplier is stable.

2. Crowding-Out and the Expenditure Function

This conflict between the Keynesians and the monetarists had to be settled by empirical investigation. Letting autonomous expenditure be denoted by E, the money supply by M, and aggregate expenditure by Y, an expenditure function

$$Y = Y(E,M)$$

could be estimated and the coefficient on E (effect of a rise in E while M is held constant) and that on M (effect of a rise in M when E is held constant) could be compared.

This equation can be thought of as a reduced form from the Keynesian model,[15] or a reduced form from the monetarist one. That is, the effect of money on total expenditure can be thought of as the indirect, Keynesian route through interest rates or as the direct, monetarist route. In this sense, the expenditure function does not commit itself to being either Keynesian or monetarist, and rather seeks to find merely the statistical fact of whether the income multiplier or the money multiplier is larger.

Attempts to estimate expenditure functions were first carried out by the Federal Reserve Bank of St. Louis using U.S. data. This was one

---

15. The Keynesian IS-LM model may be expressed in nominal terms, with an assumption of linear homogeneity, by the equations

$$I(r,Y) + E = S(r,Y)$$

$$M = L\ (r,Y).$$

Eliminating r from these two and solving for Y yields

$$Y = Y(E,M)$$

which is precisely the equation in the text.

link in the estimation of the St. Louis model, and was published in the April 1970 *Report* of the St. Louis Fed.[16] Keran applied the St. Louis model to the Japanese economy in 1972.[17] The first attempt at estimating an expenditure function in Japan was by the Bank of Japan Research Department in 1975,[18] and the work was continued by Shimpo, who published it in book form in 1979.[19] Oritani then published his expenditure function in early 1979.[20]

These expenditure functions all included lagged values of autonomous expenditure (E) and the money supply (M) in the regressions, but all except Oritani used Almon lags. Oritani used the Shiller lag, which improves over other methods by allowing more latitude for different lag patterns and lengths.[21]

Let us consider Oritani's results, the most recent attempt at estimation of an expenditure function. His equation is as follows:

$$\Delta Y = 0.028 + \sum_{i=0}^{7} m_i \, \Delta M_{t-i} + \sum_{i=0}^{7} e_i \, \Delta E_{t-1}$$

$$\bar{R}^2 = 0.694 \qquad \bar{S} = 1.07 \qquad D.W. = 1.63$$

Period of estimation: 1962/I–1977/III

Figure 6.3 shows in the upper section the parameter estimates for all lags on money and autonomous expenditure. The figure shows that the patterns and final sums of coefficients are very different for the two variables.

The parameters on money are small at first, grow larger gradually, peak in the fourth quarter, and then gradually decline. But the values remain positive until the eighth quarter, and the sum of the coefficients m_i is 1.269, a relatively high value. This value is generally consistent with average values of the money multiplier (inverse of Marshall's k).

In contrast, the values of coefficients on expenditure are largest initially, drop rapidly, and become negative in the third quarter after the initial one (i.e., in period $t-2$). This pattern shows, since money is held constant implicitly, that government spending initially has a highly ex-

16. On the expenditure function in the St. Louis model, see Anderson and Carlson 1970. Suzuki 1973 introduced this model into Japan.

17. Suzuki 1973 gives an account of Keran's work.

18. See Bank of Japan Research Department 1975. The expenditure function used in this case included as components of autonomous expenditure not only government spending but also exports (and income from abroad), autonomous plant and equipment investment, and autonomous inventory investment. Other expenditure equations referred to in the text used only government spending for autonomous expenditure. Some Keynesians have criticized the use of government spending alone as the indicator of autonomous expenditure.

19. See Shimpo 1979.

20. See Oritani 1979a.

21. For a description of Shiller lags, see Oritani 1979a, appendix 2.

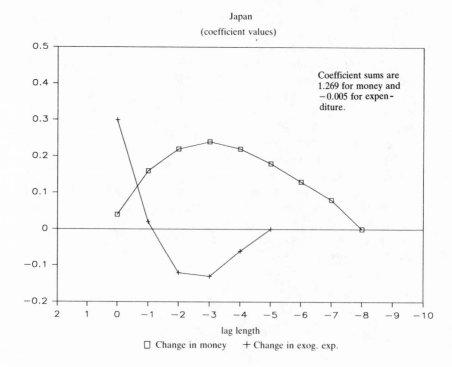

Japan
(coefficient values)

Coefficient sums are
1.269 for money and
−0.005 for expen-
diture.

lag length

☐ Change in money   + Change in exog. exp.

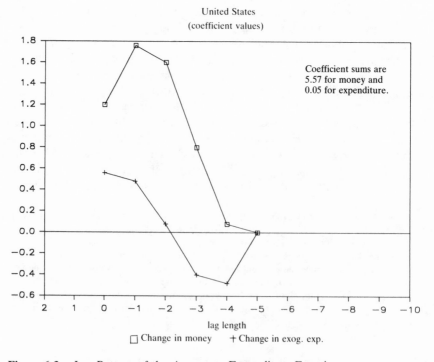

United States
(coefficient values)

Coefficient sums are
5.57 for money and
0.05 for expenditure.

lag length

☐ Change in money   + Change in exog. exp.

Figure 6.3. Lag Pattern of the Aggregate Expenditure Function

148

pansive effect on aggregate expenditure, but that it soon brings higher interest rates, and brings shrinking expenditure from crowding out. The sum of coefficients after five periods is -0.005, that is, very close to zero. Thus, the income multiplier on government spending, in the absence of supportive monetary policy, is close to zero in the long run.

The lower section of figure 6.3 shows the results of Anderson and Carlson (1970) of the St. Louis Fed. The lag pattern and cumulative coefficient sums are about the same. Shimpo's results in his 1979 study for the Japanese economy are highly similar.

In summary, these results show that the effects of money supply on the determination of aggregate nominal expenditure are stronger and more stable than those of autonomous expenditure.

III. Inflation and Output

Sections I and II considered the effects of money supply on aggregate demand. Sections III, IV, and V show that money supply affects not only the demand side, but aggregate supply as well. And since money supply affects both demand and supply sides, we will be able to evaluate in a comprehensive fashion how both prices and output are affected by changes in money.

1. Investigations of the Natural Rate Hypothesis

Friedman and Phelps pioneered ideas of the inflation augmented Phillips curve and the natural rate of unemployment. We may well ask if the reality of the Japanese economy corresponds to these theories. That is, in the long run, will the economy allow the unemployment rate to remain below the natural rate ($\bar{u}$) (or output to remain above the equilibrium rate $\bar{y}$), even with higher inflation? To put it another way, when nominal expenditure rises, will the period of simultaneous rise of prices and output be only transitional?

Ohkubo (1983) has considered this problem, and has tested for causality between prices and output using the relative power contribution (RPC) method.[22] If the Japanese economy does exhibit the tendency for higher inflation to allow higher output, then there should be a causal relation between the two. His results show that there is some power from prices to output at the extremely long periodicities, but this power is very small compared to those seen in section 1.c. Hence, even if the causality from prices to output is not exactly zero, it is extremely small; indeed it is difficult to say that it exists at all. For the period 1974/IV to 1981/IV, the power contribution at all periodicities is small enough to ignore.

22. See section I.2.c above for details of relative power contribution methods.

The results of this investigation suggest that the Phillips curve in Japan is nearly vertical. But if it were absolutely vertical, then the power contribution diagram would be identical with the horizontal axis. The slight skewness probably reflects transitional periods in which inflationary expectations are stable while actual inflation and output are simultaneously rising.

Direct investigations of whether Japan's Phillips curve is vertical have been carried out since the early 1970s, (e.g., Toyoda 1972, 1977, and 1979b, Matsukawa 1975, Shimpo 1977a and 1977b, and Kato 1982). Of these, Matsukawa, Shimpo, and Kato all conclude that the long-term Phillips curve is largely vertical. Toyoda concluded that the long-run Phillips curve was downward-sloping in the 1960s, but became increasingly steep in the 1970s, and approached the world of the natural rate hypothesis. Let us consider in detail the empirical work of Kato (1982), which includes the most recent data and is the most detailed.

Kato first uses the following formula:

$$f(U) = \dot{W} - \Theta \dot{P}_e - b\dot{r} \tag{6.1}$$

where $f(U)$ is a short-run, downward-sloping Phillips curve at a given level of expected inflation $\dot{P}_e$, where Θ is the reaction coefficient showing how $f(U)$ shifts with a change in inflationary expectations, where $\dot{r}$ is the rate of labor productivity increase, and where b is the parameter linking labor productivity to wage increases $\dot{W}$. Kato next assumes that firms set prices at a constant markup over labor costs, that is,

$$\dot{W} - \dot{r} = \dot{P}. \tag{6.2}$$

Substituting this into the equation above yields

$$f(U) = \dot{P} - \Theta \dot{P}_e - (b-1)\dot{r}. \tag{6.3}$$

Kato uses two periods, 1960/I–1980/II and 1973/I–1980/II,[23] and estimates two equations of form (6.1) and fourteen[24] of form (6.3). The results are that in virtually every case the parameter Θ on inflationary expectations is not significantly different from one. Based on this result, Kato argues that, since actual inflation and expected inflation coincide in the long run, equation (6.3) becomes

$$f(U) = -(b-1)\dot{r} ; \tag{6.4}$$

as long as labor productivity growth is constant, the unemployment rate is constant. That is, the Phillips curve is vertical. In the most convincing of Kato's cases, the natural rate of unemployment corresponds to 2.3

---

23. For exact specification of periods based on data constraints, see Kato 1982.

24. Fourteen equations were estimated to allow variation in specification of $f(U)$, $\dot{r}$, and other factors.

percent of the labor force totally unemployed. Kato also finds, most interestingly, that the slope of even the short-run Phillips curve $f(U)$ became steeper after 1973.

There is, however, room for criticism of Kato's research on technical grounds. For example, for inflationary expectations, he uses a univariate time series forecast. This approach assumes that inflationary expectations are formed rationally, just as the time series model is. Forming the series on inflationary expectations in this way forces the estimate of expected inflation to be close to actual inflation, and so the value of coefficient Θ is almost certain to be unity.[25]

But the research of Shimpo (1979) sheds light on this issue. Shimpo estimates expected inflation directly from the Economic Planning Agency's *Kigyoo keieisha mitooshi choosa* (Survey of corporate managers' forecasts), and calculates equations of form (6.1) and (6.3), although he omits the labor productivity term. Even in his results, the estimate of Θ is very close to unity.[26] This point requires further research, but for the moment we may conclude that Θ is close to unity in Japan, and that the natural rate hypothesis is hard to reject.[27]

2. Wage Flexibility in Japan Supports This Hypothesis

The above result shows that the natural rate hypothesis can at the least be applied to Japan. Why is this the case?

The critical point on which the natural rate world and the Keynesian world differ is how they treat the function of wages in balancing supply and demand. In the Keynesian system, since nominal wages are sticky, real wages remain high; labor supply is therefore permanently above labor demand, and involuntary unemployment exists. In contrast, in the natural rate world based on neoclassical theory, since the real wage is flexible and equilibrates labor demand and labor supply, involuntary unemployment does not exist.

There are two ways to consider the Keynesian assumption that nominal wages are sticky. The first is to ask whether workers are deceived by nominal wages and do not consider real wages. Here, since workers' money illusion is never corrected, nominal wages may be sticky. The other way to consider stickiness is to ask if, for institutional reasons, nominal wages may be inflexible. Wage contracts between workers and firms cover long periods and might not be changeable during the period of the contract.

After considering whether either of these situations holds in the Jap-

---

25. For the details of Kato's method of calculating inflationary expectations, see Kato 1982, appendix 2.

26. See Shimpo 1979, pp. 178–81.

27. Kato 1982 surveys literature of the natural rate hypothesis in Japan.

anese economy, it becomes clear that Japan is closer to the natural rate world than to the Keynesian world.

First, we must ask if the Japanese workers suffer from money illusion. The base wage increases demanded by workers in the annual spring wage offensive give substantial consideration to consumer price inflation (both over the previous year and expected in the coming year). Nominal quantities are not a matter of concern. On the contrary, since workers are well educated and since information from mass media is omnipresent in Japanese society, the contention that workers suffer from money illusion is ridiculous.

Next, are there institutional factors in Japan that make wages sticky? First, it is usual practice for base wages to be revised every year. Wage contracts of two or more years are not common. Thus, compared to the United States and European nations, where such contracts are quite common, base wages in Japan are flexible. Moreover, in Japan, bonuses and overtime pay account for one-fourth to one-third of annual income, and this element is even more flexible than base wages. There are firms that determine both spring and autumn bonuses simultaneously, but many firms determine them individually, for each half year. And it is traditional for the amounts to reflect the firm's performance, and hence fluctuate flexibly. Moreover, overtime pay reflects the prosperity of the business activity through extra working hours, and amounts of overtime too are of course flexible.

These facts show that both the money illusion argument and the institutional rigidity argument are hard to sustain for Japan. Rather, the natural rate hypothesis world, in which flexible real wages equilibrate labor supply and demand, is closer to Japanese reality.

Wage determination in the spring labor offensive is well known to be sensitive not only to past and expected consumer price increases (for base wages) but also to labor market conditions and corporate profits. In this sense, real wages in Japan are more flexible than those in the United States and Europe, where indexation is common. The flexibility of real wages makes it realistic to assume that the firm is in continuous equilibrium (the first proposition of neoclassical economics). This assumption is common to both natural rate and Keynesian systems, but demonstrating its validity is necessary in order to apply the natural rate hypothesis to Japan.

Japan's real growth rate fell from about 10 percent per year before the first oil crisis to 5.0–5.5 percent after it, and then to 3.0–3.5 percent after the second oil crisis, and recently to 4–5 percent. But corporate profits have been relatively stable since 1978. The situation is the result of cost cutting by corporations; but viewed in light of economic theory it implies that firms are maintaining profits through downward flexibility in real wage growth.

Another aspect of maintenance of equilibrium for Japanese corporations can be found in the high rate of growth of labor productivity. Equilibration of the real wage with the marginal product of labor of course generates the labor demand schedule but also implies that equilibrium for the firm is based on corporate profit maximization. For Japan, not only is the real wage flexible, but the marginal product of labor (which reflects capital stock growth and technological progress) on the other side of the equation is rising at speeds faster than in other nations. These factors also help the firm recover equilibrium easily.

The above discussion shows that the Japanese economy is characterized by many of the conditions that make the natural rate world, based on neoclassical equilibrium, easy to achieve. Hence, as an overall view, it is not a mistake to judge the natural rate world closer to Japanese reality than the Keynesian one.

But the natural rate world does not hold exactly. One problem, whether the proposition of neutrality of money holds precisely, is theoretical. The proposition is that when the money supply rises there is absolutely no long-term expansionary effect on the real economy. The reason full neutrality may fail to hold is found in Tobin's general equilibrium approach to portfolio selection.[28] When the supply of money, which is an asset, rises, the long-term real interest rate falls, and the demand for real capital rises; investment rises in response to the rise in demand. To this extent, a rise in the money supply has an expansionary effect on equilibrium rate of output,[29] and lowers the natural rate of unemployment. Hence, monetary policy will not be neutral.

However, we do not know if this effect is large enough to be observed empirically. But on the basis of empirical research carried out so far, it is not a mistake to think that, as a general viewpoint, money is neutral in the long run. That is, policy may be discussed on the basis of thinking that the long-run Phillips curve is nearly vertical.

IV. Effects of Money on Aggregate Supply

1. The Lucas Supply Function and Rational Expectations

The effects of money supply on aggregate expenditure (the aggregate demand curve) and hence on prices and output have been discussed in sections I and II above. But aggregate demand changes are not the only channel through which money affects prices and output.

Discussion above in Section III showed that inflationary expectations affect the position of the aggregate supply curve, and so affect prices and

---

28. See Tobin 1965, 1969, and 1980.
29. Fischer 1979 calls this production expansion effect the "Tobin effect."

output as well. Thus, if money supply directly influences inflationary expectations, then money supply can move the aggregate supply curve and affect prices and output through this channel too. That is, money can affect prices and output from both demand and supply sides. Let us consider this question in more detail.

Let the relationship between actual inflation and expected inflation be governed by the equation

$$\dot{P} - \dot{P}_e = -x(U - \overline{U}). \tag{6.5}$$

But the difference between actual unemployment U and the natural rate $\overline{U}$ corresponds to the difference between output y and the natural rate of output $\bar{y}$ (through Okun's Law). Using this, we can say

$$U - \overline{U} = -d(y - \bar{y}), \tag{6.6}$$

where d is a positive constant. Substituting this into (6.5) and eliminating $U - \overline{U}$ yields

$$y = \bar{y} + z(\dot{P} - \dot{P}_e), \tag{6.7}$$

where $z = 1/xd$.

Equation (6.7) is the so-called Lucas supply curve.[30] That is, when actual inflation exceeds expected inflation, actual output exceeds equilibrium output, and vice versa. Moreover, when $\dot{P} = \dot{P}_e$, then $y = \bar{y}$.

The next problem is how the inflationary expectations in the Lucas supply curve are formed. In Friedman's and Phelps's theories of the natural rate, inflationary expectations are adaptive. Thus, expected inflation $\dot{P}_e$ adjusts to actual inflation with a lag, and this lag generates cycles of actual output around equilibrium output. But Lucas, Sargent, and Wallace have pointed out that, when expectations are formed "rationally," an entirely different conclusion emerges from the Lucas supply curve. The application of the rational expectations hypothesis to an equilibrium macroeconomic theory like the natural rate theory yields the "macro rational expectations hypothesis."[31]

2. Formation of Inflationary Expectations

Now we come to the question of whether the macro rational expectations hypothesis (in its strong form) applies to expectations formation in Japan. Toyoda (1979b) has conducted notable research on Japanese

30. For the original statement of the Lucas supply curve, see Lucas 1972 and 1973. Lucas himself includes a random term on the right hand side of the equation.

31. Original statements of the macro rational expectations hypothesis are given in Lucas 1973, Lucas and Sargent 1980, Sargent and Wallace 1975, and Barro 1976. See Seo and Takahashi 1982 for an excellent interpretation of these.

expectations formation. He estimated expected inflation based on data in the Economic Planning Agency's *Shoohisha dookoo yosoku choosa* (Survey of consumer trends forecasts), and tested several hypotheses about expectations formation focusing on the 1972/IV to 1977/I period, which included the high inflation from 1973 to 1975. His results showed that the types of inflationary expectations consistent with Japanese experience were extrapolative expectations, overreactionary adaptive expectations, and weighted average expectations, but *not* strong-form rational expectations. That is, inflationary expectations were not an unbiased estimator of actual inflation.[32]

Extrapolative expectations are those based on the current level of inflation and past trends. Overreactionary adaptive expectations are those that derive the new expected inflation rate from correcting the past level of expected inflation by more than 100 percent of the difference between the past level of expected inflation and the past actual level. Since the usual specification of adaptive expectations has the correction below 100 percent, expected inflation always lags actual inflation. Overreactive adaptive expectations are not restricted to lag actual levels, however, and so expected inflation can actually jump ahead of actual inflation in the adjustment process. Weighted average expectations are formed through a weighted average of past inflation rates (with weights largest on most recent values). That is, these expected inflation levels are distributed lags on past inflation. This is an extremely general formulation, and in fact both extrapolative and adaptive expectations are forms of weighted average expectations.[33]

---

32. Weak-form rational expectations may be expressed by

$$_tP_{t+i} = E(P_{t+i}/I_t)$$

where $_tP_{t+i}$ is expected inflation up to time $t+i$ held as of time t, P_{t+i} is actual inflation between time t and time $t+i$, and I_t is the information set at time t. E denotes the expectations operator, and this is conditionalized by information available at time t. Strong-form rational expectations is derived from this. If u_t is a random variable of expected value zero, then we may say, under strong-form rational expectations, that

$$P_{t+i} = {}_tP_{t+i} + u_{t+i}$$

To investigate whether this holds, we may test the equation

$$P_{t+i} = a_o + a_1(_tP_{t+i})$$

for values $a_o = 0$ and $a_1 = 1$, and for the absence of serial correlation in the errors. These values for parameters correspond to the hypothesis that expected inflation is an unbiased predictor of actual inflation. Toyoda 1979b rejects this hypothesis in his investigation.

33. More precisely, these types of expectations are defined, as in Toyoda 1979b, as follows.

Using quarterly periods, let q_t be the inflation rate in quarter t measured over the same quarter of the previous year, and let $_tP_{t+4}$ be the expected inflation rate over the next four

Toyoda's research thus tested the various forms of expectations and rejected strong-form rational expectations, but he did not test weak-form rational expectations. Weak-form rational expectations are those formed with all available information at the time the expectation is formed, including money supply. This notion of expectation is treated in naive form by the Bank of Japan Research Department (1975) and in a paper by Suzuki.[34] In this paper, a model similar to St. Louis models[35] is estimated, but it differs on two points. First, as indicators of autonomous expenditure, this model used autonomous plant and equipment investment, inventory investment, and foreign demand in addition to government demand, in contrast to the St. Louis model, which used only the latter. However, this point has no direct bearing on the theoretical discussion.

The second point of difference is on expectations formation. In the St. Louis model, the expected inflation rate is included as a shift parameter for the aggregate-supply curve in the price determination equation. The form of expectations is adaptive. In both the Bank of Japan and the Suzuki models, the shift parameters for aggregate supply are import prices, wage costs, and money supply outstanding. Money supply is included as a proxy for expected inflation. That is, in line with the weak form of rational expectations, money supply is included as one of the components of the set of available information. In the results of estimation, money supply is significant, along with the other explanatory variables.

The notion that the money supply has a direct effect on formation of expectations of inflation is also emphasized by Shimpo (1977b). When he calculated his "equation of motion of inflationary expectations," he adds the deviation from trend of the Marshallian k as an explanatory variable, and this variable is significant. Shimpo therefore concludes that inflationary expectations depend not only on the past history of inflation,

---

quarters. Extrapolative expectations are given by

$$_tP_{t+4} = {_{t-4}}P_t + h(q_t - {_{t-4}}P_t)$$

where $0 < h < 2$. When this is expressed as

$$_tP_{t+4} = a_o + a_1 {_{t-4}}P_t + a_2q_t,$$

the null hypothesis is that $a_o = 0$ and $a_1 + a_2 = 1$.

34. See Suzuki, "Nihon ni okeru tsuuka no shotoku, bukka ni tai suru eikyoo" (The effects of money on income and prices in Japan), presented at the meeting of the Riron Keiryoo Keizai Gakkai (Society for Theoretical and Quantitative Economics), 15 November 1975.

35. For descriptions of the St. Louis models see Anderson and Carlson 1970. Suzuki 1973 introduced such models into Japan, but thorough analysis of the Japanese economy using one was carried out by Shimpo 1979b.

but also on the information about the excess or shortage of money in the economy. In this sense, the weak form of rational expectations may be said to hold.

3. Investigations of the Macro Rational Expectations Hypothesis

The above discussion demonstrates that past inflation rates do affect the formation of inflationary expectations in Japan, but that money supply as well, since it is part of the information set, is also influential. That is, weak-form rational expectations hold.

But we also saw above that the natural rate hypothesis also holds for Japan, in general. The next problem is whether, when people form their expectations of inflation including judgment of effects of money supply, they base their expectations on the natural rate model. If rational expectations formation of this strong form occurs, then we really are in the world of macro rational expectations. We did see above that Toyoda (1979b) rejected the strong form of rational expectations because expected inflation was not an unbiased predictor of actual inflation; however, he did not test the total macro rational expectations hypothesis directly. Attempts at this have been made by many researchers, but the pioneering one for Japan was done by Pigott (1978). Seo and Takahashi (1982) have carried out a more thorough study, and Kato and Hemmi presented similar results at the 1981 meeting of the Japan Association of Economics and Econometrics. All of these studies use the same methods that Barro used in his studies of the U.S. economy,[36] and all reject macro rational expectations for Japan. Let us consider one of these, that of Seo and Takahashi (1982), in detail.

The macro rational expectations hypothesis claims that anticipated money translates directly into price increases, and has no effect on output. Only unanticipated money affects output, and the effect is only temporary at that. Thus, to test the hypothesis, we need merely to separate money into anticipated and unanticipated components, and then test whether only the latter affects output.

Seo and Takahashi investigated for the 1960s and 1970s just what the Bank of Japan was using for final policy targets, and then used these as explanatory variables in a "money supply forecasting equation" with money supply as the dependent variable. This gave the reaction function that the Bank of Japan used in response to changes in policy target

---

36. For empirical investigations of the macro rational expectations hypothesis, see Barro 1977, 1978, and 1979; Barro and Rush 1980; and Mishkin 1980. Studies of macro rational expectations for the Japanese economy all extend the methods in these studies of the U.S. economy.

variables. If the public knew the Bank of Japan's policy rule, then the money supply based on this reaction function should have been anticipated, and the difference between actual money supply with this anticipated level would have been unanticipated. Hence, their regression provided a money supply forecasting formula.

Seo and Takahashi were extremely meticulous in their specification of these formulae for the 1960s and 1970s, and used the forecasts from the equations for anticipated money. The residuals were used for unanticipated money. The effects of these two series on output (real GNP and industrial production) were then investigated through log linear regressions. The results were as follows.

First, anticipated money had a significant influence on output. In this sense, the macro rational expectations hypothesis was rejected. As with the results of Toyoda (1979b), here too the strong form of rational expectations with respect to formation of inflationary expectations was rejected. However, the signs of coefficients on anticipated money were at times positive and at times negative, and so the effects were not stable over time.

Second, unanticipated money had a significant influence on output that was clearer than the effect of anticipated money. The effect was the same in the various equations, with a positive effect peaking one to two quarters after the occurrence of the unanticipated money, and then declining steadily for one to two years.

What do these results suggest? The fact that unanticipated money has a clear influence on output is consistent with the judgment that Japan is largely an economy for which the natural rate hypothesis holds. On the other hand, the fact that anticipated money had an influence, even though unstable, on output is consistent with the judgment that inflationary expectations are not based on the strong-form rational expectations hypothesis that includes the natural rate model as part of the available information set. But results could change with different money forecast equations. For the U.S. economy, conclusions both supporting and rejecting the macro rational expectations hypothesis have been reached, using different ways of specifying money forecasts. Thus, the results given above are provisional, and future research on the matter would be desirable.

V. The Influence of Money on Prices and Output:
A Trivariate Time Series Model

Sections III and IV have considered the relationship of money to aggregate supply, and sections I and II, the relationship of money to aggregate demand. The combination of these two relationships determines the effects of money supply on prices and output. Let us next examine, using time series methods, these overall effects of money supply on prices and output.

The contention we wish to investigate is the following: When the rate of money supply growth rises, inflation also rises, and the rate of output growth fluctuates cyclically around the equilibrium growth path. Oritani (1981) conducts statistical tests to see whether in fact money, prices, and output behave as the above theoretical model suggests. Shimpo (1979) conducts tests with the same goal, but in his case they are conducted as simulations of a St. Louis model, which assumes the natural rate hypothesis as part of the structure. Hence, the Shimpo model has a structure that imposes results from the theory, and so the results of his money supply simulations on inflation and cyclical fluctuation of output are a matter of course.

Oritani (1981) eschews a priori restrictions on the structure of the economy, and estimates a multivariate time series model using the rates of change versus same quarter previous year of M2, GNP, and the GNP deflator. He then uses conditional expectations to test how changes in money supply growth would affect inflation and output growth.[37] He conducts three tests.

The first test was to change the 12 percent rate at which money supply had been growing until 1980/I to (*i*) 15 percent and (*ii*) 10 percent, and see the effects on prices and output using conditional expectations. For the period after 1980/II, both cases (*i*) and (*ii*) slightly reduced growth rate of money in parallel with the trend. (For details, see Oritani 1981.) The results are given in figure 6.4.

First, the policy effect on prices was that inflation rose when money growth rose, and fell when money growth fell. Second, the results with respect to output were that for case (*i*) output rose and then fell, and for case (*ii*) output fell and then rose. Both generated cyclical fluctuations, and in opposite directions. These results support the contention above that an increase in money supply growth will raise inflation and cause cyclical fluctuation in output.

Oritani's second test was to gauge the marginal effects on inflation and output of a 1 percent decrease in money growth, again using the method of conditional expectations. Figure 6.5 shows the results. Reducing money growth gradually lowers inflation over the succeeding ten quarters. But output, after falling for five quarters, rebounds; after the eleventh quarter, its growth rate is even higher than originally.

37. For description of the multivariate time series model and the technique of conditional expectations, see Oritani 1981, appendix. For details on time series analysis, see Akaike and Nakagawa 1971 and Oritani 1979c.

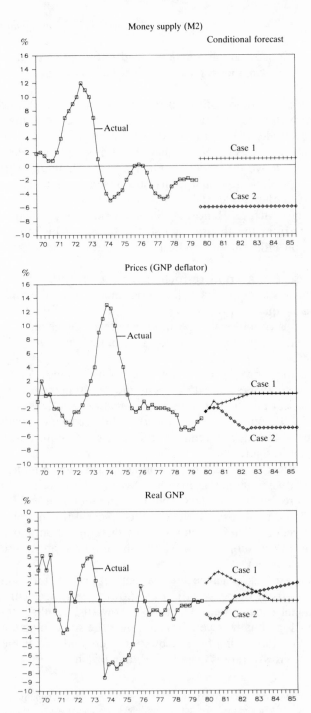

NOTE: Variables measured as differentials from linear trend of percent change versus same period of previous year. Trend computed 1956/I to 1979/III.

Figure 6.4. Offsetting Effects of Money Supply Increase on Prices and Output

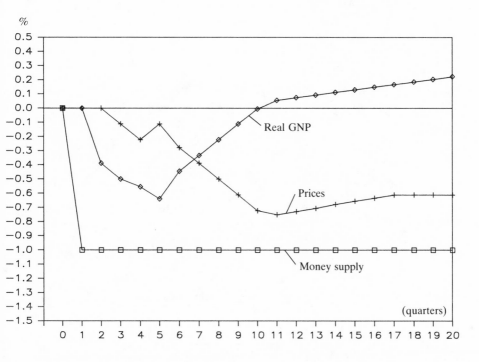

Figure 6.5. Money, Prices, and Output in a Time Series Simulation

Oritani's third test was an ex post facto, conditional expectational simulation of the period of high inflation in the early 1970s. Oritani investigates what would have happened to inflation and output if money supply had not risen sharply in 1971–72 but rather continued earlier trends throughout the period 1971–79. The results for inflation and output also include the estimated residuals from the model, in addition to the influence of the different money supply path. Figure 6.6 presents the results. The figure shows that inflation in the 1972–75 period would have been about 5 percent lower, and that a substantial reduction in inflation would therefore have been possible. Even so, the inflation rate for 1974 would have been high, reflecting the panic mentality after the first oil shock, and speculative behavior. This suggests that random elements outside the influence of money supply were quite influential. The results on real output show that growth would have been lower than actual levels for 1971–73, but that avoidance of the zero growth of 1974–75 would also have been possible. Fluctuation of the growth rate would have been narrower, and growth more stable. The results of this third test show that stablization of money growth, even when exogenous shocks such as the

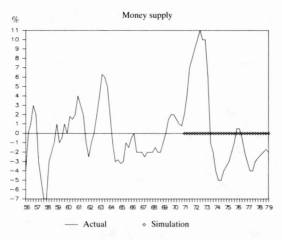

Money supply

— Actual   ◇ Simulation

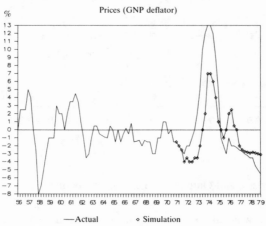

Prices (GNP deflator)

—Actual   ◇ Simulation

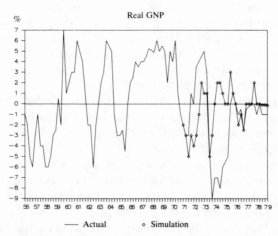

Real GNP

— Actual   ◇ Simulation

NOTE: Variables measured as deviations from trend of percent change versus same period of the previous year.

Figure 6.6. Money, Prices, and Output Simulation for the 1970s

162

oil crisis are applied to the economy, will hold inflation to the lowest level possible and keep the business cycle relatively stable.

Oritani's three tests show that there is support for the contention that a monetary business cycle exists. Moreover, the first two tests show that lowering inflation through money supply control will in the long run raise the growth rate of the economy. Or, conversely, allowing a rise in the inflation rate to stimulate the cycle will raise growth in the short run but have the contrary effect in the long run. These results testify to the contractionary effects of inflation. Similar experiences occurred in the United States, the United Kingdom, and France in the 1970s where inflation was high; their Phillips curves were actually upward sloping, with higher inflation bringing higher unemployment.

The contractionary effects of inflation are generated by harming economic efficiency and fairness through the higher uncertainty that accompanies inflation. It is hoped that further research will be carried out in this area.

7

The Yen under the
Floating Rate System

When the major industrial countries including Japan shifted to floating exchange rates, in February and March of 1973, most economists believed that, since floating would give central banks control over domestic money supply and interest rate levels, nations would be freed from consideration of external equilibrium. Hence, they would find it easier to manage policy aimed at price stability, output stability, and other elements of internal equilibrium. But how has reality evolved in the last ten years? This chapter will consider the realities of exchange market fluctuations under the floating rate system, the development of theories of exchange rate determination, and how money supply interacts with the exchange rate.

I. Theory and Experience of the Floating Rate System

1. Independence of Monetary Policy under Floating Rates

At the time the Bretton Woods system collapsed and was replaced by the floating exchange rate system, there was a difficult tradeoff in Japan between internal equilibrium (price and output stability) and external equilibrium (balance of payments equilibrium). In 1969 and 1970, when internal equilibrium was the chief goal, the external disequilibrium (BOP surplus) became extremely severe; but when BOP equilibrium was pursued in 1972 and 1973, inflation soared and the cycle overheated. Hence, when the floating rate system emerged, the goal of external equilibrium was given to the foreign exchange market, whereas management of monetary policy was for the most part assigned to achieving internal equilib-

rium goals such as price and output stability. This separation was a relief
for policymakers.

This relief was based on two optimistic beliefs. First was the belief that
smooth and small fluctuations in the foreign exchange market would
automatically equilibrate the balance of payments and achieve external
equilibrium. Second was the belief that foreign exchange rate fluctuations
would insulate Japan from foreign inflation and output fluctuations, that
is, eliminate the tradeoff of internal and external equilibrium.

Ten years have now elapsed under floating rates, and it is proper to
ask whether this optimistic forecast has been correct, and whether monetary policy aimed at price and output stability (internal equilibrium) has
become independent of external influences.

With respect to insulation from foreign inflation, the forecast has
largely proven correct. Section I of chapter 5 discussed how, under the
fixed rate system, and particularly from the late 1960s into the 1970s, the
inflation rates of the major countries accelerated simultaneously; international transmission of inflation was conspicuous. But since the advent
of floating rates, inflation has been low in Japan, West Germany, Switzerland, and Austria, but high in the United States, the United Kingdom,
France, and Italy. There were remarkable gaps between the rates. This
is immediately obvious from figure 7.1, which shows inflation rates on a
semi-log scale. Before the advent of floating in 1973, the price levels of
the United States, Japan, West Germany, France, and Switzerland were
rising at about the same rates, suggesting mutual dissemination of inflation. But after 1973, the rates for France and the United Kingdom rose
substantially, while in Switzerland the price level hardly changed at all.
The gap is tremendous. Moreover, in the last half of the 1970s, the tempo
of price level change in Japan slowed, while that in the U.S. accelerated.

The reason these divergences in inflation among countries emerged
under the floating rate system is that exchange rate adjustments naturally
halt transmission from high inflation countries to low inflation ones, since
the currencies of high inflation countries depreciate and those of low
inflation countries appreciate. To put it another way, movements of exchange rates for the most part have reflected the differences of inflation
rates across countries. That is, the purchasing power parity theory has
held in the long run.

To verify this, let us calculate real exchange rates for six major countries, by dividing the nominal exchange rate by the ratio of the price
indexes of the country in question and the United States. Graphs are
presented in figure 7.2. The figure shows that in the ten years of floating,
real exchange rates have fluctuated substantially. If exchange rates continuously reflected purchasing power parity, then the lines on the graph
would be horizontal. Thus the graph shows that exchange rates deviate

log scale

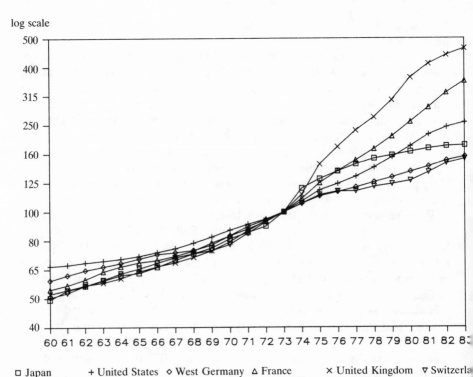

□ Japan   + United States   ◇ West Germany   △ France   × United Kingdom   ▽ Switzerla
  GNP deflator   GNP deflator   GDP deflator   GDP deflator   GDP deflator   GDP de

Figure 7.1.   Price Movements in Major Industrial Countries

from purchasing power parity in the short and medium runs, i.e. do not
always exactly reflect inflation differentials.

However, the yen, the German mark, the French franc, and the Italian
lira real rates versus the U.S. dollar were all about the same in the 1981–
82 period as they were in the first few years of the floating rate system.
Hence, in the long run of ten years, exchange rates do reflect purchasing
power parity, and do prevent international transmission of inflation. For
the Swiss franc, the level of 1975–77 and the most recent levels are about
the same, so that, depending on where one chooses the point of reference,
purchasing power parity might be said to hold here as well. The only
exception is the British pound; but North Sea oil improved the terms of
trade for the United Kingdom, so there was a special structural reason
for a rise in the British real exchange rate. Hence, if we exclude cases in
which structural changes on the real side generated changes in the terms
of trade, it seems that the foreign exchange market does reflect inflation
differentials in the long run. To the extent this is true, floating rates do
guarantee independence of monetary policy for nations.

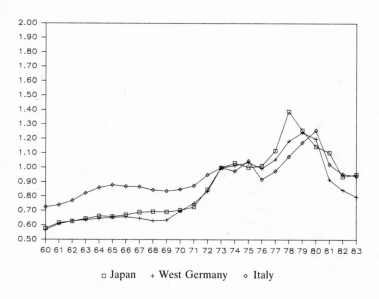

□ Japan   + West Germany   ◇ Italy

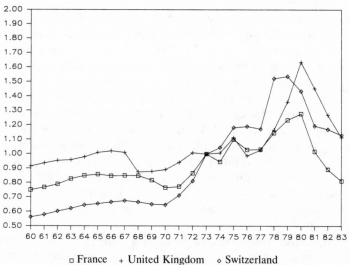

□ France   + United Kingdom   ◇ Switzerland

NOTE: Rise indicates appreciation. Real exchange rate index is defined as dollar price of a unit of each currency, deflated by the ratio of domestic prices to U.S. prices where the value of the index in 1973 is set to 1.   The formula is: $rx = e_i p_i / p_i^*$, where rx is the real exchange rate, e_i dollar price of home currency, p_i domestic prices, and p_i^* foreign prices.

Figure 7.2.   Real Exchange Rate Index Movements versus the U.S. Dollar

2. New Problems under the Floating Rate System

To the extent that international transmission of inflation was halted, the forecast of the economics profession about floating rates was accurate. But the forecast was not accurate about various problems that policy management faced in the short and medium runs.

First, fluctuations in the exchange market have not been smooth and narrow, but rather volatile and wide. These gyrations have destabilized the profitability of international trade and capital transactions, and have disrupted prices and output in the domestic economy of every nation. Many central banks must be concerned with the exchange market when managing monetary policy. And because of this concern, the major nations including at times the United States have intervened in the foreign exchange markets, conducting smoothing operations to stabilize markets. That is, even with the shift to floating, monetary policy in most countries has not concentrated exclusively on achievement of internal equilibrium. Japan is no exception.

Second, it has become clear that the adjustment period between exchange market changes and reachievement of equilibrium in the balance of payments, and particularly the current account, is two to three years, much longer than expected. In the meantime, deficits or surpluses accumulate, push exchange rates away from purchasing power parity, and generate real exchange rate fluctuations in the medium term. For this reason, vicious cycles of depreciation and inflation or virtuous cycles of appreciation and price stability can continue. For the period 1976–78, the former group included the United States, the United Kingdom, France, and Italy, and the latter group included Japan, West Germany, and Switzerland. Hence, monetary policy cannot be carried out ignoring the medium-term movements of the balance of payments; and so, even with a floating rate system, it cannot concentrate exclusively on internal equilibrium.

Third, interest rate levels, particularly for long-term real interest rates (nominal interest rate minus expected rate of underlying inflation), are transmitted internationally through the exchange market, so that a nation's monetary policy may be constrained for international reasons. Economists once believed that the advent of floating would raise exchange rate risk, so that uncovered interest rate arbitrage would all but cease. It was thought that fluctuations of the interest rate spreads between countries would reflect mostly the spot-forward spread in the exchange market, and have no effect on the exchange market.[1]

In reality, however, when the interest rate differential between nations expands beyond the differential of expected inflation—or in other words,

---

1. For a statement of this view, see Komiya and Suda 1980.

when a differential of real interest rates occurs—the pressure for international capital flows mounts, and the exchange market is affected. The inordinate strength of the dollar from 1981 to 1985 was to a large extent due to the high real interest rates in the United States; nominal interest rates in the United States were high despite the decline in expected inflation. In response, both Japan and Western European nations either kept or pushed their own interest rates high, in order to prevent weakening of their currencies and the imported cost-push pressure on domestic prices that would result from such weakening. In this sense, even under a floating rate system, the level of interest rates is transmitted internationally, and monetary independence of nations is constrained.

II. Empirical Analysis of the Yen Market

We have seen above that the advent of the floating rate system did not bring total independence of domestic monetary management from considerations of the exchange market, the balance of payments, and foreign interest rates. But what is the proper balance between concern about external equilibrium and concern about internal equilibrium? To answer this, let us survey empirical analysis of the yen market, keeping in mind both the experiences since the 1970s under floating rates and the theories of exchange rate determination that have developed so rapidly since the 1970s. Let us remember that long-run movements of the yen are largely explained by purchasing power parity. Hence, here we will consider the short- and medium-run movements of the yen.

1. Short-Term Volatility and Intervention

Seo (1981) has analyzed the short-term movements of the exchange market under the floating rate system from a variety of viewpoints. First was to compare the change versus previous month of the exchange rate, equities, and wholesale prices. The average of the absolute value of changes in the exchange rate was 2.69 percent versus 2.98 percent for equities and 1.43 percent for wholesale prices. Moreover, the direction of movement of wholesale prices often was the same for several months at a time, whereas directions of both the exchange rate and equity price movements changed from month to month and were random. Calculation of autocorrelation coefficients for these series reveals that those of equities and the exchange rate were virtually nil, but that of wholesale prices was very large.

Another part of Seo's study considered the forecastability of the yen market. First he studied how well the forward rate (F_{t-1}) one month ahead predicted the actual spot rate (S_t) for that period. Of course, the current forward rate is supposed to equal the expected spot rate. If this is not the case, then, for example in the case when the forward rate is weaker than the expected spot, one can buy forward in the current period, collect these yen one month hence, and sell them with the expectation of a speculative profit of exactly the amount by which the forward rate is weaker than the expected spot.[2] If all agents tried to do this, then demand in the forward market would expand tremendously, and the forward rate would strengthen and eventually equal the expected spot rate. Under these circumstances, the forward rate is, from a statistical point of view, an unbiased predictor of the future spot. The regression

$$ln\ S_t = a_o + a_1\ ln\ F_{t-1}$$

should yield $a_o = 0$ and $a_1 = 1$, with no serial correlation left in the residuals. When these conditions are met, the market is called an efficient market, and strong-form rational expectations hold.

There is, however, another factor to consider, which is that holding of assets denominated in foreign currency carries a risk not borne when domestic currency-denominated assets are held. Thus, the forward rate should equal an unbiased estimate of the future spot rate plus a risk premium. However, discussion here ignores the risk premium, which will be taken up again below.

Seo's results using monthly data from 1973/10 to 1980/6 are as follows. The regression came out as

$$ln\ S_t\ =\ 0.105\ +\ 0.963\ ln\ F_{t-1}$$
$$(1.062)\quad (41.901)$$

$R^2\quad =\ 0.956$

$SE\quad =\ 0.031$

$D.W.\ =\ 1.702$

(numbers in parentheses are t-statistics).

nobs = 80

2. More precisely, the transaction would go as follows. Say you have $100, and you expect the yen/$ rate to be ¥250/$ one month hence. But also say you can sign a forward contract to deliver dollars for yen one month hence and get ¥275/$ at that time. Say you sign this contract. Then you would pay your hundred dollars to the other party in the contract, and receive ¥27,500 (¥275/$ x $100) one month hence. But if your expectation turns out to be correct, then you can take the ¥27,500 that you will receive, go to the foreign exchange spot market at that time, and exchange these yen for dollars at the rate of ¥250/$. Hence you would receive $110 (¥27,500 ÷ ¥250/$) in this spot transaction one month hence. The whole process yields you an expected profit of $10, or 10 percent of your original $100. This is also a 10 percent profit when the difference of the forward rate and the expected spot (275 − 250 = 25) is taken as a percentage of the expected future spot, ¥250/$.

These results show that the hypothesis that $a_o = 0$ and $a_1 = 1$ is supported at the usual level of 5 percent significance. The Durbin-Watson level of 1.702 indicates absence of serial correlation (The D.W. bounds are $d_1 = 1.54$, $d_u = 1.59$). Thus this analysis could not reject the hypothesis that the forward rate is an unbiased predictor of the future spot, and hence it could not verify the existence of a risk premium.

The coefficient of determination ($\bar{R}^2$) for this equation appears at first glance to be high, at 0.956. But the remaining 0.044 corresponds to about ¥10 on the ¥/$ rate. Hence there is ¥10 of uncertainty in forecasting one month out, so that the ability to forecast based on strong-form rational expectations is extremely low, due to the large random element.

If we take the spot rate and the future rate, and divide them by the previous period's spot rate, then we can recalculate the change in the spot rate (S_t/S_{t-1}) as a function of the spot-forward spread (F_{t-1}/S_{t-1}). The results are as follows:

$$ln\ (S_t/S_{t-1}) = \quad -0.003 \quad + \quad 0.420 \quad ln\ (F_{t-1}/S_{t-1})$$
$$(-0.600) \qquad (0.673)$$

$$\bar{R}^2 = 0.003 \qquad SE = 0.032 \qquad D.W. = 1.768$$

The hypothesis that $a_o = 0$ is supported at the usual level of confidence. The hypothesis that $a_1 = 1$ cannot be rejected at the 90 percent confidence level, since the t-statistic on that hypothesis is 0.929. Moreover, the errors are not serially correlated. Hence, these results cannot strongly reject the hypothesis that the forward rate is an unbiased predictor of the future spot. The problem is that the coefficient of determination is extremely low at 0.003. This means that the forward market has very low predictative power for the future spot market; that is, the spot-forward spread of today is a poor predictor of the rate of change of the spot rate.

Thus, there is some evidence[3] that the forward rate is an unbiased predictor of the spot rate, though the probability of the forecast rate actually occurring is extremely low. This is because the future spot rate includes not only the currently available information in the forecast but also new information that becomes available only in the future. In today's economy, in which the weight of new information coming in every second is so high compared to that of currently available information, it is no surprise that there is only a low probability that the actual future spot rate will correspond to the forecast of it by the current forward rate.

Thus, new information available second by second causes wide swings in both spot and forward rates. When these short-term fluctuations in the yen market widen further through expectations generating further

---

3. There is also some evidence in the other direction, if one uses monthly instead of quarterly data or changes the period of estimation. A risk premium should also exist.

expectations (i.e., bandwagon effects), then the risk associated with all international transactions rises, and clearly stunts their development.

In an effort to prevent extreme short-term fluctuations, many central banks now engage in "smoothing operations." So long as this exchange market intervention does not reach the level at which it would seriously affect portfolio balances, it will not be a major source of transactions. This is clear, since today we realize the inapplicability of the flow approach to exchange rate determination. The goal of intervention is to give new information in the form of central bank intentions, or marginal movements of the market that accompany it, which will affect determination of the short-run level of the market. The effectiveness of intervention therefore depends to a great extent on how market agents interpret the fact of central bank intervention or the marginal movements that accompany it. If it is viewed as an unexpected offset to shocks, then the effect can be large. But if it is interpreted as evidence that the yen is weak, then it may be ineffectual or even counterproductive. The effectiveness of central bank intervention therefore depends on extremely psychological factors, and the uncertainty associated with it is extremely large. Still, renouncing it altogether is probably not appropriate. The very uncertainty over whether the central bank will intervene at all guarantees effectiveness on rare occasions of intervention.

2. The Yen in the Medium Term: The Monetary Approach

Let us next consider one approach to determination of the level and movements of the yen in the medium term, and its policy implications. Until about 1977, the value of the yen did not depart substantially from purchasing power parity, and so the monetary approach to exchange rate determination explained medium-term movements well. This was shown by Shirakawa (1979a). His argument is as follows.

First he posits a standard money demand function, in which demand for real balances depends on real income and the interest rate. He expresses monetary equilibrium as follows,

$$M = P \cdot l(y,r) \tag{7.1}$$

where M is money and P is the price level. The same holds true in the foreign country, where the latter is denoted by an asterisk. Hence

$$M^* = P^* \cdot l^*(y^*,r^*) \tag{7.2}$$

Letting the spot rate be denoted by S, adherence to purchasing power parity implies that

$$P = P^*S \tag{7.3}$$

Solving for P and P^* from (7.1) and (7.2), and substituting the results into (7.3) yields

$$S = \frac{P}{P^*} = \frac{M}{M^*} \cdot \frac{l^*(y^*,r^*)}{l(y,r)} \tag{7.4}$$

Taking natural logs on both sides yields

$$ln\ S = ln\ M - ln\ M^* + ln\ l^*(y^*,r^*) - ln\ l(y,r)$$

Once we specify money demand in the two countries as $ln\ l = k(ln\ y) - hr$ and $ln\ l^* = k^*\ (ln\ y^*) - h^*r^*$, and substitute these into (6.5), we get the equation Shirakawa uses:

$$ln\ S = ln\ M - ln\ M^* - k(ln\ y) + k^*(ln\ y^*) + hr - h^*r^*. \tag{7.6}$$

The actual form of (6.6) that Shirakawa estimated was

$$ln\ S = a_o + a_1\ ln\ M + a_2\ ln\ M^* + a_3\ ln\ y + a_4\ ln\ y^* + a_5 r + a_6 r^*. \tag{7.7}$$

The exchange rate used is that versus the U.S. dollar, and the period of estimation is from the time floating began in 1973/3 to 1978/1, with monthly data. The results were as follows:

$$ln\ S = 3.59 + 0.85\ ln\ M - 1.77\ ln\ M^* - 0.74\ ln\ y + 0.87\ ln\ y^*$$
$$\ \ \ \ \ (4.89)\ \ (5.09)\ \ \ \ \ \ \ \ \ (-5.92)\ \ \ \ \ \ \ (-5.04)\ \ \ \ \ \ \ (3.99)$$

$$+\ 0.61\ r - 0.01\ r^*$$
$$\ \ (6.37)\ \ (-3.27)$$

$\bar{R}^2 = 0.813$ $SE = 0.03$ $D.W. = 1.28$ ( ) indicates t-statistic

All coefficients fulfill sign conditions, and all are of high significance as seen by their t values. Considering that the data are monthly, the coefficient of determination also indicates high explanatory power.

Using this estimation, a factor analysis of the movements of the exchange rate from the advent of floating until 1978/1 was performed. This is given in table 7.1. We see that the weakness of the dollar between 1976 and 1978 was due to two factors, the excess of money supply growth in the United States over that in Japan and the relatively higher inflationary expectations (the rise of interest rates through the Fisher effect) in the United States. The trend in the U.S. money supply was discussed in chapter 5, referring to figure 5.1; M1 growth rose from 5 percent in 1976 to 8 percent in 1978. In contrast, Japanese money growth (M2) fell from 15 percent to 10 percent. Considering the facts that Japan's real growth rate was higher and that the ratio of M2 to nominal GNP has been rising on trend at 1–2 percent per year in Japan, then even if money growth in Japan were a bit higher, this would still indicate contractionary monetary policy in Japan and expansionary monetary policy in the United States.

Table 7.1. Causes of Yen Fluctuation According to the Monetary Approach

	Log of actual exchange rate 1/	Log of forecast exchange rate			
		Total 1/	Monetary effect 2/	Real GNP effect 3/	Interest rate effect 4/
1973 I	5.596	5.596	1.075	0.733	0.240
II	5.585	5.617	1.070	0.744	0.247
III	5.617	5.617	1.055	0.740	0.253
IV	5.783	5.658	1.058	0.722	0.280
1974 I	5.700	5.692	1.058	0.744	0.347
II	5.700	5.742	1.078	0.767	0.313
III	5.825	5.825	1.045	0.744	0.347
IV	5.825	5.813	1.063	0.760	0.380
1975 I	5.775	5.783	1.050	0.744	0.413
II	5.792	5.800	1.055	0.767	0.413
III	5.825	5.783	1.075	0.784	0.363
IV	5.825	5.792	1.075	0.778	0.370
1976 I	5.817	5.804	1.080	0.767	0.370
II	5.804	5.800	1.090	0.762	0.377
III	5.817	5.742	1.088	0.762	0.380
IV	5.742	5.742	1.055	0.760	0.383
1977 I	5.700	5.650	1.025	0.784	0.387
II	5.658	5.554	1.013	0.789	0.330
III	5.617	5.554	1.000	0.793	0.280
IV	5.492	5.575	0.995	0.789	0.280

1. A higher figure indicates a weaker yen.
2. The monetary effect is $0.85 \ln M - 1.77 \ln M^*$. A higher figure indicates Japanese monetary policy more expansionary than U.S. monetary policy.
3. The real GNP effect is $-.74 \ln y + 0.87 \ln y^*$. A higher figure indicates Japanese growth weaker than U.S. growth.
4. The interest rate effect is $0.06 r - 0.01 r^*$. A higher figure indicates expectation of weak yen.

This empirical work eloquently shows that the reasons for the strength of the yen and the weakness of the dollar during these years were the differences in money growth and the inflationary expectations that reflected the monetary growth differences.

3. The Yen in the Medium Term: The Portfolio Balance Approach

Around 1978, when the medium-term deviation of the exchange market from purchasing power parity became obvious, the monetary approach (or more precisely monetarist approach), which assumes purchasing power parity, ceased yielding good empirical results. It was replaced by the portfolio balance approach, which does not assume purchasing power parity in the short or medium runs.

Fukao (1981, 1982a, 1982b) applied a formula for exchange rate de-

termination from the portfolio balance approach to the markets for the
yen and the European currencies. The form of the equation is

$$e - f = \frac{1}{z}[(r^* - \dot{P}^*_e) - (r - \dot{P}_e)] - \frac{1}{z}(X) \qquad (7.8)$$

where e is the spot rate, f the forward rate, r and r^* nominal interest
rates in the domestic and foreign currencies, $\dot{P}_e$ and $\dot{P}^*_e$ the expected
inflation rates in the two, and X is a risk premium associated with holding
foreign assets.[4] The actual equation that Fukao estimated was

$$e + P_{us} - P_j = c + \frac{1}{z}[(r_{us} - \dot{P}^{us}_e) - (r_j - \dot{P}^j_e)] - \frac{1}{z}\Sigma\, m_i B_i$$

where e is the log of the yen/\$ exchange rate, P_{us} and P_j are logs of the
price levels of the United States and Japan respectively. Thus, $e + P_{us} - P_j$
is the log of the real exchange rate versus the U.S. dollar. The constant
is labeled c, and both z and k are coefficients. Nominal interest rates are
r_{us} and r_j for the United States and Japan respectively, and $\dot{P}_e^{us}$ and $\dot{P}^j_e$
are their respective expected inflation rates. The terms B_i are the cu-
mulative current account balances of countries i (in U.S. dollars) and
these are weighted by weights m_i representing substitutability of the yen
with the currencies of countries i. Hence, the sum $\Sigma\, m_i B_i$ is the weighted
average of cumulative current account surpluses.

Fukao's estimations used the GNP deflators for price levels, and three-
month money market rates for interest rates. For expected inflation,

4. This equation is derived as follows. Start with the usual interest parity condition,

$$r = r^* + d,$$

where d is expected depreciation of the domestic currency. The left hand side gives the
attractiveness of domestic assets and the right hand side the attractiveness of foreign assets.
Foreign assets are more attractive when the domestic currency is expected to depreciate,
so the variable d is added to r^* to adjust the attractiveness of foreign assets for exchange
rate changes. But foreign assets also carry more risk than domestic assets, so we must
subtract something from the right hand side to adjust the attractiveness of foreign assets
for their higher risk. This risk premium is subtracted from the right hand side to yield the
risk-adjusted interest parity condition

$$r = r^* + d - X$$

where X is the risk premium.

Next we introduce a theory of expected depreciation, after Frankel 1979. Expected
depreciation is held to be the inflation differential between the two countries plus a proportion of the current spot-forward spread. More precisely, we specify that

$$d = (\dot{P}_e - \dot{P}^*_e) + z(f - e).$$

That is, expected depreciation is high when domestic inflation exceeds foreign inflation and
when the forward rate is weaker than the spot. Substitution of this theory of expected
depreciation into the risk-adjusted interest parity condition yields equation (7.8) in the text.

perfect foresight one year out was assumed, so that ex post GNP deflator changes a year ahead were used. For the weights m_i, Fukao used the covariances of the real exchange rate of the yen versus the dollar with the real exchange rates of other countries versus the dollar (calculated over 1973/1 to 1981/1). The other countries were the United Kingdom, West Germany, France, Italy, Canada, Switzerland, Belgium, the Netherlands, Norway, and Sweden. With Japan included, this comes to eleven countries. Quarterly data were used, and the period of estimation was 1975/1 to 1981/3. The results were as follows:

$$e + P^{us} - P^j = -5.6554 + 1.4967 [(r_{us} - \dot{P}_e^{us}) - (r_j - \dot{P}_e^j)] - 0.3485 \Sigma m_i B_i$$
$$(-166.3) \quad (4.13) \quad\quad\quad\quad\quad\quad\quad\quad\quad (4.83)$$
$$\bar{R}^2 = 0.91 \quad SE = 0.041 \quad D.W. = 1.28 \ (\ ) \text{ indicates } t\text{-statistic}$$

All signs are correct, and all t-statistics indicate significance. The $\bar{R}^2$ of 0.91 indicates relatively high explanatory power. According to the results here, a 1 percent change in the real interest rate gap between the United States and Japan will cause about 1.5 percent change in the yen market (about 4 yen if the rate starts at ¥250/$). And though this cannot be read directly from the results presented here, an extra $10 billion current account surplus versus the United States while trade with the EMS countries remains balanced will yield about a 6 percent rise in the yen (about 15 yen on a rate of ¥250/$). However, if at the same time the EMS countries are running an overall deficit of $10 billion, there will also be downward pressure on the yen in sympathy with the European currencies, and the net effect on the yen will be a strengthening of only 3 percent or so.

Figure 7.3 shows the actual movements of the variables used in this estimation. According to the diagram, the reason for the large deviation of the yen/$ rate from purchasing power parity in the 1977–78 period was the large accumulation of current account surpluses by Japan and other nations. These large expansions of current account surpluses meant a tremendously expanded supply of risky dollar-denominated assets to Japanese residents and a tremendously expanded supply of risky yen- (or other currency-) denominated liabilities to U.S. residents. Until the dollar had weakened enough to generate expectations of substantial appreciation, voluntary holding of these cumulating assets or liabilities could not occur. In contrast, the weakening of the yen from 1978 to 1980 reflected the shrinking of the cumulative current account balances of Japan and other nations in the face of the second oil crisis.

In mid-1980, U.S. interest rates fell temporarily, and the Japanese current account deficits began to shrink; the result was a stronger yen and a weaker dollar. But once 1981 began, even though the Japanese current account swung into surplus, the surpluses of the European countries did not improve quickly, so that the weighted average of their cu-

Index (1973 = 100)

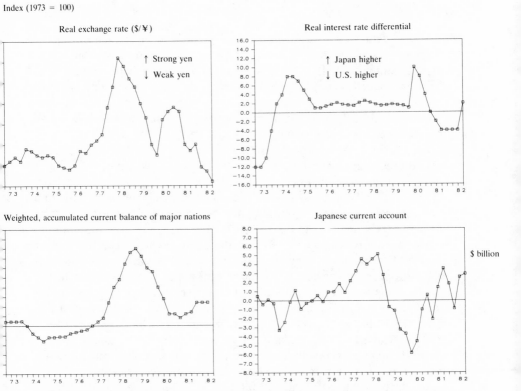

Figure 7.3. Causes of Yen Fluctuation in a Portfolio Balance Model

mulative values did not rise very much. On top of these factors was the forceful raising of interest rates by the Reagan administration in the United States from 1981 to 1984, coupled with the cut in interest rates in Japan once the battle with the second oil crisis was over. The real interest rate differential reversed and saw U.S. rates much higher than Japanese rates. This factor dominated the influence of the cumulative current account, and brought a weak yen and a strong dollar.

Moreover, risk factors not even included in the estimated equation above are exceedingly important in explaining the weakness of the yen and the strength of the dollar in the latter period. The risk factor X from equation (7.8) is represented in the equations only by the cumulated current account. The risk that investors feel about holding foreign assets or liabilities is included in this measure, but other risks are not. Both the Soviet invasion of Afghanistan and the Polish crisis raised the risk of holding European currency–denominated assets, depressed the values of the European currencies, and caused weakening of the yen due to the strong complementarity relations. Rumors of international liquidity problems also put yen- or European currency–denominated assets at a disadvantage, due to the relative confidence in the U.S. financial system, and thus caused a strong dollar and a weak yen. Moreover, foreign knowledge of Japan is relatively limited, so for example the uncertain outlook for the Japanese government budget deficit and methods of funding it might lead to unease about the future of the Japanese economy, raise the risk associated with yen-denominated assets, and thus cause weakness of the yen.

III. The Money Supply and the Yen

Let us now summarize the relationships of money supply to the experiential, theoretical, and empirical evidence presented above.

In the pure theoretical models, the existence of a fixed rate system means that the central bank has the duty to intervene to support the market; in this sense, the money supply is not an independent, exogenous variable, but rather an endogenous one. The exogenous variable is the exchange rate. On the other hand, in a floating-rate system, determination of the exchange rate may be left to the market, so the money supply may be determined independently by the central bank as an exogenous variable. In this case, the exchange rate is the endogenous variable.

In theory this situation is all very well and good. But in the reality of policy management, is it in fact appropriate for the central bank to ignore the movements of the exchange market or to determine the money supply independently of the exchange rate, with consideration only of internal equilibrium?

In the long run, it probably is. The reason is that in the long run, purchasing power parity will hold. If money is supplied in concordance with the long-run equilibrium growth path, then long-term output fluctuations will be smoothed and inflation will be controlled at a low level, just as we saw in chapter 6. Corresponding to this long-term picture of the domestic economy, the exchange value of the yen will exactly reflect the differential between domestic and foreign inflation, and insulate the domestic economy from invasion by foreign inflation. Then monetary policy can rely on the automatic equilibrating mechanism of the exchange market, leave exchange rate determination to that market, and exert its own efforts at appropriate money supply with a view to only the domestic economy.

But the reality of policymaking is that the long run is not so important as the short and medium runs. It is not acceptable to do nothing for five or ten years on the grounds that in these long runs adjustment will occur. There is of course the viewpoint of "nonactivism," which holds that whatever policymakers do only increases uncertainty, so they should keep quiet and sit on their hands. But short-term fluctuations of the yen disrupt both trade and capital transactions, whereas medium-term fluctuations disrupt both the price level and output. These negative effects are probably greater than the negative effects that may accompany disruptions caused by policy decisions, so the policy of sitting on one's hands is probably not correct.

There is no doubt that the short-term fluctuations of the exchange market disrupt international transactions. But short-term risks can be avoided by covering in the futures market. Hence, the only undesirable fluctuations are those of such short duration that they prevent profitable international transactions. To avoid such troubles, smoothing operations are desirable. But intervention over a period of days attempting to lead the market to a given level is virtually useless. When the exchange rate is being determined by turnover many times the level of assets outstanding, any attempt to change the outcome with a flow of intervention funds, except at the most extreme levels, would be doomed from the start.[5] Moreover, the larger the intervention, the closer the central bank would be to acting as if under a fixed-rate system with endogenous money supply. The controllability of money as an exogenous variable would be lost. The goal of intervention is to seem like unusual behavior or a surprise on the part of the central bank. To the extent that it counteracts bandwagon effects, it may have some effectiveness. It is no more than this, but no less either. With this realization, intervention should be kept to moderate levels.

5. Recall the calculation in Fukao 1982b that $10 billion would bring only a ¥15 change in the exchange rate. This $10 billion would correspond to about 10 percent of high-powered money for 1981.

But how should monetary policy respond to medium-term deviations of the exchange rate from purchasing power parity? When the short-term (daily or monthly) fluctuations of the yen are annualized, the rates appear enormous; but medium-term fluctuations (quarterly or semiannual) are much smaller even when annualized. The former generate a great deal of risk and make the profitability of short-run fluctuations very uncertain, whereas the latter are far less severe and leave some room for maneuver. Hence the problem with medium-term yen fluctuations is not their disruption of international transactions, but rather their disruption of the domestic economy. For example, when the yen departs from purchasing power parity and falls over the medium term, foreign inflation spreads to the domestic economy through imported cost-push, bringing higher domestic prices and lower output.

To prevent such inflation, appropriate control of money supply is necessary. The investigations above suggest that the following three rules of monetary control will put upward pressure on the real exchange rate in the medium term. First, monetary restraint will drive up domestic interest rates, cause the differential to move in favor of the domestic economy (i.e., move domestic rates relatively higher), and thus strengthen the real exchange rate. Second, as seen in chapter 6, weak-form rational expectations will come into play, lower expected inflation, and raise domestic real interest rates. Again the interest differential (in real terms) will move in favor of the domestic economy, and help recovery of the real exchange rate. Third, appropriate control of the money supply will reduce the amplitude of the monetary business cycle, and avoid expansion of uncertainty about the future of the economy. This will reduce the risk that nonresidents associate with holding of yen-denominated assets, and also help strengthen the real exchange rate.

Let us now summarize the short-, medium-, and long-term arguments about the relationships of money supply control and the yen market. First, if money supply is stable and appropriate in amount, domestic prices and output will be stable; then, since purchasing power parity holds in the long run, transmission of foreign inflation and the disruptions of the domestic economy due to it will be prevented. Second, if the yen market's medium-term deviations from purchasing power parity are kept to a minimum by appropriate monetary control, then imported inflation and disruption of the domestic economy will also be kept to a minimum. Third, although exchange market intervention is necessary to deal with short-term fluctuations in the market, it is essential that fluctuations be kept within limits so that they do not affect the medium- and long-run controllability of the money supply. Fourth, current balance surplus due to the yen's deviation from PPP will diminish in the medium run as the accumulated current balance and equalized real interest rates by capital movements will eventually strengthen the yen.

8

Money-Focused Monetary Policy

Implementation of monetary policy can focus on one of two indicators, money or interest rates. Japanese monetary policy for the last decade has focused in the medium and long term on money. Though the relationships of the two are of course intimate—they are after all price and quantity from a single market—Japanese authorities have come to view the money focus as more effective, for reasons that will be made clear below.

I. Choosing and Achieving Intermediate Objectives

1. Final Goals and Operating Targets

Monetary policy affects many variables, even those not intended to be affected. Hence it is necessary to focus attention on variables relating to economic stabilization, the final goal of monetary policy. For other goals, other tools may be assigned.

But the phrase "economic stabilization" has many aspects, among them price stability, stable output growth, and external balance. As seen in chapter 6, however, it is not proper to give equal weight to prices and output as the primary goals of monetary policy. Output stabilization is impossible without price stability, so it is best to give much more weight to prices. Moreover, as seen in chapter 7, price stability in the long run generates exchange market stability, and helps strengthen the exchange rate and isolate the economy from foreign inflation when it occurs.

Once price stability has been established as the final goal of monetary policy, the next problem is the specific means of implementing it. The channels from the policy tools used by the central bank to the final targets

181

are extremely long. The central bank manages policy tools while simultaneously paying close attention to financial variables along this long channel and judging the effects of policy on targets. The indicators along the transmission path are called operating targets. A further differentiation of them into two groups is useful, and these two groups are the operating variables, which are financial variables easily manipulated by the central bank, and intermediate objectives, which are financial variables farther from the central bank but closer to final goals.

Since operating variables are easily manipulated by the central bank, they are directly affected by policy tools. For this very reason they are easier to control, but on the other hand their relationships to final goals are somewhat unstable. On the other hand, the intermediate objectives are so far from the central bank that they can be influenced only indirectly by policy tools, but their relationships with goals such as the price level are relatively stable.

The financial variables chosen as operating targets can be roughly divided into two groups. One is market conditions indicators, best represented by interest rates. The other is monetary aggregates, such as quantities of money and credit. Through the 1960s, most central banks of advanced nations conducted monetary policy paying most attention to indicators of market conditions. For example, in the United States, the operating variables were free reserves (a market balance indicator equal to bank reserves, both vault cash and deposits at the central bank, less the sum of required reserves and borrowings from the central bank) and the Federal Funds rate (interbank interest rate). The intermediate objectives in the United States were interest rates on bank loans and yields on long- and short-term bonds. In Japan, the operating variable was the same, that is, the interbank rate (called the "call rate"), and it was tracked closely as monetary adjustments were made. But Japan's intermediate objective was different; it was the increase in lending, especially that of city banks, compared to the same period of the previous year.

There were two reasons for Japan's choosing this indicator as its intermediate objective. First, since the artificially low interest rate policy kept stated interest rates to customers low, there was no interest rate at the intermediate range that could reflect market conditions with any sensitivity. Deposit rates and yields to subscribers on bonds were extremely sticky, and even loan rates were not very flexible. The only interest rate with any sensitivity was the call rate, which was an operating variable very closely influenced by policy. The repurchase and secondary bond markets were thin during the 1960s and early 1970s, and were insufficient as medium-term indicators of market conditions.

The second reason was that corporate liquidity was low during the investment/export-led high growth years, with corporate borrowings far in excess of own-captial (i.e., "overborrowing," as defined in Suzuki

1974). Bank lending went directly into plant and equipment or inventory investment, so that the rise in bank lending itself was an indicator of corporate investment. Since corporate investment was the engine of growth, the rise in bank lending served very well as an intermediate objective. Moreover, since the lending shares of various banks did not change substantially in the short run, the lending increases of city banks could be used as representative of the total. These data were available with very short reporting lag, and hence were very valuable as indicators.

2. Shift in Intermediate Objectives from Interest Rates to Money

a. The U.S. Experience.   But in the 1970s, with the United States as icebreaker and the European nations following, the movement of intermediate objectives from interest rates to money supply became general. The shift from market conditions indicators to quantitative indicators was closely related to the rise in chronic inflation. That is, when the inflation rate rises, fluctuates, and causes swings in inflationary expectations, market conditions and interest rates become difficult to interpret. For example, a rise in interest rates might indicate higher demand for funds due to speculation from higher inflation's generation of higher expected inflation, or might indicate spreading effects of tight money policy as funds supply is lowered. Judgment cannot be made on the basis of interest rate movements alone. But the central bank must have operating indicators that can distinguish between the cases, since in the former case a tightening of policy is needed whereas in the latter it is not.

But money supply gives clear information, and can be used as a medium-term operating objective, for the following reason. Examination of the relationship of money supply to the ultimate goals of price level or nominal income reveals that money supply increases always lead to higher prices or nominal income, and never the opposite. This is not true for interest rates.

In fact, interest rate movements can be interpreted in three ways. The first is the liquidity effect interpretation, whereby higher rates indicate lower supply of money and credit, and financial tightness. The second is the income effect interpretation, in which higher interest rates are interpreted as signs of financial tightness due to higher demand; if expectations about the future become more sanguine, investment demand rises, leading to higher money demand or nominal income, which in turn results in higher money demand or nominal income, which in turn results in higher interest rates. The third is the Fisher effect interpretation, whereby higher interest rates result from higher inflation or expected inflation, which generates investment, speculative demand, and hence higher money demand. Interest rate movements always give information about these three effects, but they are chronologically distinct.[1] Hence, when interest rates rise, we never know exactly which of the effects is revealing itself. If the liquidity effect is leading to higher rates, then tightening of policy is being felt, and policymakers need not adjust further. If the income effect is being felt, then there is worry that the cycle is overheating. If the Fisher effect is being felt, then decisive countermeasures are required. Since the policy response in the three cases must differ, the inability of interest rates to distinguish which is occurring means that interest rates are wholly unacceptable as operating targets for monetary policy.[2]

The failure of the United States to realize this fact in the late 1960s was very painful. The high interest rates of that time were interpreted to be the result of liquidity effects due to tight policy, and further tightening was postponed since policymakers thought they were being successful. But in fact the high interest rates were due to the Fisher effect, while inflation was accelerating. In the reevaluation that followed this experience, the Board of Governors of the Federal Reserve System changed its intermediate objective in the early 1970s to money supply, and began announcing targets. And today, the central banks in European nations focus on money supply or similar quantitative indicators as their intermediate objectives, and many announce targets.

b. The Japanese Experience. Japan too shifted to a money focus as its intermediate objective in the last half of the 1970s. An article entitled "On the Importance of the Money Supply in Japan" appeared in the Bank of Japan's monthly bulletin (*Choosa geppoo*) in July 1975. Moreover, "forecasts" of average money (M2 + CDs) growth for a quarter

1. Narukawa 1982 uses Japanese data to show how money supply changes influence interest rates through the liquidity, income, and Fisher effects.

2. The simple IS-LM model includes only one of the three effects; when the IS and LM curves are both stable, a change in the interest rate can only occur due to a shift in the LM curve, i.e., the liquidity effect. But a liberal interpretation of the IS curve would include shift parameters for marginal efficiency of investment, based on expectations of inflation and output, along with expected future income effects. Particularly in the 1970s, when the uncertainty of expectations grew and when inflationary expectations began to fluctuate, shifts of the IS curve due to these factors became common. The shifts of the IS curve due to changing expectations about the course of the cycle generated income effects on the interest rate, whereas the IS curve shifts due to changes in inflationary expectations were Fisher effects.

Interest rate movements in the 1970s lost the ability to convey whether liquidity, income, or Fisher effects were at work because of expanded instability of the IS curve, increased uncertainty about inflation, the cycle accompanying the Great Inflation, and inability of the central banks to forecast IS curve shifts.

In more general theoretical terms, we may say that money is a better indicator than interest rates in times when the IS curve is relatively unstable, whereas interest rates are a better indicator when the LM curve is relatively unstable. Poole 1970 was the first to point this out clearly. See also Poole 1978. An accessible explanation is given in Tachi 1982, pp. 212–14.

Table 8.1. Actual and "Forecast" Levels of Money Supply Growth

	Announced "Forecast" (%)	Actual[1] (%)
1978/III	about 12	12.1
IV	12–13	12.2
1979/I	12–13	12.3
II	12–13	12.3
III	about 12	11.7
IV	about 11	11.2
1980/I	about 10	10.6
II	10–11	10.1
III	below 10	8.4
IV	about 8	7.8
1981/I	about 7	7.6
II	6–7	7.9
III	9–10	9.6
IV	10–11	10.6
1982/I	about 11	10.6
II	about 10	9.2
III	about 9	9.0
IV	about 8	8.1
1983/I	7–8	7.6
II	7–8	7.6
III	about 7	7.1

1. Average growth of M2 + CDs versus that of same period previous year.

versus the same quarter previous year began to be announced at the start of each quarter in July 1978. Table 8.1 compares the announced "forecast" and the actual levels achieved, and shows the latter closely controlled by the former.

There were several circumstances surrounding the Bank of Japan's switch to focus on money. The first was the theoretical factor mentioned above. Interest rate movements could no longer distinguish what information was being given about the effects of monetary policy. This was the main reason that most central banks shifted from interest rates to money as their intermediate objectives in the 1970s. Second, Japan had allowed an excessive increase in the money supply in 1972–73, and had experienced a great inflation. The lesson of the importance of the money supply was learned in a school with very high tuition. Third, the growth rate of the Japanese economy changed at about this time. The structure of flow of funds in the economy began to change gradually, with the deficit of funds of the corporate sector shrinking as reliance on outside funding fell, and with the deficit of the public sector growing, as seen in the large flotations of government securities. These changes meant that money was supplied not only through loan increases to the private sector as in earlier years, but also through large bond absorptions by banks. Hence, whereas money and loan increases had moved together in earlier years, now the change in the money supply also came to depend on absorption of public bonds. The money supply generated by the bond flotations accumulated in the form of own-capital liquid balances of corporations, and it became the source of funding of their activities. A cushion between the business activity of firms and bank credit emerged, and hence activity and lending ceased necessarily to move in the same direction. The easiest way to grasp the trend of business activity of firms ceased to be focus on loan increases and started to be focus on money outstanding. Moreover, statistical investigation showed that the strong correlation between loan increases and prices or nominal income completely disappeared in the early 1970s. But the correlation between money and prices or nominal income remained strong.

3. The Method of Targeting

We have thus seen that the United States, European nations, and Japan all switched from interest rates to money as the intermediate objective of monetary policy. But there are major differences among the countries on three points, namely, (a) which monetary indicator is considered most important as the intermediate objective, (b) the time period over which the intermediate target is to be achieved, and (c) whether the target should be announced.[3]

a. Choice of Monetary Indicator. In rough terms, there are four types of monetary indicators from which to choose the intermediate objective. These are narrow money (M1),[4] broad money (M2 or M3),[5] central bank money,[6] and the monetary base.[7]

---

3. For the world situation relating to monetary targeting, see Meek 1983, published by the Federal Reserve Bank of New York. This book is the proceedings of a nonpublic conference at the New York Fed held in May 1982 on the subject of monetary targeting. Policymakers from the world's central banks, including Chairman Volcker of the Federal Reserve Board, President Solomon of the New York Fed, Chairman Schlesinger of the Bundesbank, and Vice Chairman Lefort of the Banque de France, gathered with economists to discuss the state of money-oriented monetary policy. Participants from Japan were Director Shimamoto, Foreign Department Director Ohta, and the author (at the time, Vice Director of the Monetary and Economic Studies Division). For Japan's contributions to this conference, see the paper by Shimamoto in the conference proceedings and Suzuki 1981a.

4. Narrow money, defined as the nonbank public's holdings of currency and demand deposits, is labeled M1.

5. Broad money is defined as narrow money plus the nonbank public's holdings of time deposits. Hence, it is the sum of currency and all deposits held by the nonbank public.

Narrow money is the main intermediate objective in the United States and Canada. The central banks of these countries give three reasons for this. First, M1 is the monetary aggregate with the highest correlation with income and expenditure. Second, it is more controllable, since it is composed of zero-yielding currency and deposits, which are strongly affected by interest rate changes. M2 and M3 both contain assets such as money market certificates, savings certificates, and money market mutual funds, which carry rates closely reflecting market rates; hence, these aggregates are more difficult to control with interest rate movements. Third, both M2 and M3 include portions that reflect savings motives; these portions are not controllable in the short term by monetary policy, and neither should they be.

Countries focusing on broad money are Japan, West Germany, the United Kingdom, and France. One reason is that, in contrast to the United States and Canada, these nations show a higher correlation of income and expenditure with M2 or M3 than with M1. The causality is viewed as being of great importance here, with these measures of money moving before income and expenditure, and hence influencing their future values. That is, even in these countries, M1 has the highest correlation with current income, but movements of M1 reflect only income or expenditure that either already has been or is currently being realized. But for a central bank the important thing to control is the monetary indicator with the closest relationship to potential income and expenditure in future periods. M2 and M3 have stronger correlations with future income than does M1. Chapter 6 already showed that the correlation between current quarter nominal expenditure and M1 was higher than that with M2 + CDs, and the correlation of two-quarter earlier M2 + CDs with current nominal income was higher than that of earlier M1 with current income. But the highest correlation is seen between M2 + CDs four to six quarters behind current nominal expenditure.

The second reason that countries that use broad money give for doing so is that M2—and even M3, given time—are in fact controllable. These countries do admit that M2 and M3 are influenced by savings behavior, and they also admit that the influence of interest rates on M1 is greater than that on M2 or M3. (However, in Japan, the interest rates on assets included in M2 and M3 are almost controlled rates, so that interest rate changes have less effect on shifts among M1, M2, and M3 than in the United States and Europe.) But the important point is to control M2 or

---

When deposits in banks only are included, the aggregate is labeled M2, and when savings-type deposits in nonbank financial institutions are included the aggregate is labeled M3.

6. Definition of central bank money is treated in detail below.

7. The monetary base is the sum of currency outstanding and deposits at the central bank, and is alternatively known as base money or high-powered money. This is the quantity that is multiplied to get the money supply, whence the terms "base" and "high-powered."

M3, which have the closer relationship with future potential income and expenditure, and not M1, which is most closely affected by current income and expenditure. (More on this below.)

Both West Germany and Switzerland are somewhat special in their emphases on central bank money and the monetary base, respectively. In Germany's case, the reason to focus on central bank money is the combination of its close relationship to M3 and its very short reporting lag. That is, since central bank money is used as a proxy for M3, Germany may in fact be said to focus on M3.

Central bank money is defined as currency in circulation plus required reserves (excluding changes in reserve requirements). The difference between central bank money and the monetary base is excess reserves and variations due to changes in reserve requirements. Hence, central bank money can be separated into three components—required reserves, currency held by banks, and currency in circulation outside banks. Since the series that measures required reserves excludes effects of reserve requirement changes, the former two bear a fixed relation to the deposit component of M3, whereas the latter component constitutes the currency component of M3. Hence, central bank money moves as does M3, and can act as its proxy. Moreover, both required reserves and currency outstanding are accounts on the central bank's balance sheet, so that there is very little reporting lag in obtaining them.

Finally, Switzerland is unique in that it is the only country to use the monetary base as an intermediate objective rather than as an operating target. Switzerland is a highly internationalized nation with a highly developed financial system, but it is also small. Hence, massive capital flows occur when exchange rate expectations change, given the floating exchange rate. These flows are tremendous when compared to the money supply of a small nation such as Switzerland, so the money supply is subject to large fluctuations. But as long as the central bank does not intervene in the exchange market, it can control the monetary base. (In this case the net foreign asset position of private banks will change, and hence the change in the money supply. That is, even though the monetary base is constant, the money multiplier is moving, which changes the money supply.) Investigation of the influence of the monetary base on income and expenditure contrasting it with that of the highly variable money supply shows that even in the medium term the monetary base has a more stable, and closer, relationship. For this reason National Bank of Switzerland is not concerned with movements of the money supply, which are so highly influenced by international factors, but rather uses medium-term control of the monetary base as its intermediate objective.

b. Period of Targeting. Next let us consider the period over which the chosen monetary indicator is to achieve its target. On this matter, there is a great difference between U.S. practice and that of other nations. The United States determines desired annual rates of growth for M1 (and also for the now-emphasized M2) outstanding, and announces quarterly growth (in annual rates) that will achieve this target. The Federal Reserve also publishes weekly and monthly outstandings or growth rates (seasonally adjusted, versus previous week or month). The public converts these to annual rates, compares them to the quarterly targets, and has a tendency to react wildly to them. Each time the weekly figure is announced, people revise their expectations of tightening or loosening monetary policy, and as a result substantial volatility of interest rates, and hence of the exchange rate, occurs.

In contrast, the European central banks announce only annual targets for money supply growth of the selected monetary indicators. In Japan, the central bank announces a forecast of money growth in the first month of each quarter for that quarter, the forecast being of M2 + CDs growth versus the same period previous year. There is a difference between targets in Europe and the forecast in Japan, but all are annual figures. What is important from the viewpoint of stabilizing income and expenditure—and therefore prices—is that monetary control not be over short-term figures for a week, month, or quarter, but rather at an appropriate level measured over the longer term of a year.

We saw in detail in chapter 6 that M2 + CDs, which in Japan's case has the highest correlation with nominal expenditure, influences the latter over nine quarters. In other words, the money supply in any given quarter has only a 1/9 influence over future nominal income. A more precise measurement was given in the aggregate expenditure function of chapter 6. Here the total effect of money outstanding in the current and previous seven quarters on current nominal GNP was used as the explanatory variable. Hence, it is rather meaningless to attempt to control money supply strictly over a period shorter than a quarter, from the viewpoint of stabilizing income and expenditure, and hence prices. It is important to stabilize the average growth over a one- or two-year period at an appropriate target level.

The U.S. approach focuses people's attention on the short-run movements of volatile narrow money, disrupts market psychology, and causes gyrations of interest rates and the exchange rate; to do so is meaningless from the viewpoint of price stabilization, and the economy. As an exercise, let us compare money growth rates (quarterly averages) for the United States and Japan, divide these by their standard deviations, and compare the sizes of fluctuation. Table 8.2 gives the results. In both nations, the fluctuations of narrow money (seasonally adjusted versus previous quarter) are the largest. In contrast, fluctuations of broad money over the same period previous year were the smallest. Hence, in the

Table 8.2. Fluctuations in Money Growth in Japan and the United States, 1975/I–1981/I

		Size of Fluctuation* (Standard Deviation/Mean)	
		Japan	U.S.
M1 Growth† (%)	Change vs. previous period (seasonally adj.)	0.88	0.46
	Change vs. same period previous year (not seasonally adj.)	0.51	0.22
M2 Growth† (%)	Change vs. previous period (seasonally adj.)	0.22	0.28
	Change vs. same period previous year (not seasonally adj.)	0.18	0.21

*Size of fluctuation is $SQRT (E (X_t) - \chi)^2) / \chi$ where E is the expectations operator, X_t is M_t/M_{t-1} (for seasonally adjusted series) or M_t/M_{t-4} (for not seasonally adjusted series), χ is the mean of X, and M_t is the level of M1 or M2 at time t.
†For the U.S., M1 is M_1B, and for Japan, M2 is M2+CDs.

United States, attention is drawn to the most volatile indicator, whereas in Japan it is drawn to the most stable one.[8]

The reason the United States has come to pay such close attention to short-run fluctuations of narrow money is to be found in the failures of monetary policy in the 1970s. Ever since money supply targets were first announced in the United States, the actual money supply had overshot the targets, with inflation worsening even to double-digit levels from the late 1970s to 1981. Thus, the American people had deep doubts about the will and ability of the Federal Reserve to control the money supply. In response to this loss of credibility of monetary policy, Chairman Volcker has led the Federal Reserve since October 1978[9] in strict adherence to achievement of short-term targets, and he has shut his eyes to the wide swings of interest rates and the exchange rate, considering them necessary evils.[10]

   8. For a discussion of international comparisons of money supply, see Friedman 1983.
   9. Board of Governors of the Federal Reserve System 1979 gives a formal interpretation of the shift of policy management by the Federal Reserve.
   10. According to the *Wall Street Journal*, in a speech to the Business Council on 8 October 1982 Chairman Volcker said that due to technical reasons and effects of financial innovations, the movements of M1 were becoming disrupted, so (*a*) more emphasis would

From both Europe and Japan strong criticism has come that the wide swings of interest rates and exchange rates are an important disruption to the world economy. In the final analysis, the critical feature in money-oriented monetary policy is how to achieve credibility simultaneously in both will and ability for monetary control and flexibility in the period over which control is exercised.

c. How to Determine and Whether to Announce Targets

(1) The European and U.S. Cases.   Harmonization in achieving both credibility and flexibility is closely interrelated with the method of choosing targets and the way they are announced. The European central banks choose their growth targets for the selected monetary indicator by common sense methods rather than by reliance on econometric methods. This is called the "EC formula," and the money growth target is calculated from the expected rate of real growth plus unavoidable GNP deflator increase plus trend and cyclical movements of the Marshallian k.[11] Since each of these elements is determined within a given range, the annual target is given in the form of x percent plus or minus some range.

Targets set and announced in this fashion have three important policy implications. First, the central bank obtains the trust and support of the populace when it sets the target already allowing for some given level of inflation, thus showing its will and ability to control inflation through control of money supply. Second, as long as other things are equal, the target levels for succeeding years can be lowered gradually, meaning a gradually declining level of allowable inflation. This causes year-by-year decline in inflationary expectations. Third, all elements in society have their interest aroused in the monetary targets. Since understanding by the people of the relationship at the macro level between target money growth and income or expenditure growth is obtained, a general consensus can be formed about the interrelationships of business and labor income expectations, politicians' and bureaucrats' notions of the scale of fiscal spending, and so on. Achievement of these three objectives does not require strict econometric calculation of monetary growth targets. The important point is to achieve the targets, and thereby to establish a track record of reducing the inflation rate.

The situation is somewhat different in the United States. Annual target

---

henceforth be put on M2 and M3, and (*b*) short-term deviations of M1 from its target level would be permitted.

11. The Marshallian k is the ratio of the money supply to nominal GNP, and hence a different Marshallian k can be calculated for each money supply measure. The Marshallian k can rise, remain stable, or fall on trend due to the character of the monetary aggregate used (e.g., the relative weights of transactions vs. investment elements in it), the course of financial innovation (e.g., development of competing assets), or the level of development of the financial system (e.g., the degree of intermediation in the system). The Marshallian k also moves to reflect financial prosperity.

growth rates in the United States are calculated from economic forecasts based on an econometric model and successive approximations, and the quarterly growth targets used to achieve the annual target are based on many econometric techniques starting with estimates of the money demand function. Every time new money supply data become available, the equations of estimation are improved and forecasts revised, so the targets are moved.

It is difficult to set interest rate targets in the same way. As we have seen above, it is difficult to calculate appropriate interest rate levels with econometric methods when changes in inflationary expectations or increased economic uncertainty lead to large fluctuations in forecasts of the cycle, and hence to shifts of investment and savings functions. Moreover, there are often political demands for low interest rates, and income distribution arguments also become sharper.

Hence, in the U.S. case the announcement of monetary targets is done to avoid the economic difficulties of determining appropriate interest rate levels and to decrease the social and political pressures involving interest rates. So long as the Congress in representing the people believes in the method of determining the monetary targets and agrees to them, the populace cannot put any pressure on monetary policy when the level of interest rates is determined by supply and demand in the market reflecting these monetary targets.

This is the situation that has generated the strict adherence to short-term targets in the United States, as discussed above. That is, if short-run flexibility with respect to targets were allowed in the United States, then political and social demands with respect to interest rates would inevitably interfere.

(2) The Japanese Case. In the Japanese case, control of the broad money supply is focused on, but no target is set. The figure announced to the public is a "forecast." But since the "forecast" includes consideration of the behavior of the Bank of Japan, there is implicit Bank of Japan approval for the forecast level of money growth. The Bank of Japan continuously reexamines what effects the forecast money growth will have on income and expenditure growth, and hence on price-level growth. And when it is judged that undesirable effects may occur, policy is changed without delay, and money growth controlled. In such cases, the "forecast" money growth rate of course falls.

Repetition of such events has generated the stable, controlled growth of the money supply and falling inflation. The important factor is the successive achievement of lower inflation through money supply control, and the acquisition of public support in the Bank of Japan's will and ability to control money. Setting and announcement of actual targets is not necessary for this. Indeed, targets must necessarily be related to

government economic forecasts, and might even prove harmful by shack-
ling monetary policy and causing disruption. Announcement of "forecasts" is sufficient to provide the public with information about policy.

Is the Bank of Japan's operating procedure a rule? Not in Friedman's
sense of a fixed rate of money supply growth (an x percent rule).[12] Ad-
vocacy of an x percent rule is based on the belief that the automatic
recovery mechanisms will stabilize growth and will reestablish long-run
equilibrium at a point on the long-run Phillips curve (at the natural rate
of unemployment and an inflation rate of x percent) if the money supply
growth rate is fixed. But the Bank of Japan does not believe in a continuously fixed rate of money supply growth. First, the Bank of Japan, as
already mentioned, continuously considers what effects the money supply
is expected to have on future income and expenditure and hence on prices.
When adverse effects are expected, the money supply growth rate is
gradually corrected. But when unexpected but temporary changes in
money supply occur but are within the range in which adverse effects on
prices will not occur, they are allowed to pass. In terms of the model of
chapter 6, the equilibrium growth path of full employment income is
subject to unforeseen change, and monetary policy must recognize this
uncertainty.

Second, the Bank of Japan does believe in the spontaneous recovery
mechanism in the market economy, but there are cases when extraordinary circumstances result from unexpected, exogenous shocks to the
economy or from extremely skewed expectations due to increased uncertainty. In such cases, waiting for the spontaneous recovery mechanisms
to work would extend the period of uncertainty excessively. But such
cases are rare, the only recent examples being the first postwar revaluation
of the yen and the first oil crisis.

The increased importance of stable money growth can best be understood by referring to figure 8.1, which shows rates of change in money
stock, nominal GNP, and real GNP over the same quarter of the previous
year. A marked contrast is apparent from the figure. During the 1956–
73 period, the high-growth era, money growth fluctuated widely. It declined to around 15 percent during periods of tight money, and rose to
around 25 percent during periods of easy money. With a lag of a few
quarters, the same pattern of fluctuation occurred in growth of both real
and nominal GNP and of the GNP deflator (the latter of which may be
read from the figure as the gap between nominal and real GNP lines).
In this period, the discretionary changes in monetary policy helped to
sustain rapid though variable economic growth, but at the same time
resulted in average inflation of around 6 percent.

12. See Friedman 1960.

(percentage change from previous year)

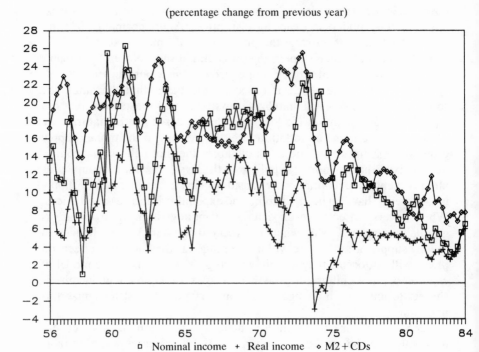

Figure 8.1. Nominal Income, Real Income, and M2 + CDs

During the period since 1973, real growth has dropped to one-half its former level. At the same time, fluctuations in the growth rate of the money stock have become small, and the rate of monetary growth itself has been declining gradually, from 15 percent to 7 to 8 percent. Consequently, the rate of growth of nominal GNP also declined. However, the decline in nominal GNP growth has been fully reflected in declines in GNP deflator growth. In contrast, real GNP growth has stayed around 5 percent throughout this period (except for a temporary decline after the second oil crisis, which is considered below).

This experience testifies that low inflation and macroeconomic stability can be achieved through stabilizing the rate of monetary growth and reducing it gradually over time. And it contrasts sharply with the pre–oil crisis period, in which radical changes in money growth destabilized both inflation and real growth. One may therefore conclude that stabilizing monetary growth is an effective way to stabilize both inflation and real activity.

The mechanism by which monetary stability encouraged spontaneous adjustment is illuminated in figure 8.2, which shows the growth of real GNP together with the contribution to growth of each of its components, that is, domestic private demand, government demand, and foreign demand. Growth rates apply to seasonally adjusted fiscal year semesters (April–September and October–March), and are measured versus the previous semester and annualized. The growth rate became negative after the first oil crisis and stayed there for three semesters from the second half of FY 1973 to the second half of FY 1974. But in the first semester of FY 1975, real growth recovered to 5 percent. Since then, the economy has deviated from the 5 percent path significantly only in two semesters after the second oil crisis, the second semesters of FY 1981 and FY 1982. The growth rate recovered in the first half of FY 1983, and was back on track by the second half.

Both of these deviations from stable growth occurred because of shocks from fiscal policy and the current account. In both cases, the contribution of fiscal expenditure was negative, as public investment was front-loaded in the first half of the fiscal years. And in the first instance, the situation was worsened by a negative contribution from the current account. On the other hand, private domestic demand began to recover spontaneously in the second half of FY 1981, after an adjustment period of the second oil crisis that lasted from the second half of FY 1979 to the first half of FY 1981. Recovery of private domestic demand provided the major force that pulled the economy back to the 5 percent stable growth path.

This spontaneous recovery of private domestic demand was possible only because monetary policy stabilized inflationary expectations, reduced uncertainty, and allowed both corporations and workers to adapt rationally to external shocks. Fiscal policy, as we see in figure 8.2, was destabilizing.

In summary, the Bank of Japan's approach to monetary control is neither that of post-Keynesian fine tuning nor that of the monetarist *x*-percent rule. It is discretionary in that it allows for gradual tuning, and it conforms to a rule in the sense that it stabilizes money growth as much as possible and gives information to the public about policy in the form of announcements of forecasts. An appropriate term is "eclectic gradualism."

II. Money Supply Controllability and Operating Variables

The above paragraphs have discussed the meaning of money as an intermediate objective, the choice of monetary indicators, and the methods of targeting. Next, let us examine the controllability of the money supply.

1. Choice of Operating Variables

Earlier in the chapter, we used the term "operating variable" to describe policy variables easily influenced by authorities in order to control the intermediate objectives. We also noted that there has been a shift of

Real growth
(in percent, semiannual periods)

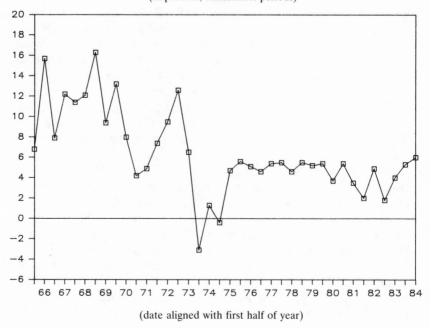

(date aligned with first half of year)

Contributions to growth
(in percentage points)

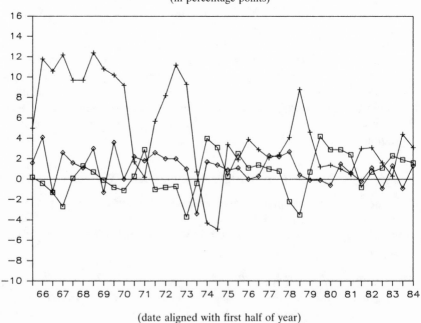

(date aligned with first half of year)

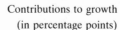
□ Foreign   + Private domestic   ◇ Government

Figure 8.2. Real Growth and Contributions to Growth

the intermediate objectives from interest rates to money supply; but conditions with respect to the easily influenced operating variables are somewhat different. The candidates for operating variable that are quantitative indicators are high-powered money (i.e., the monetary base) and reserves held by banks. The only nation setting and announcing targets for monetary base at the moment is Switzerland, and in the Swiss case it is an intermediate objective, not an operating variable. The West German central bank defines an aggregate called central bank money that is close to high-powered money, and sets and announces targets for it. But in this case, too, it acts as a proxy with short reporting lag for money supply, and is an intermediate objective.

For many years the United States used the Federal Funds rate as its operating variable, and announced targets for it. But since October 1979, the Federal Reserve has declared that it focuses on total reserves, nonborrowed reserves, and monetary base as operating variables, and has announced targets for these.[13] And since that time, the Federal Funds rate has fluctuated widely. Thus, with the exception of the United States there are no nations that use quantitative indicators as operating variables.

At the theoretical level the same factors mentioned with respect to intermediate objectives apply to operating variables. That is, the information included in the movement of interest rates is difficult to discern. The reasons that so many nations—Japan, West Germany, the United Kingdom, et cetera—use interbank interest rates as operating variables despite this difficulty are as follows.

First, in order to control high-powered money or reserves directly, the central bank must refuse to lend even a single cent when targets are in danger of being exceeded. It would create tremendous problems if, because of such a refusal, a bank somewhere became insolvent or suffered a run. The central bank's function as lender of last resort and guardian of orderly credit conditions is vital to the smooth functioning of an economy. In Switzerland, since banks hold about 10 percent of the value of deposits in cash reserves and are closely tied to foreign markets, refusal of the central bank to lend anything at all as it tries to control the monetary base will not cause panic. The wide swings in interest rates in the United States show that there are extreme swings in demand and supply conditions even when no bank is failing. If these swings raise the uncertainty with which people hold expectations, then they are a problem. They lower financial efficiency and may even lower efficiency of the economy. Does it make any sense to pay such costs? Or will bearing these fluctuations cause development of the custom of holding high cash reserves as Swiss

13. For an account of the change, see Board of Governors of the Federal Reserve System 1979.

banks do? For the moment, we can only watch the results of the experiment.

Second, interbank interest rates can be flexibly adjusted while watching bank behavior at current interest rate levels and movements of money supply. When exceeding the intermediate objective seems likely, then all one needs to do is raise interbank interest rates, and vice versa. In these cases, there will be a time lag between the time when the under- or overshooting is seen and when the change of interest rates will make itself felt in the money supply. But a short time lag of this nature is not a serious problem for money supply control. The problem is control of the money supply over the one- to two-year period, so that the interbank rate should suffice to guide the money supply toward its target. Hence the interbank rate should be controlled flexibly and with successive approximation, rather than by announcing a target for the operating variable and sticking to it. This flexible approach enables us to avoid the problem of having to distinguish the various strands of information included in the interest rate.

Third, the demand function for high-powered money is highly unstable in the short run. In short, daily events that are difficult to forecast, such as a snowstorm, change the desired cash holdings of individuals and the desired reserves of banks. The theoretical argument was that highly unstable money demand implies interest-rate control to be better than money control. Over short periods of days or weeks, the investment and savings functions are more stable than the money demand function, so that when we consider the problem of short-term money control through the operating variable we must conclude that monetary adjustment based on fixing targets for quantitative indicators is more disruptive to the economy.

2. Japan's Operating Variables and Controllability of Money

a. The Interbank Rate as Operating Variable.   Japan's operating variables for monetary policy throughout the high-growth period and even today have always been interbank interest rates. Earlier, the call rate was used, whereas today the bill rate is most important. The reason that the Bank of Japan is able to control interbank rates is that the path of accumulation of bank reserves over the month-long accumulation period can be adjusted by direct lending or by bill operations. This method of control was first pointed out to academic audiences in Suzuki 1966, and was expanded on in detail in Suzuki 1974.[14] More recently, exact theoretical models have been built by Yamamoto (1980) and Yasuda (1981).

14. See Suzuki 1966, pp. 93–94, and Suzuki 1974, pp. 182–83, 209.

The reserves system in Japan requires that banks use the average level of deposits from the first of the month to the last of the month as the basis for average level of reserves (deposits in the Bank of Japan only—vault cash is not included) held from the sixteenth of that month to the fifteenth of the succeeding month. Since reserves held are calculated as the average over the half-lagged period of a month, the actual level on any one particular day may be whatever a bank wishes. Of course a negative figure for reserves of the banking system as a whole would mean that somewhere a bank was insolvent and that the orderly credit conditions had been disrupted; hence, the Bank of Japan as lender of last resort supplies credit so that the total does not go negative. Moreover, even in the positive region, it is possible to adjust monetary policy so that an amount less than the average daily required reserves is held. In this case, since the actual accumulation path is below what an average accumulation path would be, interbank conditions grow increasingly tighter and interest rates rise. It is also possible for the Bank of Japan to lend or to buy bills so that the actual accumulation path lies above the average path; in this case, the interbank market would see gradual loosing of conditions, and interest rates would fall.

Suzuki 1966 performs a regression on the call rate that uses the ratio of excess reserves (which are high when accumulation is faster than normal or low when it is slower than normal) to required reserves as an explanatory variable. The estimated parameter on this variable showed high excess reserves leading to a low call rate and vice versa, with high significance for the coefficient.[15] More direct methods are also used, such as regression analysis of the call rate using the rate of reserves accumulation itself. In this case, the explanatory variable was the accumulation ratio (actual reserves divided by required reserves) at month-end, the exact center of the accumulation period. Again results showed the call rate moving inversely with the accumulation rate, with high significance.[16]

b. Influence of Interbank Rates on Money Supply. Above we considered how the Bank of Japan controls the interbank rate as its operating variable. Next let us consider the influence of the operating variable on the intermediate objective, the money supply.

Ohkubo 1982 has used the relative power contribution method, described in earlier chapters, to investigate the causal relationships between the intermediate objective money supply (M2 + CDs) and two potential operating variables, the interbank rate and the monetary base. The results show clear, unidirectional causality from the interbank rate to money supply. In contrast, it seems that reverse causality from M2 + CDs to monetary base is quite strong. This reverse causality makes it clear that

15. See Suzuki 1966, p. 95.
16. See Suzuki 1974, p. 121.

for Japan the interbank rate is better than the monetary base as the operating variable for control of the intermediate objective, money supply. There are three transmission channels that give rise to the estimate of unidirectional causality from interbank rates to money supply.

The first is the influence of bank portfolio selection. Loan rates in general are free rates, but the prime rate is sticky, due to de facto connections between it and the controlled discount rate, and due to the difficulty of moving it quickly from the viewpoint of maintaining good long-term relations with bank customers. As a result, loan rate changes are small relative to interbank market rate changes, so bank portfolio selection favors interbank market assets over loans when rates are rising. The obvious result is lower money supply due to suppression of lending. This path of causality was given its first theoretical and empirical presentation in the model of bank behavior in Suzuki 1966, and has since been developed by Royama 1982, Tachi and Hamada 1972, Suzuki 1974, Hamada and Iwata 1980, and Horiuchi 1980.

The second influence is that of interest rate changes on expenditure behavior. Arbitrage relations mean that a rise in interbank rates spreads into repurchase, CD, secondary bond, and other money markets, and raises interest rates in them. And, though the strength of the effect is less, even the sticky loan rate is influenced. For borrowers, the cost of borrowing has risen, and for lenders the yield on assets has risen. In other words, the former see a rise in the cost of investment, whereas the latter see a rise in the opportunity cost of investment. Both forces work to hold down investment and thus lower income. As a result, money demand falls, and money supply falls with it.

Third is the influence of disintermediation. The deposits offered by banks are subject to guidelines on upper limits of interest rates; thus, when interbank rate strengthening leads to arbitrage pulling open market rates upward, deposit rates are left at relatively low levels. As a result, the nonbank public shifts its assets from deposits to open market assets. Banks face difficulty in raising funds, and so have no choice but to restrain lending. This is financial disintermediation, and it results in a fall in the money supply.

All the description above of these three influences has been for the case of a rise in interbank rates, but the reverse case of a cut in interbank rates would yield an identical causal chain with a rise in the money supply.

As mentioned in chapter 4, the relative importance of the three channels depends on how interest rates are determined. For example, as the interest rates on loans and deposits become more flexible, the first and the third path become less important and the second path more important. The critical point here is that no matter how interest rates are determined, the aggregate effect of the three influences leads to unidirectional causality from the interbank rate to money.

The reasons for the reverse causality from money to the monetary base are as follows. As I stated above in reference to the path of reserves accumulation, the Bank of Japan performs its adjustments of money markets by changing the monetary base enough to influence the accumulation path of reserves. To this extent, monetary base changes would show up in interbank rate changes, and be causally prior to the money supply. But the portion of the monetary base so affected is small relative to the total.[17] Movements of the overall base are dominated by currency demand, which reflects income and expenditure. And since, as we saw in chapter 6, income and expenditure are influenced by money, in the end the monetary base is influenced by the money supply through income and expenditure.

17. In Japan, required reserves are about 10 percent of the monetary base, but excess reserves are only 0.1 percent. Hence, adjustment of the accumulation path of reserves is statistically minute relative to the total but can still control excess reserves.

References

Akaike, Hiroshi, and Tooichiroo Nakagawa. 1971. *Dainamikku shisutemu no tookeiteki kaiseki to seigoo* (Statistical analysis and control of dynamic systems). Saiensu Sha.

Anderson, L. C., and K. M. Carlson. 1970. "A Monetarist Model for Economic Stabilization." *Federal Reserve Bank of St. Louis Review*, vol. 52, April.

Bank of Japan Research Dept. 1961. "Wagakuni bukka koozoo no hendoo ni tsuite" (On changes in Japan's price structure). Bank of Japan, *Choosa geppoo*, March.

———. 1963. "Tsuuka to bukka no kankei ni tsuite" (On the relationship of money and prices). Bank of Japan, *Choosa geppoo*, October.

———. 1973. "Waga kuni ni okeru sho kinri no hendoo ni tsuite" (On interest rate fluctuations in Japan). *Choosa geppoo*, May.

———. 1975. "Nihon ni okeru manee sapurai no juuyoosei ni tsuite" (On the importance of the money supply in Japan). Bank of Japan, *Choosa geppoo*, July.

Bank of Japan. 1981a. "Seisan kansuu no keisoku ni tsuite" (On estimation of the production function). *Choosa geppoo*, September.

Bank of Japan. 1981b. "Saikin no setsubi tooshi dookoo ni tsuite" (On recent movements of plant and equipment investment). *Choosa geppoo*, November.

Barnett, W. A. 1980. "Economic Monetary Aggregates." *Journal of Economics*, vol. 14.

———. 1983. "The Optimal Level of Monetary Aggregation." *Journal of Money Credit and Banking*, February.

Barnett, W. A., and P. A. Spindt. 1982. "Divisia Monetary Aggregates." Federal Reserve Board, *Staff Studies*, no. 116, May.

Barro, R. 1976. "Rational Expectations and the Role of Monetary Policy." *Journal of Monetary Economics*, vol. 2, January.

———. 1977. "Unanticipated Money Growth and Unemployment in the United States." *American Economic Review*, March.

————. 1978. "Unanticipated Money, Output, and the Price Level in the United States." *Journal of Political Economy*, vol. 86, August.

————. 1979. "Unanticipated Money Growth and Unemployment in the United States: A Reply." *American Economic Review*, vol. 69, December.

Barro, R., and M. Rush. 1980. "Unanticipated Money and Economic Activity." In Fischer, S., ed., *Rational Expectations and Economic Policy*. University of Chicago Press.

Baumol, W. J. 1952. "The Transaction Demand for Cash: An Inventory Theoretic Approach." *Quarterly Journal of Economics*, vol. 66, No. 4.

Board of Governors of the Federal Reserve System. 1979. "Record of Policy Actions of the Federal Open Market Committee." *Federal Reserve Bulletin*. December.

Bruno, M. 1981. "Raw Materials, Profits, and the Productivity Slowdown." NBER Working Paper no. 660, April.

Bruno, M., and J. Sachs. 1979. "Macroeconomic Adjustment with Impact Price Shocks: Real and Monetary Aspects." NBER Working Paper no. 34, April.

————. 1979. "Supply versus Demand Approaches to the Problem of Stagflation." NBER Working Paper no. 382; and in *Weltwirtschafts Archiv*, 1981.

Cagan. P. 1972. *The Channels of Monetary Effects on Interest Rates*. NBER General Series no. 97. Columbia University Press.

Cockerline, J. P., and J. D. Murray. 1981. "A Comparison of Alternative Methods of Monetary Aggregation." Bank of Canada, *Technical Report*, no. 28, November.

De Kock, M. H. 1954. *Central Banking*. 3rd ed., Staples Press (London).

Economic Planning Agency. 1981. *Nenji keizai hookoku* (Annual economic report).

Fischer, S. 1979. "Anticipation and the Nonneutrality of Money." *Journal of Political Economy*, April.

————. 1980. "On Activist Monetary Policy with Rational Expectations." In Fischer, S., ed., *Rational Expectations and Economic Policy*. University of Chicago Press.

Fisher, I. 1930. *The Theory of Interest*. Macmillan.

Frankel, J. 1979. "On the Mark: A Theory of Floating Exchange Rates Based on Interest Rate Differentials." *American Economic Review*, September.

Friedman, M. 1960. *A Program for Monetary Stability*. Fordham University Press.

————. 1968. "The Role of Monetary Policy." *American Economic Review*, vol. 58, March.

————. 1977. "Nobel Lecture: Inflation and Unemployment," *Journal of Political Economy*, vol. 85, June.

————. 1983. "Monetary Variability: The United States and Japan." *Journal of Money, Credit, and Banking*, August.

Friedman, M., and S. Okita. 1963. "Nihon keizai wa infure e no michi" (The Japanese economy on the road to inflation). Japan Economic Research Center, *Nikkei Sentaa kaihoo*, July.

Friedman, M., and A. Schwartz. 1963. "Money and Business Cycles." *Review of Economics and Statistics*, vol. 45, February.

Fukao, Mitsuhiro. 1981. "The Risk Premium in the Foreign Exchange Market." Ph.D. dissertation, University of Michigan.

———. 1982a. "Kawase reeto to risuku puremiamu" (The exchange rate and the risk premium). Bank of Japan, *Kin'yuu kenkyuu shiryoo*, no. 13, June.

———. 1982b. "Saikin no kawase reeto to sono kettei yooin" (Recent exchange rates and their determinants). *Shuukan tooyoo keizai*, Kindai Keizaigaku Shiirizu, no. 63, October.

———. 1982c. "Hendoo soobasei no keiken to kawase reeto kettei riron no henkoo" (Experience with the floating-rate system and changes in exchange-rate determination theory). Bank of Japan, *Kin'yuu kenkyuu*, vol. 1, November.

Goldfeld, S. M. 1976. "The Case of the Missing Money." *Brookings Papers on Economic Activity*, no. 3.

Goodhart, C., et al. 1976. "Money, Income, and Causality: The UK Experience." *American Economic Review*, June.

Granger, C. W. J. 1969. "Investigating Causal Relations in Econometric Models with Cross Spectral Methods." *Econometrica*, July.

Gurley, J. G., and Shaw, E. S. 1960. *Money in a Theory of Finance*. Brookings.

Hamada, Koichi, et al. 1976. "Waga kuni no kashidashi shijoo koozoo: Toshi ginkoo to chihoo ginkoo to no kashidashi kinri wo chuushin ni" (The structure of the Japanese loan market: Focusing on city bank and local bank loan rates). Economic Planning Agency, *Keizai bunseki*, March.

Hamada, Koichi, and Fumio Hayashi. 1983. "Monetary Policy in Postwar Japan." Bank of Japan, *First International Conference Papers* (mimeo).

Hamada, Koichi, and Kazumasa Iwata. 1980. *Kin'yuu seisaku to ginkoo koodoo* (Monetary policy and bank behavior). Tooyoo Keizai Shimpoo Sha.

Harrod, R. 1948. *Towards A Dynamic Economics*. Macmillan.

Heller. H. R., and M. S. Khan. 1979. "The Demand for Money and the Term Structure of Interest Rates." *Journal of Political Economy*, February.

Hicks, J. R. 1974. *The Crisis in Keynesian Economics*. Basil Blackwell.

Horiuchi, Akira. 1980. *Nihon no kin'yuu seisaku—Kin'yuu mekanizumu no jisshoo bunseki* (Monetary policy in Japan: Empirical analysis of the monetary mechanism). Tooyoo Keizai Shimpoo Sha.

Inagaki, Hiroshi. 1974. "Waga kuni shihon shijoo ni okeru rimawari koozoo ni tsuite: Kitai moderu ni yoru kentoo" (On the yield curve in the Japanese capital market: An investigation based on the expectations model). *Shooken kenkyuu*, March.

Judd, J. P., and J. L. Scadding. 1981. "Liability Management, Bank Loans and Deposit 'Market' Disequilibrium." Federal Reserve Bank of San Francisco, *Economic Review*, Summer.

Kato, Hirotaka. 1980. "Keizei riron ni okeru yosoo keisei kasetsu no kentoo" (An examination of expectation formation hypotheses in economic theory). *Shuukan tooyoo keizai*, Special Issues, nos. 49–54.

———. 1982. *Monetarisuto no Nihon keizai ron—Gendai infure to kahei shugi* (A monetarist theory of the Japanese economy—Modern inflation and currency-ism). Nihon Keizai Shimbun Sha.

Kawase Seisaku Kenkyuu Kai. 1972. "En reeto no kokizami choosei ni tsuite no teigen" (A proposal on a crawling peg for the yen exchange rate). July.

Keynes, J. M. 1936. *The General Theory of Employment, Interest, and Money*. Macmillan.

Klein, L. R. 1947. *The Keynesian Revolution*. Macmillan.

Komiya, Ryutaro. 1969. "Economic Growth and the Balance of Payments: A Monetary Approach." *Journal of Political Economy*, vol. 77, January/February.

———. 1976. "Shoowa 48–9-men infureeshon no gen'in" (Causes of the 1973–4 inflation). *Keizaigaku ronshuu*, April.

Komiya, Ryutaro, and Miyako Suda. 1980. "Kanri furooto ka no tanshi idoo— Sono riron to saikin no keiken" (Short-term capital movements under managed floating—Theory and recent experience), Tokyo University, *Keizaigaku ronshuu*, April.

Komiya, Ryutaro, and Yoshio Suzuki. 1977. "Inflation in Japan: 1960–74." In Krause, L. B., and W. S. Salant, eds., *Worldwide Inflation: Theory and Recent Experience*. Brookings.

Kosai, Yutaka. 1981. *Koodoo seichoo no jidai* (The high-growth era). Nihon Hyooron Sha.

Kumagai, Hisao. 1963. "Setsubi tooshi to infureeshon" (Business investment and inflation). *Keizai seminaru*, August.

———. 1966. "Wagakuni no bukka mondai to kakaku riron" (Japan's price problem and price theory). In Kumagai, H., and T. Watanabe, eds., *Nihon no bukka mondai* (Japan's price problem). Nihon Keizai Shimbun Sha.

Kuroda, Akio. 1982. *Nihon no kinri koozoo: Kokusai rimawari no riron to jisshoo* (Interest-rate structure in Japan: Theory and empirical investigation of government bond yields). Tooyoo Keizai Shimpoo Sha.

———. 1983. "Expected Inflation Rates and the Term Structure of Interest Rates." Bank of Japan, *Monetary and Economic Studies*. vol. 1, no. 1, June.

Kuroda, Akio, and Takashi Ohkubo. 1981a. "Waga kuni ni okeru kokusai ryuutsuu shijoo no rimawari kettei mekanizumu ni tsuite: Kitai riron ni yoru apuroochi" (On the mechanism of determination of yields in the secondary market for government bonds in Japan: An approach based on expectations theory). Bank of Japan, *Kin'yuu kenkyuu shiryoo*, no. 9, September.

———. 1981b. "On the Determination of Yields in the Japanese Secondary Bond Market." Bank of Japan, *Discussion Paper Series*, no. 7, August.

———. 1982. "An Empirical Investigation of the Term Structure of Japanese Government Bond Yields." Bank of Japan, Discussion Paper Series, no. 11, January.

Kuroda, Iwao. 1979a. "Waga kuni ni okeru kashidashi kinri kettei ni tsuite: Juurai no giron no saikentoo to arantana shiten" (On the determination of loan rates in Japan: A reconsideration of debate heretofore and a new view). Bank of Japan, *Kin'yuu kenkyuu shiryoo*, no. 2, April.

———. 1979b. "Kin'yuu seido bunseki no rironteki wakugumi: Asymmetric information no riron to kin'yuu seido" (The theoretical framework of financial system analysis: Asymmetric information theory and the financial system). Bank of Japan, *Kin'yuu kenkyuu shiryoo*, no. 2, April.

———. 1981. "Kin'yuu ron no sai-koochiku wo semaru 'kin'yuu shakai ka' " (Socialism in the financial system forces a restructuring of financial theory). *Shuukan zaisei jijoo*, July.

Kuroda, Iwao, S. Namba, and Y. Oritani. 1980. "Money, Income, and Government Expenditure." Bank of Japan, Discussion Paper Series, no. 1, April.

Lucas, R. E. 1972. "Econometric Testing of the Natural Rate Hypothesis." In

Eckstein, O., ed., *The Econometrics of Price Determination*. Board of Governors of the Federal Reserve.

———. 1973. "Some International Evidence on Output Inflation Tradeoffs." *American Economic Review*, vol. 63, June.

Lucas, R. E., and T. Sargent. 1980. "After Keynesian Macroeconomics." In Federal Reserve Bank of Boston, *After the Phillips Curve*. Conference Series, no. 19, June.

Matsukawa, Shigeru. 1975. "Infureeshon ni okeru kitai no yakuwari" (The role of expectations in inflation). *Kikan riron keizaigaku*. December.

Meek, P. 1983. *Central Bank Views on Monetary Targeting*. Federal Reserve Bank of New York.

Minobe, Ryookichi. 1967. *Bukka mondai nyuumon* (An introduction to the price problem). Ushio Shinsho.

Mishkin, R. 1980. "Does Anticipated Monetary Policy Matter? An Econometric Investigation." NBER Working Paper no. 506, July.

Moriguchi, Chikashi. 1970. "Kooru roon juyoo kansuu to kyoshiteki kin'yuu moderu no seigoosei" (The call loan demand function and consistency of macroscopic monetary models). *Kikan riron keizaigaku*, August.

Nakamura, Takafusa. 1962. "Bukka jooshoo ron" (Inflation theories). *Chuuoo kooron*, July.

———. 1963. "Konkyo nai kosuto-infure ron" (Cost-push inflation theory has no basis). *Ekonomisuto*, 23 July.

Narukawa, Ryoosuke. 1982. "Manee sapurai to kinri no kankei ni tsuite" (On the relationship of money supply and interest rates). Bank of Japan, *Kin'yuu kenkyuu shiryoo*, no. 13, June.

Nihon Keizai Shimbun Sha, ed. 1973. *Infure ronsoo* (The inflation debate). Nihon Keizai Shimbun Sha.

Nihon Shooken Keizai Kenkyuu Sho. 1980. "Keisoku shitsu tekunikaru peepaa" (Estimation Department technical paper), no. 52, December.

Niida, Hiroshi. 1971. "Bukka no kin'yuuteki bunseki" (A monetary analysis of prices). In Shimano, T., and K. Hamada, eds., *Nihon no kin'yuu*. Iwanami Shoten.

Ohkubo, Takashi. 1982. "Manee sapurai to sho-keizai hensuu-kan no inga kankei" (Causality among money supply and economic variables). Bank of Japan, *Kin'yuu kenkyuu*, no. 1, November.

———. 1983. "Money, Interest, Income, and Prices." Bank of Japan, *Monetary and Economic Studies*, vol. 1, no. 2, October.

Oritani, Y. 1979a. "Manee sapurai oyobi zaisei shishutsu to meimoku GNP no kankei ni tsuite" (On the relation of money supply and fiscal expenditure with GNP). Bank of Japan, *Kin'yuu kenkyuu shiryoo*, no. 1, January.

———. 1979b. "Infure kitai to kinri: Fisshaa kooka no kentoo to sono inpuri-keishon" (Inflationary expectations and interest rates: A consideration of the Fisher effect and its implications). Bank of Japan, *Kin'yuu kenkyuu shiryoo*, no. 4, September.

———. 1979c. "Jikeiretsu bunseki ni tsuite" (On time series analysis). Bank of Japan, *Kin'yuu kenkyuu shiryoo*, no. 4, September.

———. 1981. "The Negative Effects of Inflation on Economic Growth in Japan." Bank of Japan, Discussion Paper Series, no. 5, April.

Patinkin, D. 1948. "Price Flexibility and Full Employment." *American Economic Review*, vol. 38.

——. 1965. *Money, Interest, and Prices*. Harper & Row.

Patrick, H. 1962. *Monetary Policy and Central Banking in Contemporary Japan*. University of Bombay.

Phelps, E. S. 1970. *The Microeconomic Foundation of Employment and Inflation Theory*. Norton.

——. 1972. *Inflation Policy and Unemployment Theory: The Cost Benefit Approach to Monetary Planning*. Macmillan.

Pigott, C. 1978. "Rational Expectations and Countercyclical Monetary Policy: The Japanese Experience." Federal Reserve Bank of San Francisco, *Economic Review*. Summer.

Pigou, A. C. 1943. "The Classical Stationary State." *Economic Journal*, vol. 53.

Poole, W. 1970. "Optimal Choice of Monetary Policy and Instruments in a simple Stochastic Macro Model." *Quarterly Journal of Economics*, May.

——. 1978. "The Theory of Monetary Policy under Uncertainty." In Teigen, R., ed., *Readings in Money, National Income, and Stabilization Policy*. Irwin.

Royama, Shoichi. 1969. "Wagakuni no tsuuka kyookyuu to kin'yuu seisaku" (Currency supply and monetary policy in Japan). Hitotsubashi University, *Keizai kenkyuu*, July.

——. 1982. *Nihon no kin'yuu shisutemu* (The Japanese financial system). Tooyoo Keizai Shimpoo Sha.

Sachs, J. 1979. "Wages, Profits, and Macroeconomic Adjustment in the 1970s: A Comparative Study." *Brookings Papers on Economic Activity*, vol. 2.

——. 1980. "Energy and Growth Under Flexible Exchange Rates." NBER Working Paper, no. 682, November.

Sachs, J., and D. Lipton. 1981. "Kyookyuu moderu ni yoru sekiyu kiki go no Nihon keizai bunseki" (An analysis of the Japanese economy after the oil crisis using a supply side model). *Shuukan tooyoo keizai: Kindai keizaigaku shiiriizu*, no. 57, July.

Saito, S. 1981. *Keizaigaku wa gendai o sukueru ka?* (Can economics save us?). Bungei Shunjuu Sha.

Sakakibara, Eisuke, et al. 1980. *Zaisei kin'yuu seisaku no kooka to Firipusu kaabu* (Fiscal and monetary policy effects and the Phillips curve). Economic Planning Agency.

Sargent, T. 1979. *Macroeconomic Theory*. Academic Press.

Sargent, T., and N. Wallace. 1975. "Rational Expectations, the Optimal Monetary Instrument, and the Optimal Money Supply Rule." *Journal of Political Economy*, October.

Schultze, C. L. 1959. "Recent Inflation in the United States." U.S. Congress, Joint Economic Committee, *Study Paper*, no. 1.

Seo, Junichiroo. 1981. "Wagakuni kawase shijoo no kooritsusei to saikin no en reeto hendoo no sho tokuchoo" (The efficiency of the Japanese foreign exchange market: Some characteristics of recent yen rate movements). Bank of Japan, *Kin'yuu kenkyuu shiryoo*, September.

Seo, Junichiroo, and Wataru Takahashi. 1982. "Gooriteki kitai to wagakuni no manee sapurai seisaku—Makuro gooriteki kitai kasetsu no kenshoo" (Rational expectations and Japanese money supply policy—An examination of the macro rational expectations hypothesis). Bank of Japan, *Kin'yuu kenkyuu shiryoo*, no. 11, February.

Shimomura, Osamu. 1963. *Nihon keizai wa seichoo suru,* Koobundoo. (The Japanese economy grows), chapter two.

Shimpo, Seiji. 1977a. "Firipusu kyokusen to infure bunseki (II)" (The Phillips curve and inflation analysis, part II). *ESP*. March.

———. 1977b. "Monetarisuto moderu ni yoru sutagufureeshon no kaimei" (Analysis of stagflation in a monetarist model). *ESP*, December.

———. 1979. *Gendai Nihon keizai no kaimei* (A study of the contemporary Japanese economy). Tooyoo Keizai Shimpoo Sha.

Shinkai, Y. 1971. "Infureeshon no kokusaiteki hakyuu to heika chooseisaku" (International transmission of inflation and parity adjustment policy). *Kikan gendai keizai*, no. 2, Fall.

———. 1973. "Infureeshon no kokusaiteki sokumen" (International aspects of inflation). *Kikan gendai keizai*, no. 9, Summer.

Shirakawa, Hoomei. 1979a. "Monetarii apuroochi ni tsuite" (On the monetary approach). Bank of Japan, *Kin'yuu kenkyuu shiryoo*, no. 4, August.

———. 1979b. "Gooriteki kitai kasetsu ni tsuite—Kin'yuu seisaku e no inpuri-keeshon o chuushin ni," (On the rational expectations hypothesis—The implications for monetary policy). Bank of Japan, *Kin'yuu kenkyuu shiryoo*, no. 4, September.

Sims, C. A. 1972. "Money, Income, and Causality." *American Economic Review*, September.

Suzuki, K., and M. Otaki. (1984). "Setsubi tooshi to hendoo ni tai suru shuueki ritsu to rishi ritsu no eikyoo—Tobin no *q* riron no hatten" (The influence of rates of return and interest rates on fixed investment—Development of Tobin's *q* theory). Japan Development Bank, *Keizai keiei kenkyu*, vol. 5, no. 1.

Suzuki, Yoshio. 1964. *Nihon no tsuuka to bukka* (Money and prices in Japan). Tooyoo Keizai Shimpoo Sha.

———. 1966. *Kin'yuu seisaku no kooka: Ginkoo koodoo no riron to keisoku* (The effects of monetary policy: Theory and measurement of bank behavior). Tooyoo Keizai Shimpoo Sha.

———. 1968. "Nihon no kinri hendoo to kashidashi, tooshi" (Interest-rate fluctuation, lending, and investment in Japan). *Kikan riron keizaigaku*, March.

———. 1973. "Kin'yuu men kara mita bukka jooshoo mekanizumu" (The mechanism of inflation viewed from the financial perspective). *Kikan gendai keizai*, no. 9, Summer.

———. 1974. *Gendai Nihon kin'yuu ron* (Money and banking in contemporary Japan). Tooyoo Keizai Shimpoo Sha.

———. 1980. *Money and Banking in Contemporary Japan.* Yale University Press.

———. 1981. *Nihon keizai to kin'yuu: Sono tenkan to tekioo* (Finance and the Japanese economy: Change and adaptation). Tooyoo Keizai Shimpoo Sha.

———. 1981a. "Monetary Control and Anti-Inflation Policy: The Japanese Experience Since 1975." Bank of Japan, *Discussion Paper Series*, no. 8, September.

———. 1983a. "Interest Rate Decontrol, Financial Innovation, and the Effectiveness of Monetary Policy." Bank of Japan, *Monetary and Economic Studies*, vol. 1, no. 1, June.

————. 1983b, "Changes in Financial Asset Selection and the Development of Financial Markets in Japan." Bank of Japan, *Monetary and Economic Studies*, vol. 1, no. 2, October.

————. 1983c. *Nippon kin'yuu keizai ron* (Treatises on finance in Japan). Tooyoo Keizai Shimpoo Sha.

Tachi, Ryuichiro. 1965. "Kin'yuu seisaku no yuukoosei" (The effectiveness of monetary policy). *Keizai gaku ronshuu*, Tokyo University, July.

————. 1982. *Kin'yuu seisaku no riron* (Theory of monetary policy). Tokyo University Press.

Tachi, Ryuichiro, and Koichi Hamada. 1972. *Kin'yuu* (Finance). Iwanami Shoten.

Tachi, Ryuichiro, Ryutaro Komiya, and Hiroshi Niida. 1964. *Nihon no bukka mondai* (Japan's price problem). Tooyoo Keizai Shimpoo Sha.

Takasuga, Yoshihiro. 1972. *Gendai Nihon no bukka mondai* (Inflation problems in contemporary Japan). Shin Hyooron Sha.

Teranishi, Juuroo. 1982. *Nihon no keizai hatten to kin'yuu* (Finance and the economic development of Japan). Iwanami Shoten.

Tobin, J. 1956. "The Interest Elasticity of Transactions Demand for Cash." *Review of Economics and Statistics*, vol. 38, no. 3.

————. 1965. "Money and Economic Growth." *Econometrica*, October.

————. 1969. "A General Equilibrium Approach to Monetary Theory." *Journal of Money, Credit, and Banking*, February.

————. 1980. *Asset Accumulation and Economic Activity*. Blackwell.

Toyoda, Toshihisa. 1972. "Price Expectations and the Short-run and Long-run Phillips Curve in Japan, 1956–1968." *Review of Economics and Statistics*, August.

————. 1977. "Sutagufureeshon to 'infure kitai' no yakuwari" (Stagflation and the role of inflationary expectations). Shuukan Tooyoo Keizai Kindai Keizaigaku Series, no. 39, February.

————. 1979a. "Wagakuni no infureeshon to shitsugyoo no kankei" (The relation of inflation and unemployment in Japan). *Kikan gendai keizai*, no. 36.

————. 1979b. "Dai infureeshon ki ni okeru kitai no keisei" (Expectations formation in periods of great inflation). *Kikan riron keizaigaku*, December.

Wakita, Y. 1981. "Good customer relationship to ginkoo koodoo" (Good customer relationships and bank behavior). Bank of Japan, *Kin'yuu kenkyuu shiryoo*, no. 7, February.

Watanabe, Tsunehiko. 1966. "Chingin-kakaku no kankei to sono seisakuteki imi" (The relationship of prices and wages, and its policy implications). In Kumagai, H., and T. Watanabe, eds., *Nihon no bukka mondai*. Nihon Keizai Shimbun Sha.

Wojnilower, A. 1980. "The Central Role of Credit Crunches in Recent Financial History." *Brookings Papers on Economic Activity*, vol. 2.

Yamamoto, Yasushi. 1980. "Wagakuni ni okeru manee sapurai kontorooru mekanizumu ni tsuite" (On the money supply control mechanism in Japan). Bank of Japan, *Kin'yuu kenkyuu shiryoo*, no. 5, May.

Yasuba, Yasukichi. 1970. "Infureeshon no shin kyokumen" (A new stage of inflation). In Tatemoto, M., and T. Watanabe, eds., *Gendai no keizaigaku*. Nihon Keizai Shimbun Sha.

Yasuda, Tadashi. 1981. "Manee sapurai kontorooru no arikata" (The state of money supply control). Bank of Japan, *Kin'yuu kenkyuu shiryoo*, no. 10, November.

Yoshino, Toshihiko, ed., 1962. *Keizai seichoo to bukka mondai* (Economic growth and the inflation problem). Shunjuu Sha (3rd ed., 1973).

Subject Index

Author Index

217